BEYOND WILD AND TAME

INTERSPECIES ENCOUNTERS

The last decade has seen significant theoretical advances in critical animal studies, posthumanism, science and technology studies, perspectivism, and multispecies anthropology. This groundbreaking series offers innovative works in the social sciences, which have risen to the challenge of engaging across species boundaries: humans, animals, insects, plants, and microbes, and expands methodological and theoretical approaches in the course of ethnographic engagements with other species. Questioning the distinction between human and non-human through innovative narrative and methodological strategies, books in the series address a range of pressing social and environmental issues.

Volume 2
Beyond Wild and Tame: Soiot Encounters in a Sentient Landscape
Alex C. Oehler

Volume 1
Wolf Conflicts: A Sociological Study
Ketil Skogen, Olve Krange, and Helene Figari

BEYOND WILD AND TAME
SOIOT ENCOUNTERS IN A SENTIENT LANDSCAPE

Alex C. Oehler

berghahn
NEW YORK · OXFORD
www.berghahnbooks.com

First published in 2020 by
Berghahn Books
www.berghahnbooks.com

© 2020, 2025 Alex C. Oehler
First paperback edition published in 2025

All rights reserved. Except for the quotation of short passages for the purposes of criticism and review, no part of this book may be reproduced in any form or by any means, electronic or mechanical, including photocopying, recording, or any information storage and retrieval system now known or to be invented, without written permission of the publisher.

Library of Congress Cataloging-in-Publication Data

A C.I.P. cataloging record is available from the Library of Congress
Library of Congress Cataloging in Publication Control Number: 2020002030

British Library Cataloguing in Publication Data

A catalogue record for this book is available from the British Library

ISBN 978-1-78920-678-4 hardback
ISBN 978-1-80539-725-0 paperback
ISBN 978-1-80539-915-5 epub
ISBN 978-1-78920-679-1 web pdf

https://doi.org/10.3167/9781789206784

To my sister,
Elisa

CONTENTS

List of Illustrations — viii
Preface — ix
Acknowledgments — xii
Notes on Transliteration and Translation — xiii
List of Abbreviations — xiv

Introduction — 1

Chapter 1. Mirrored Homes — 19

Chapter 2. Sacred Enfolding — 39

Chapter 3. Dreaming of Deer — 65

Chapter 4. Khainak between Worlds — 93

Chapter 5. In the Society of Horses — 116

Chapter 6. Reading Wolves — 142

Conclusion — 161

References — 173
Index — 187

ILLUSTRATIONS

Illustration 0.1. Borzhon and Ranzhur's home at Uro. Photograph by the author.   14
Illustration 0.2. Moving a horse group to summer pasture. Photograph by the author.   16
Illustration 1.1. Brick oven and bark floor. Photograph by the author.   23
Illustration 1.2. Fishing with Borzhon on the Upper Sorok River. Photograph by the author.   37
Illustration 2.1. Badma makes an offering at Shaman tree. Photograph by the author.   44
Illustration 2.2. Sacred caves of Oka. Photograph by the author.   55
Illustration 3.1. Tofa reindeer camp. Photograph by the author.   67
Illustration 3.2. Tofa riding bulls near reindeer camp. Photograph by the author.   72
Illustration 4.1. Yak grazing at winter pasture. Photograph by the author.   97
Illustration 4.2. Yak herd at summer pasture. Photograph by the author.   100
Illustration 5.1. Laying down a horse, steps a to j. Photographs by the author.   132
Illustration 5.2. Horse castration sequence, steps k to t. Photographs by the author.   134
Illustration 6.1. Freshly shot and skinned wolf at Uro. Photograph by the author.   144
Illustration 6.2. Ruins of a Tofa wolf trap. Photograph by the author.   152

PREFACE

The story of this book begins with the last Inuit-owned reindeer herd of Arctic Canada. In a land teeming with wild caribou, where did these docile reindeer come from? Of course the reindeer found today in the Inuvialuit Settlement Region are immigrants from Alaska, descending from herds across the Bering Strait in Chukotka, Russia. But their historical journey to North America begins in the very heart of southern Siberia, a region famed as the prehistoric cradle of Eurasian reindeer domestication. In spite of the area's fame, little is known today about the descendants of the people who first domesticated reindeer in this region, and shrouded deeper in mystery are their prolific relations with animals other than reindeer. Following early twentieth-century explorers of the Eastern Saian Mountains, the introduction recounts the convoluted history of Soiots of Buriatia, concluding with an introduction to the Uro Valley and its ten mountain households among whom the majority of the events described in this book take place.

Chapter 1 introduces the reader to some of the key literature on animal domestication with which this book dialogues. But before doing so, it explores how Soiot households position themselves in a sentient landscape. Because I am working with the domus as a model for the household, the chapter consults Greco-Roman ideas about dominance over members of the house before turning to Soiot ways of dwelling with others. I argue that the Soiot household, centered on key pastures, is a mirror image of spirit households of the taiga. Spirit households are centered on valleys, streams, and mountain peaks. In an inversion of perspective, spirit masters share their game animals as stock with human households while wild predators are sent by spirits to feed on human-owned herd animals as game. This reversal of "wild" and "domestic" not only opens up reciprocal material exchanges between spirit and human households but also allows animals to move back and forth between pastured and forested home places. Rather than seeing domestic human-animal associations solely as the outcome of human control, they are understood as the product of mutual negotiation, opening up new possibilities in a shared environment.

The second chapter takes a deeper look at the sacred aspects of this sentient landscape. Drawing on observation, participation, and interviews with Soiot and Buriat shamanic practitioners, the chapter introduces divergent approaches to mountains as spirit masters. The argument is made that balanced reciprocity in the landscape is possible only as long as spirits and animals remain free to engage in an open and reciprocal dialogue with human herder-hunters. Following descriptions of shamanic communication, which range from spirit manifestations in animals to ways of speaking through trees, the chapter turns to the historical arrival of Buddhism. Through conversations with local Buddhist lamas, I recount how clergy sought to tame spirit masters of the Eastern Saians, and how Soiot herder-hunters not only moved back and forth between shamanic and Buddhist perceptions of the landscape but also how they adapted Buddhist ritual to the needs of people and animals in an economy based on the taking of life.

Chapter 3 focuses on historical and contemporary movements of neighboring Soiot and Tofa reindeer herds. It opens with waking to Tofa reindeer caravans silently winding their way through thick snowy forest, followed by quite another caravan: the scholars who have variously hypothesized the domestication of a species that seems to thrive on dwelling between wild and tame spaces. The chapter juxtaposes Soiot and Tofa herding practices, emphasizing historical fluctuations in human-herd dynamics alongside the presence of other species, showing both the flexibility of households and the seasonal entanglements of diverse species within it. Revisiting the 1963 loss of all Soiot reindeer, the chapter invokes Soiot herders' living memory and diaries of a time they attempted to re-introduce reindeer to their cattle-dominated herding practices in the mid-1990s. The chapter concludes on the present state of a Soiot reindeer herd, kept in a remote valley as living potential for another way of being Soiot.

Chapter 4 examines the pivotal role of yak and hybrid cattle in Oka. Among the four quadrants of the Saian Cross, each of which shares the Saian Style of reindeer herding, Oka is the only place in which Indigenous residents took up yak breeding. The chapter opens with some ideas for why this may be so before it delves into a more detailed analysis of the transition that occurred from pure yak herding to the breeding of dairy cattle and its effects on nomadic movement and local land management. It then traces the roots of yak herding back to Tibet, exploring the sacred meaning of this highly self-willed species. As Oka is seeking new ways to participate in the markets of nearby metropoles, contemporary attempts at engineering a marketable and patented Oka breed are contrasted with ongoing Indigenous preference for the so-called khainak hybrid. Various hybrid breeding techniques are explored, including dairying.

The chapter ends with a note on the impact of predators on yak and hybrid populations today.

Salt and smoke-based invitational herding constitutes one side of animal-human pastoral relations in the Saians. The other side relies on material objects that may seem more restrictive. Observing horse roundups, chapter 5 explores how herders interpret animal volition through seasonal fluctuations of proximity between herds and herders. What does it mean to round up a group of free ranging horses in spring? Are these animals invited or coerced to rejoin human encampments after a long self-sufficient winter? Focusing on material implements, such as ropes, corrals, horseshoes, and saddles, but also on implements of more invasive encounters, such as castration, the coercive connotations of pastoral implements are problematized, calling attention to their communicative qualities. In this context, selective breeding is shown not only as a process intended to increase docility in animals but also as a way to foster fierceness and self-reliance in select herd animals. Ultimately, materials become incubators for the negotiation of new sociality.

Apprenticing with an elder blacksmith, I show how pedagogy and knowledge of wolves are inseparable in the Saians. Good learners are like wolves in that they are able to learn from observation, developing a capacity to accurately predict another's movements. At once fiercely hated and deeply admired, wolves are sometimes seen as inherently autonomous and other times as emissaries of a spirit master. As keen observers of human and other livelihood, their treks crisscross domains of practice and property. Chapter 6 juxtaposes human-built traps with wolf-designed dens, showing how two thinking parties employ design to conceal intent. As intent is disclosed through experience and reflection, these material structures attain new histories. In contoured land, the author explores how wolves disclose and reveal their bodies through empathetic emplacement, anticipating the human gaze. And while stock roam afar, wolves venture into the heart of the encampment, thus inverting range and proximity and problematizing what is domestic.

As the title *Beyond Wild and Tame* suggests, the focus is not on the ethnos of ethnography, but on the concept of domestication beyond an increase of predictability and efficiency in human-animal relations through commodification, domination, and/or willful habituation of animal dependency upon ourselves. The conclusion reiterates a counterdomesticity that relies on perpetual negotiation. Reflecting on examples of animal-human interaction in the Saians, it ponders what it means to share thought in collective acts, and how such collective thinking and acting may affect the future of domestication relationships.

ACKNOWLEDGMENTS

My foremost gratitude goes to the herder-hunters of Uro, the lamas and shamans of Oka, and to the administration of Okinskii Raion and Sorok Somon. Their openness to me, my family, and a multitude of creatures at large made this book possible. I am deeply indebted to Beth and our children who have moved around the globe with and without me to enable this work. Together we have become a band of global nomads. I am deeply grateful to the many colleagues, especially in the United Kingdom, France, and the Russian Federation who have played integral roles in advising the direction of my research while sharing their own insights from many years of working on human-animal relations in Siberia. In Scotland, my special thanks go to David G. Anderson, Rob Wishart, and Tim Ingold for their inspiration, guidance, and friendship on this journey. In Aberdeen, I also thank Martin Mills for his assistance with research on early Buddhist activities in Western Buriatia. In France, I would like to thank Grégory Delaplace, Charlotte Marchina, and Charles Stépanoff. Their critiques and ideas have been pivotal. In the Russian Federation, I am deeply thankful to Artur V. Kharinskii, Arkadiy D. Kalikhman, and Igor V. Rassadin whose introductions and field support were indispensable. Countless other people have been instrumental—too many kind souls to list here. I am grateful to the European Research Council, the Arctic Domus project, and The North Theme at the University of Aberdeen, which together enabled me to spend many months working with herder-hunters in remote mountain valleys, as well as in the vaults of numerous Siberian archives. My gratitude goes out to the peer reviewers of the initial manuscript for their meticulous and helpful comments. Finally, I would like to thank Anastasia Kvasha for preparing the map and Kathy Plett for her work on the index.

NOTES ON TRANSLITERATION AND TRANSLATION

Almost all of the conversations with the people of Oka were conducted in Russian, one of the official languages of the Republic of Buriatia. Where Russian, Buriat, Soiot, or Tofa terms are used, I try to follow the simplified transliteration guide of the Library of Congress for these languages as has been the practice of other Siberianists (e.g., Ulturgasheva 2012). For the sake of accessibility, diacritics are omitted in the transliteration of commonly used place names and personal names. Plural forms of commonly used foreign transliterations are written by adding "-s" to the singular word to simplify often complicated conventions in the original languages. All Russian and German terms, citations, and quotations, unless otherwise noted, are the translations of the author.

ABBREVIATIONS

b. ca.   born circa
Bur.   Buriat
Col.   Colloquial language
Eng.   English
Pers. comm.   personal communication
Rus.   Russian
Soi.   Soiot
Tof.   Tofa

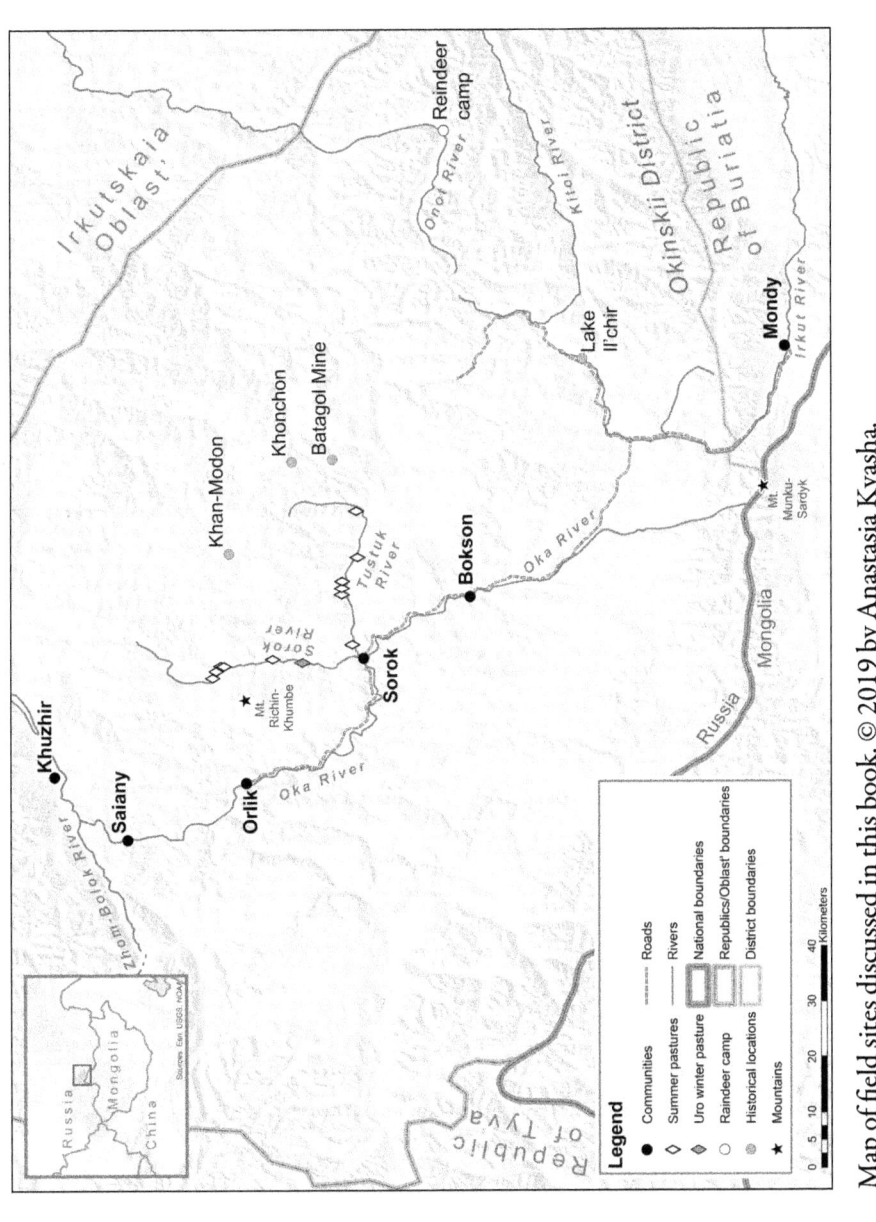

Map of field sites discussed in this book. © 2019 by Anastasia Kvasha.

INTRODUCTION

Russian anthropologist Larissa Pavlinskaia's (2002) book *Kochevniki Golubykh Gor* (Nomads of the Blue Mountains) was the first-ever comprehensive ethnography of Soiot society. She accomplished what anthropologist and archaeologist Bernhard E. Petri (see Sirina 2003) may have wished to do in the later 1920s had he not died prematurely. Pavlinskaia produced an ethnography in the truest sense, abiding by the outline of other Soviet and post-Soviet ethnographers. But her work is ethnographic not only in its more or less Malinowskian form but also because at its core lies the concerted effort of retracing—even constructing and re-defining with and for the people—what may be the Soiot ethnos. Pavlinskaia does this carefully and meticulously, and her work has been foundational for Soiot political activism of the early post-Soviet period.

My own work has departed significantly from this classical model of ethnography. On the one hand, it is perhaps too early to produce another comprehensive account of Soiot life. On the other hand, my departure from the classic paradigm follows other developments in our discipline. As anthropologist Tobias Rees (2018) points out in his book, *After Ethnos*, other concepts of fieldwork have emerged since the late 1990s. One of them has been a shift in focus from "difference in space" (i.e., comparing lifeways between places) to "difference in time." The latter follows the transformation of experiences, recurring events, consumables, labor practices, concepts, or microbes through time, ever asking: what is different, what is new? (Rees 2018: 80). Without losing interest in the meaning of Soiot identity, I have sought to ask what is wild, what is tame?

FROM THE CANADIAN ARCTIC TO SIBERIA

One of the most memorable sights for any visitor to the Canadian Western Arctic are its massive caribou herds. Peary, Dolphin, and Union caribou populate Canada's Arctic Archipelago, as well as much of its High Arctic mainland, while tall-standing Northern Mountain and Boreal woodland caribou are found further to the south. The largest population are barren-ground caribou. Like a silver-grey carpet, they flow elegantly over hills and across shallow waters as they migrate between wintering and summering grounds. Fluctuating in herd size, and divided into genetically and geographically distinct populations, these *Rangifer tarandus* are known by their calving sites to which they migrate long-distance each year. During their migrations, they pass through Inuvialuit, Sahtú, Gwich'in, and Tłı̨chǫ lands. For each of these North American Indigenous peoples, caribou have been an essential component for nutrition, shelter, clothing, and cultural identity.

While living in the Mackenzie Delta town of Inuvik, an Arctic Canadian community that is home to Inuvialuit (Inuit) and Gwich'in (First Nations) in the Northwest Territories, I frequently visited my neighbor and local meat seller, Lloyd Binder. Binder's soup cuts, which he kept in several freezer chests outside his home, tasted much like caribou. In actuality, however, they came from reindeer belonging to Canada's last private, open-range reindeer herd. These reindeer belong to the common species *Rangifer tarandus*, which is known as caribou in North America and as reindeer in Eurasia. Yet locals of the northern Northwest Territories clearly differentiated between the activities of "hunting caribou" and "herding reindeer." Both animal types share common tundra grounds in the summer, and it was not uncommon to hear complaints about subsistence hunters who had "mistaken" a reindeer for a caribou. In terms of taste, Indigenous elders seemed to prefer caribou over reindeer, even though both types belong to the same species. In a way, elders' taste preferences may have reflected the significant differences in allele frequencies known to exist between caribou and reindeer populations in the Western Arctic, differences that suggest limited gene flow between the two populations (Cronin et al. 2003). As an outsider newcomer, I was naturally intrigued to learn about the origins of Binder's reindeer in a land crawling with caribou.

Fortunately, the history of North American reindeer breeding is quite well recorded. I soon learned the need for reindeer meat had first arisen among Alaskan Inuit who had suffered a sharp decline in caribou herds, largely due to overexploitation by European and American commercial whaling crews in the mid-nineteenth century (Treude 1975: 121). A similar trend was affecting Canadian Inuit in the Western Arctic where alterations in caribou migratory routes had further exacerbated the situation brought about by the whalers (Conaty and Binder 2003: 9). In Alaska, Presbyterian missionary and US

General Agent for Education Dr. Sheldon Jackson is said to have first imported "semi-domestic" reindeer from Chukotka in an attempt to alleviate the shortage in caribou (Miller 1935: 21; North 1991: 6). As part of Alaska's aim for Inuit to transition from caribou hunting to a more stable and predictable reindeer breeder's way of life, a total of 1,280 reindeer were purchased between 1891 and 1902, primarily from communities in Chukotka (Treude 1975: 121). To enhance the resilience of these animals, 254 of them were of the tall-standing Tungus breed purchased separately at Okhotsk in 1901 (North 1991: 8).

By 1925, some 350,000 reindeer belonging to 110 herds could be seen roaming the north Alaskan coast (North 1991: 8). The evident success of this US experiment convinced the Canadian government to follow suit, making their own purchase of reindeer in Alaska. The Canadians invited experienced Sámi herders from Scandinavia to train Inuit in reindeer breeding techniques. In 1935, after the famous "five-year trek" from Alaska, 2,370 reindeer arrived in the Mackenzie Delta (Treude 1975: 121). Although a significant number of Mackenzie Delta Inuit would spend the next quarter century herding reindeer along the Beaufort Sea, the pastoral practice fell into decline by the late 1960s. By the mid-1970s, the remnant herd had gone through several private hands—Binder's ownership being the most recent. As a descendant of two intermarried herding families—the Sámi Pulk family of Norway and the Inuvialuit Binder family—his ownership is testimony to a regional heritage rooted in Sápmi, the Fennoscandian homeland of Sámi, and by extension in Far Eastern Siberia from where the Tungus breed of reindeer had originally come.

THE CRADLE OF REINDEER DOMESTICATION

My attempt to trace reindeer domestication back to Siberia was by no means novel. Scholars, scientists, and explorers have been in search of the origins of Eurasian reindeer domestication for well over a century, a journey we will examine more closely in chapter three. My own curiosity in the area lauded as the "cradle of Eurasian reindeer domestication" peaked after reading anthropologist Tim Ingold's (1980) book, *Hunters, Pastoralists, and Ranchers: Reindeer Economies and Their Transformations*. In this book, Ingold hypothesizes human-reindeer relations started out as predatory (humans hunting reindeer), then became pastoral and protective (humans guarding reindeer from other predators), and finally resumed a predatory character in ranchers who predate on their own herds as much as economically feasible to market meat.

Although Ingold's main argument in this early work concerns the changing economic relations of hunters, herders, and ranchers, and the transition from one economic model to another, he also touches on the finer details of how such changing relations may be reflected in the nature of reindeer as a species.

This latter part speaks directly to the questions of "what is domestication?" and "at what point can we speak of an animal as having become domesticated?" These questions touch on the beginnings of physical transformations resulting from changes in the relationships between people and other animals.

Having long moved beyond the Marxist economic framework of his earlier work, Ingold turned to the phenomenology of Martin Heidegger and Maurice Merleau-Ponty to advocate for animals as fellow beings-in-the-world (Ingold 2000: 173). For him, this is a world that arises from attention to "movements, sounds and gestures of animals" (2000: 25). In the words of anthropologist David G. Anderson, such a world is best described as a sentient ecology, or "the mutual interrelation of person and place" (2002: 116). This theoretical shift, from quasi autonomous individuals shaping an outside world to agents as co-constituents of their environment, does not detract from Ingold's original concern with domestication. It does however surrender its urgency with origins to a new emphasis on the perpetual becoming of social relations as part of a "meshwork" of "co-responding lifelines" (Ingold 2011: 63–94, 2017: 14).

In this meshwork, reindeer have been especially elusive when it comes to definitions of domestication, particularly in the archaeological record. Even under conditions of domestic breeding, their morphological traits remain much the same as those of their nondomestic counterparts (Ingold 1974: 523). However, we know that Indigenous breeders in Siberia are well aware of distinct behavioral and phenotypic differences between living wild and tame populations, differences they deliberately maintain through their breeding, and are evident also in each population's distinct genetic signature (Anderson et al. 2017: 6,799).

On the whole, however, the phenotypic variation between wild and tame reindeer remains minimal enough to ensure domestic reindeer stay as hardy as their cousins in the wild, while not losing their unique behavioral traits. Several Siberian reindeer breeding peoples seem also to lack a unanimous account of the origins of domestication. Instead they will argue "there have been [domestic] reindeer for as long as there have been people" (see Shirokogorov 1966: 29). Of course, this is where the very root argument of this book lies. It does not have to do with reindeer per se, but with the notion that not all forms of domestication must result in tangible morphological changes, nor would domestication result in gradually increasing dependence upon human care. As Ingold (1980: 82) has pointed out so aptly:

> Tame animals may be "domestic," in the sense of their incorporation as members of human households, but need not be morphologically "domesticated." Conversely, selectively bred animals may run wild, as in emergent ranching systems, while the herds of pastoralists need be neither "domestic" nor "domesticated." It will not do to refer to such combinations as states

of "semi-domestication," for the implication that they are in the process of evolution towards "full" domestication is not always warranted.

There needs to be a distinction, then, between definitions of domestication based on deliberately or serendipitously introduced morphological changes, and domestication defined by the maintenance of wild-like qualities in combination with unique behavioral traits. One way these two approaches can be contrasted in southern Siberia is in terms of residence. Intermittent cohabitation with humans allows for extensive periods of absence, which fosters self-reliance in animals. Permanent human care, on the other hand, can result in a species' greater reliance on the human household, as we see in many farm animals.

At this point it is necessary to distinguish between domestication as an adaptive, evolutionary process and domestication in the sense of the domestic animal. The latter shares a "home," or domus, with humans, the prior is a large-scale process whereby species adapt to changing environments. Of course all animals, whether they live with humans or not, are subject to adaptive, evolutionary processes, but in an Inner Asian context—as we will see—the domestic animal forms an accepted category, even if this category is somewhat more flexible than in most Euro-American models. This flexibility has to do with the fluctuating distance between animals and humans.

Fellow anthropologists Charles Stépanoff et al. (2017) have come to a similar conclusion in their study of "animal autonomy and intermittent coexistences." Based on extensive ethnographic research on nomadic and semi-nomadic animal husbandry practices in North Asia, including South Siberia, they outline a model of pastoralism in which herders rely on their herds' abilities to feed and protect themselves. Here the bond between animals and people is enabled by way of a shared landscape in which animals and humans balance their autonomous movements with mutual engagements through patterns of intermittent contact.

In many of the cases described in this book, the adaptive physical features of animals found in the wild already match the requirements for survival in a mountainous taiga setting, domestic or not. Where species belonging to the human household have no counterpart in the wild—as is the case with dairy cattle—they will be bred to best suit the requirements for survival in an unsheltered environment. In south central Siberia, this may mean interbreeding relatively vulnerable dairy cattle with hardy yak. In either case, what makes a breed a good "domestic" candidate in this northern context is a fine-tuned balance between self-reliance and an ability to respond and relate to people.

By allowing animals to roam freely, finding their own food and defending themselves against predators, stock owners ensure that their animals survive even in remote locations and under hostile circumstances. At the same time, routine interaction with their animals in commonly shared spaces allows herders to maintain approachability in their animals. This approachability can be described as an animal's ability to recognize and make use of the benefits that come with human encounters while maintaining a degree of autonomy that enables a measure of resistance to human volition. The delicate management of these habituated encounters is perhaps what best describes domestication relationships in southern Siberia.

TOWARD A MULTISPECIES ETHNOGRAPHY

So far I have primarily discussed reindeer. Much of the ethnographic literature depicting Indigenous human-animal relations in mountainous South Siberia emphasizes human-reindeer relations. This does not come as a surprise, especially from the perspective of European explorers who were intrigued by the uniqueness of the Saian style of reindeer breeding, and especially by its tradition of equestrian-like riding. As one reads through the accounts of explorers and researchers of the region, however, one also finds mention of hunters and herders interacting with other species in households and the taiga.

One of the first European visitors to the Eastern Saians was British explorer Douglas Carruthers, who in the summer of 1910, together with fellow explorers John H. Miller and Morgan P. Price, visited Tozhu reindeer herders on Ala-Su River in eastern Tyva. Excited to find wild and domestic reindeer as far south as the northern border of Mongolia, Carruthers presents his Tozhu informants as householders concerned almost exclusively with reindeer breeding. Only in a side note does he mention "wiry horses" being used in a summer hunt or hunting dogs tied down near tents (Carruthers 1914: 226–28). In spite of encountering horsehair fishing nets, the British explorer argues that in most cases "Uriankhai [Tozhu] are no fishermen" (1914: 229). Although his account could be written off as unbalanced travel writing, Carruthers's publication stirred the scholarly community and revived an interest in the origins of reindeer domestication.

One of the people attracted by Carruthers's discovery was Norwegian zoologist Ørjan Olsen. Fueled by a pan-Scandinavian curiosity about the origins of the Sámi way of life, Olsen organized a well-funded expedition to the Eastern Saians in the summer of 1913. In his 1914 travel report, "Til Jeneseis Kilder" (To the Inenisei's sources), he recalls being greeted not by reindeer but by a large group of free-running dogs before reaching the bark-covered conical lodges of a Tozhu summer encampment. Inside the tents, he found horsehair fishing nets waiting to be used in surrounding rivers and lakes, and for transportation, people relied on horses alongside reindeer. In his second and more focused book, *Los Soyotos* (1921: 72–73) [*Et Primitivt Folk: De Mongolske Rennomader* 1915], Olsen goes on to describe in more detail the fishing nets as well as the technique used by Tozhu to drive fish into them. Unlike Carruthers, Olsen soon realized that Tozhu transhumance depended on orchestrating herding, hunting, and fishing schedules (1921: 121). He even mentions cattle theft (1921: 138), which was common among Tozhu who had settled more to the west and who were holding cows, sheep, and goats (1921: 99). Although it is not his focus, one cannot read Olsen's work without noticing that early twentieth-century Eastern Saian mountain households incorporated multiple species side by side.

The expeditions of Carruthers and Olsen penetrated a remote and little-explored region of Inner Asia. Some scholars have referred to this area as the "Saian Cross" because it is home to four distinct yet historically related peoples, all of whom share the heritage of a common Saian style of reindeer breeding. The Tozhus of Carruthers's and Olsen's accounts still reside in the western part of the Eastern Saians in what is now called the Todzhinskii District of the Republic of Tyva. Their immediate neighbors to the north are the Tofas of Tofalariia in Nizhneudinsk District of Irkutsk Oblast, and to the southeast, they shoulder with the Dukhas who dwell just across the border in the Khövsgöl Aimag in Mongolia. Edged in between their Mongolian and Tofa neighbors, reside the Oka-Soiots of Okinskii District (a district also known simply as "Oka") in the westernmost part of the Republic of Buriatia.

In recent years a number of anthropologists have produced highly insightful work on human-animal relations with Tozhu, Dukha, and Tofa communities (e.g., Donahoe 2004; Endres 2015; Küçüküstel 2018; Mel'nikova 1994; I. V. Rassadin 2005; Stépanoff 2012). Soiots, by comparison, seem to have been passed over by this renewed attention. This may be in part due their reputation as "the most assimilated" of the four groups to settler ways of life. It may also have to do with the fact that Soiots were not officially recognized as an Indigenous people during the Soviet period, and even after the demise of the Soviet Union, little was known about them. The first ethnographer to write in-depth about Soiots was Larissa Pavlinskaia (2002). In her work she describes Soiot and Oka-Buriat ways of life, relying in part on the testimony of elders able to recall pre-Soviet experiences and who have since passed away. Her book became an active aid in the official reinstatement of Soiots as a distinct Indigenous people, and it inspired me to base my own doctoral work in an Oka-Soiot community. The account that follows is based on a first visit to Soiot communities in 2012, followed by ten months of ethnographic and archival research conducted primarily with the Soiot community at Uro in 2013 and 2014, as well as subsequent visits to Oka and Tofalariia in the autumn of 2014 and the spring of 2018.

SOIOT HISTORY

The archaeological record for Oka is sparse, and the beginnings of Soiot presence in these mountains is limited to fragmented oral memory and scholarly speculation. Because many residents of Oka are hostile to the idea of disturbing the ground, archaeologists have been limited to surface surveys. Fear of "stealing from the earth" is reflected in a common utterance I overheard many times among Buriats and Soiots alike. "What is in the ground belongs to Burkhan [the local mountain deity], and nothing good comes from moving it." In spite of this belief, Soiots have a long history of encounters with geological exploration. There are stories about Soiot ancestors who, "a hundred years ago," worked for a foreigner by the name of M. J.-P. Alibert—a French prospector who discovered high quality graphite on Mt. Krestovaia in 1847 (see Radde 1865: 51–61). Having set up camp above the Batagol River, Alibert hired Soiot men and their reindeer from Khonchon River as porters. In later years, Soiot herders and their reindeer were hired to transport countless Soviet geological expeditions. Although an eyesore to many Soiot elders, today's corporate gold mines employ younger Soiot men, while at the same time moving tons of often contaminated soil and poisoning the fish in a number of streams.

Although Oka has long been known for its rich mineral deposits, the region has been much less at the center of early ethnographic focus. Few explorers of the tsarist period ever ventured directly into the territory, which explains the lack of prerevolutionary depictions of Soiot life. Commissioned to explore the Saian Mountains in 1772, German naturalist Peter Simon Pallas found them inaccessible, and he soon returned to Krasnoiarsk (Henze and Pallas 1967: xii). A survey of nineteenth- and early twentieth-century explorers' maps and itineraries for south-central Siberia reveals how travel routes repeatedly bypassed Oka on all sides, running instead through eastern Tyva, northern and northwestern Mongolia, Karagassia in the Irkutsk Governorate, and even through the Tunka Valley of Buriatia. Among the few explorers who did travel into Oka were German naturalist Gustav Radde (1863, 1865: 58), and young geographer, later famed Russian anarchist, Piotr Kropotkin (1867). Radde, who had stayed with Alibert at the mine while studying birds in the area, described Soiots as "nomadic savages" whose lives to him starkly contrasted the cultured ways he had witnessed at the Frenchman's mine. By the time Kropotkin (1867: n.p.) came through Tustuk Valley, Alibert had already abandoned his mine. Not venturing toward the Khonchon River, where Alibert had hired Soiot porters, Kropotkin encountered only a single Soiot man in a yurt at Batagol. As Kropotkin ventured along the Oka River, he saw Tofa (Karagass) moving along the ridges above Buriat camps. He reasoned that in the past Soiots would have done likewise. Yet Kropotkin's actual encounters with local residents were evidently limited to Buriat settlers.

Two decades earlier, in 1848, Finnish scholar Alexander Castren had visited Tofa hunter-herders of Tofalariia who had told him about distant Soiot relatives that had settled in the Tunka Valley. That same year, Castren decided to travel to Tunka, desiring to meet these people for himself. He writes (1856: 396–397):

> These [Soiots], according to legend, once lived in the Verkhneudinsk District [Tofalariia] on the Sikir River, but later migrated to Tunka where they split into two branches, of which the one resides in the mountains on rivers Oka, Gargan, Halbi, and Hoshun, while the other [branch] stays in the flatlands of the Buriat Ulus of Bukha-Gorkhon. . . . The Steppe Soiots are nowadays pure Buriats, while the Mountain-Soiots remain in part faithful to the practices of their ancestors . . . Not long ago Mountain-Soiots are said to have spoken the same Turkic dialect as the Karagass. . . . [b]ut in regard to Samoyed ancestry of Soiots, all memory has disappeared . . .

As one of few scholar-explorers who encountered Soiots outside of Uriankhai [Tyva], Castren nevertheless failed to venture up the rivers he describes as the homeland of Mountain-Soiots. Thus it seems Castren himself never encountered the men and women who are most likely the ancestors of present day Oka-Soiots.

The first scholar to conduct work specifically with Oka-Soiots, albeit just after the revolution, was Swiss-born Russian anthropologist and archaeologist Bernhard Eduardovich Petri (1884–1937). Based at the University of Irkutsk, Petri amassed both archaeological and ethnographic data for several indigenous peoples of southern Siberia, including Tofas. In 1926, he ventured into Oka for the first time. Together with his colleagues, and in the service of the Soviet Northern Committee (Rus. *komitet severa*), he visited all known Soiot settlements while conducting a systematic demographic medical survey (Petri 1927a: 12–20). With the exception of a "preliminary" report (Petri 1927a), all detailed results, including his personal archives, are believed lost. His preliminary report provides a glimpse into the locations of Soiot households, their composition, and stock ratios in the mid to late 1920s prior to complete collectivization by the Soviet state. Given the lack of prerevolutionary data on Soiots, historians, anthropologists, and archaeologists have relied on materials from neighboring regions in their efforts to reconstruct earlier Soiot lifeways. In what follows, I will rely on the work of Pavlinskaia (2002: 27–34) who brings together in her work several of the sources speaking to the complicated developments in the demographic composition of the Eastern Saian Mountains.

Near Oka's regional center, located on the Zhombolok River, there is an archaeological site that Buriat archaeologist Bair B. Dashibalov dates to between 3000 and 2000 BCE (2000: 4–6). Historian Sevian Vainshtein (1980b: 69, 87) and archaeologist Valeri Chernetsov (1973: 12) were convinced this site was once inhabited by the easternmost proto-Samoyed tribes belonging to the Finno-Ugrian Samoyed branch of the Uralic language family. But the picture is further complicated by discoveries of Samoyed material culture infused with a series of Tungus features along the central and upper Enisei River. Museologist Natalia Prytkova (1970: 54) and Vainshtein (1980b: 87) interpreted these finds as a blend of early Tungus peoples with Samoyed in-migrants who would have lived here as early as the Neolithic Age. By the Bronze Age (2000 to 1000 BCE), signs of semi-settlement and pastoralism, including cattle, sheep, and horses for meat production appear. Archaeologist Mikhail Kosarev (1991: 22–23) describes yet another wave of Samoyedic peoples populating the Saian Region, this time familiar with pastoralism, at the time of the early Iron Age (1000 BCE to 1000 CE).

A series of toponyms found in both Eastern Tyva and Tofalariia suggest that as the Hun Empire expanded, Ket-speaking people arrived in the Saians (Alekseenko 1980: 129). It would seem that although Samoyeds may have had a stronger presence, Ket and ancient indigenous Tungus populations were present at the same time. Anthropologist Maxim Levin and famous linguist Glafira Vasilevich (1951: 63–87) saw these later populations as introducing the domestication of reindeer to the Tozhu region of eastern Tyva, as well as to Tofalariia and Oka, thus enabling local Samoyed and Tungusic peoples to migrate further into the northern taiga. At the same time, these diverse peoples must have come together to form what linguist Valentin Rassadin (1971: 93–94) saw as a common "southern Samoyedic" language, incorporating both Ket and Evenk (Tungus) elements. In this view, Southern Samoyedic would have served as a foundation for contemporary Tofa and Tozhu languages.

Although pastoralism is likely to have come to the Saians around 500 BCE, it may well have been introduced to Western Tyva as early as 1000 BCE along with the arrival of early Indo-Iranian mobile populations (Pavlinskaia 2002: 30). Turkic peoples of Central Asia, to whom are attributed the ancient rock engravings found along the Oka River, are most likely to have introduced pastoralism to the Saians, their language influencing local speech as early as the second half of the first millennium (Pavlinskaia 2002: 30; V.I. Rassadin 1971: 96). Seventh-century Chinese Tan-Shu texts refer to "Duba" tribes located in Duba, Milige, and Echzhi *aimags* (districts) that likely encompass present-day Tozhu, Tofa, and Oka territories, all part of the Turkic Khanate at the time (Pavlinskaia 2002: 31–32). These Tan-Shu sources speak of Duba as having no calendar, cattle, or agriculture, living in tree bark shelters and possessing large numbers of good horses.

By the eighth century, the Uighur take over the Turkic Khanate from Altai to Manchuria, and after 750 CE central and western Tyva and the Khakass fell to them as well (Bichurin 1950: 355). Not much is said about the residents of the Saians during this time, but their furs appear in Chinese registers via taxes collected by Uighur rulers (Pavlinskaia 2002: 33). We know from archaeologist Leonid Kyzlasov that by the ninth century mobile tribes from the Saians joined the Khakass in battle against the Uighur, which may confirm that the Saian Mountains were under Uighur taxation (1969: 93). A powerful government, backed by Imperial China, emerged under the Khakass and its envoys gave gifts of Eastern Saian sable and chipmunk to the emperor (Bichurin 1950: 352). By the thirteenth century, the Khakass government weakened and a new Mongolian power rose under Ghengis Khan, which soon included the Saians, the inhabitants of which were now referred to as "forest peoples" along with all other southern Siberians under Mongol rule (Pavlinskaia 2002: 33). Several crushed uprisings mark this period, during which local populations repeatedly withdrew into Mongolia (Kyzlasov 1969: 135–37). For Pavlinskaia (2002: 33), this demographic mobility helps explain why several clan names are shared between Mongolia and the Saians, and why medieval traces of Mongolian are found in the ancestral languages of Tofas and Soiots.

Between the fourteenth and sixteenth centuries, at the time when the Mongol Empire grew weak, the Saians once again fell under the power of the Khakass. The historical record is silent on the Saians for these two centuries, and Pavlinskaia speculates that the peoples encountered by Russians in the Saians of the seventeenth century were formed precisely during this time (2002: 34). By the seventeenth century, the Turkic influence of the preceding centuries culminated in a language shift for Samoyeds, with Tofalars and Soiots joining the Uighur group of Turkic languages (V. I. Rassadin 1971). Meanwhile, the Saians were subjected to two new powers: the Russians and the Manchurians.

A new border divided the two empires following the Treaty of Kiakhta (1727). It ran through the southern flanks of the Saian Mountains, and was lined with border sentry posts (Rus. *karauly*), two of which were located in Oka—one at the mouth of the Zhombolok River and the other at Narin-Kholoiskii in Gargan (Sharastepanov 2008: 9). The Mongolian-speaking Buriat settlers who came to staff these sentry posts quickly established themselves among indigenous Soiot Turkic speakers and eventually pushed for a second language shift in the local population—this time from Turkic-Soiot to Mongolian-Buriat. As Pavlinskaia (2002: 34) points out, it is likely that this shift of the eighteenth and nineteenth centuries progressed so rapidly because of the preexisting linguistic and cultural similarities Soiots shared with Mongolia since the thirteenth century.

Local historian Dashi Sharastepanov (2008: 6–8) describes contemporary Oka-Buriats as the descendants of clans and subclans who had come from the Tunka and Alar' regions. Sent to staff the new border sentry posts, they encountered Soiots belonging to Khaasut, Irkit, and Onkhot clans. We know from historian Bair Dugarov (1983: 97) that these three unrelated clans were at the time living in the mountainous taiga of the upper Oka River. The Khaasut clan is thought to have arrived in Oka first. According to a Sorok elder, the late Dezhida Dambaevich Sonopov, this clan descended from a man by the name of Khuruldai, who had come to Oka from eastern Tyva some eleven generations ago (ca. 360 years). Together with his Uriankhai wife, he had settled near Lake Il'chir, following a disagreement with his relatives in Tyva (Dugarov 1983: 97–98). The Irkit clan emigrated more recently from the village of Zhemchug in Tunka, also settling in the area around Lake Il'chir. Based on the genealogy of Darma Khontoevich Khusaev (b. 1888) of Engorboi in Tunka, Dugarov (1983: 98) establishes that they had come from the shores of Lake Khubsugul to settle in the Tunka Valley before moving into Oka. Finally, the Onkhot clan is said to have originated from among the Bulagats of Prebaikalia at a later time (Sharastepanov 2008: 7). This kaleidoscopic vision of Oka-Soiot origins, in conjunction with subsequent intermarriages between Soiots and Buriat settlers, provides us with some background to contemporary Soiot identity in Oka.

LIFE AT URO

When I first arrived in Oka, I was met by Badma Khorluevich Dondokov, a well-respected Soiot elder in his sixties, working as the representative for indigenous minorities at the regional administration in Orlik. At our first meeting, he was sitting behind his desk on the first floor of the administration building, dressed in a black suit with polished black shoes. In spite of his official attire, it soon became clear that as a hunter and herder, Badma much preferred to be in the forest. Hearing of my hopes to find a Soiot herding family that might take me in for a year of fieldwork, he immediately organized a van and driver to take us around Oka to visit with various families and to see his youngest brother Baianbata at Uro.

Uro is one of many winter pastures (Rus. *zimniki*) strategically positioned among a series of connected valleys and mountain ridges, forming part of a larger transhumant landscape, similar to those found in the European Alps with dairy cattle or the South Asian Himalaya with its yak herds. Uro is a seasonal home to several extended families who herd their stock here from late August until early May. Like all other Uro residents, Baianbata left the valley each year between June and August to migrate his household and stock to his summer pasture (Rus. *letnik*) at higher elevation. Located 1,550 meters above sea level, Uro lies just below its corresponding summer pastures on the Tustuk River, located at 1,700 meters—a long day's hike from the winter pastures. The difference in elevation is sufficient to reduce insects pestering stock, and it allows yak to easily reach pastures at elevations of 2,000 to 2,500 meters.

In August, before the animals are allowed to return to their winter pastures, families come to harvest hay patches around their winter homes in Uro, as well as in a number of inherited spots scattered around other valleys. Once the hay is safely stacked and fenced away, cattle and sheep are returned to Uro. Because families spend a greater number of months at their winter pastures each year, and because warmer summer months require fewer comforts, the winter locations serve as the primary residence for most families. This is evident in slightly more substantial homes, coupled with greater storage capacity for seasonal items. Neither summer nor winter locations had any municipal services during my stay, although Uro was connected to the village of Sorok with a power line, allowing more or less reliable electricity for television sets, light bulbs, mobile phone chargers, milk separators, and a small number of other electrical devices.

On our tour of Oka, I was able to make contact with a number of herding families, but nowhere did the fit seem as ideal as at Uro, where Baianbata (b. 1970) kindly invited me to stay with him, beginning the following autumn. It served him well to have someone at the cabin, since his family had moved to the village for their children's education. Although Baianbata shared much work with his neighboring elder brother Borzhon (b. 1966), it was difficult to be away from his wife and children while herding his yak in the hills near Uro. On a visit to their home in Sorok, his wife, Beligte, told me how she missed having Baianbata by her side. Yet, not only did the children need an education and someone to look after them in the village, Beligte had also taken the job of running the local post office, which came with a government salary that greatly helped make ends meet. In spite of Baianbata's unwillingness to let go of his yak herd for a more settled life, it was not difficult to see Beligte's affection for this man, whom she revered for "maintaining such a strong herd of yak all by himself." Beligte clearly recognized her husband as the master (Rus. *khoziain*) of their household, but given his quiet and reserved manner, I never saw Baianbata assert himself over her in any way.

During his visits to Sorok, Baianbata would help their fifteen-year-old daughter, Andama, with her homework, while his five-year-old daughter, Balma, would sit on his lap or lay beside him watching television. Andama milked the family's two dairy cows and assisted her mother in all other household tasks, ranging from baking bread to cooking supper and cleaning house. Her ten-year-old brother, Dugdan, would be allowed to play with his friends after school, but before long, he too would be called in to complete his chores, which included hauling water, chopping wood, making fire, or peeling potatoes. At Uro, and also at the summer pasture, children learned by watching and participating in their parents' tasks. Boys learned how to drive yak, round up and saddle horses, cut hay, butcher stock, and hunt for game with dogs. In their free time, they fished in local streams and shared their catch with their families. Daughters joined their mothers and elder sisters in milking cows, shearing sheep, knitting with sheep and yak wool, cooking, processing dairy products, and cleaning and preparing intestines after a slaughter.

Illustration 0.1. Borzhon and Ranzhur's home at Uro. Photograph by the author.

The winter pastures at the center of the valley at Uro were divided between two intermarried clans. One of the two clans was headed by Badma Khorluevich Dondokov, the elder who had invited me to the community. In his absence, he was represented by his younger brother Borzhon and wife Ranzhur (b. 1963). The couple shared a house with their son Buinto (b. 1990), daughter Balma (b. 1989), and Balma's two-year-old daughter. Borzhon's adoptive son, Regbi (b. 1984), his wife Norzhima, and their two children lived next door in a newly completed cabin of their own making. Baianbata and I lived in an older house just past Borzhon's winter stables. To the south, across a small stream called Urda-Uro, their youngest brother Vandan (b. 1974) with his wife Ochigma (b. 1980) and their five children resided in the middle of the valley. The Dondokov brothers and their wives frequently visited each other and collaborated on various projects.

The second clan was headed by Aunty Vera (b. 1965), whose husband had passed away, but whose son Tseden (b. 1986) was handling most of his late father's responsibilities. Vera was the sister of Ranzhur, Borzhon's wife, and she lived in one house with her unmarried sons Dagba and Tseden, as well as their disabled sister, Masha. Across the pasture from their house lived Iumzhap (b. 1974) with his wife Tserigma (b. 1983) and their three boys, aged five to nine. A stone's throw to the west lived Tsydyp (b. 1977) with his wife

Dagzama (b. 1981) and their two boys, aged five and ten. Although members of both clans would visit each other, the majority of interhousehold collaboration occurred within rather than between clans. Larger tasks, such as construction projects, stock inoculations, and log preparation were usually accomplished with the help of members from within one's own clan.

The collaborative relationship within each clan could also be seen in the herds each household held. Any given horse group, or yak or sheep herd, was likely to be comprised of animals belonging to other members of the clan. Some of their owners held jobs in the village, lived in Orlik, or had moved to the capital city of Ulan-Ude. If one inherited a herd, it did not mean that one became sole owner of all its head. More likely one became a steward of many animals, some of which belonged to members of the wider clan. Clan members living in the city could come to pick up their riding horses at Uro to go hunting in autumn, and often all the sheep and horses of one clan were held together during the summer. Because of the free-roaming nature of yak herds and horse groups, much of the conversation during visits between households was concerned with the location of animals in the landscape.

At Uro, households were centered on a main residence, usually a log cabin or wooden house with a brick-built stove used for cooking, baking, and heating located in the center. Thin boarded walls or curtains divided the living space into quarters for parents, children, and other kin, each sharing a section of the rear hearth wall for warmth. The cooking side of the hearth would open up to a kitchen space where all meals were prepared and bread baked. A lean-to, or separate front room, served as storage space for hunting and herding equipment and as a meat cellar in winter. A boarded outhouse and log cabin-style wash house were located twenty to thirty meters from each residence. Wash houses had a steel stove on which to heat water for the family's weekly bath and laundry session for which water would be hauled from the river in buckets suspended from a wooden yoke. Firewood was brought from neat stacks of up to twenty cubic meters of ready-chopped larch, prepared by the family in April, harvested from government allotted sections in the forest.

Wooden corrals were built adjacent to or immediately onto log-style stables with grass sod roofs, housing sheep and cattle during the coldest months of the year. Many corrals consisted of two or more rectangular or round forcing pens for the sorting of horses and cattle, usually with an attached milking pen. A straight single-file chute connected corrals for biannual stock inoculations. Sheep pens were positioned in view of residence windows to protect against wolves and they were movable to prevent foot rot. The harvestable pasture surrounding the compound sometimes had a wooden fence around it. Most summer compounds were similar in design, although families usually shared a single room without dividers, and their stoves were not as sophisticated.

When Uro's residents left for the summer, they did so in staggered fashion to prevent livestock from mingling, as each household set out in direction of their respective summer pastures. Combined, ten of Uro's households owned roughly 465 cattle and yak, 173 horses, 155 sheep, 15 goats, 23 dogs, and 32 chickens. Establishing these figures was not easy, as people considered it improper to speak about the number of stock one owns, especially in relation to yak and hybrids. This may have been considered a kind of superstition. By numbering one's stock, it would be exposed to greater danger in what were already volatile conditions, considering predation and sickness. At the same time, silence about numbers prevented people from comparing each other's property. Additionally, some herders seemed to keep disclosed and undisclosed counts, allowing them to minimize fees arising from mandatory inoculations without which it was illegal to sell meat. A certain number of yaks could thus be hidden in the mountains during a zoo technician's visit. With all disclosed stock inoculated, undisclosed animals could rejoin the heard once the veterinary workers had left.

When all residents returned from the summer pastures in August, many of the school children would be with their families for the hay harvest, causing the valley's population to swell for a short time. Between 2013 and 2014, Uro experienced a low of thirty-three residents and a high of sixty-nine across twelve households. The swell served as a happy reunion after summer migration, which

Illustration 0.2. Moving a horse group to summer pasture. Photograph by the author.

had taken each household in a different direction. In summer, people became part of a different community, a fact everyone seemed to look forward to. While the winter valley was more densely populated, some of the summer pastures rendered households somewhat more isolated. Visits between camps became all the more important with some residents preferring the sociality of their summer residence to that of their winter residence. Summer was generally associated with a better atmosphere, greater joy, and perhaps less strained relations.

AN ANTHROPOLOGICAL APPROACH

The methodology of anthropological fieldwork differs in many ways from other disciplines involving empirical field research. As a qualitative researcher, I was primarily interested in long-term observations of animal-human interactions achieved by way of triangulation. It is one thing to watch someone interact with an animal, and then to write down this observation. Triangulation, by contrast, calls for repeated long-term cross-checking of such observations. To prevent misinterpretation or misrepresentation, the field-worker must interview the participants, which often involves going over previously taken field notes together with them. In some cases, this can be done by recording an interaction on video and watching the footage step-by-step with the actors later on. During this process, further notes of clarification or correction can be made.

At the same time, the anthropologist will be interviewing and observing similar processes in different locations and with different individuals, allowing for a comparative element. This comparative work yields insight into regional variation, while it can also serve as a corrective, identifying initial misunderstanding. Another way of comparison comes through a detailed study of ethnographic literature from neighboring areas. As cultural practices usually come to be shared across neighboring populations, certain continuities will come to the fore. A third research strand takes place in archives: here the field-worker consults every available historical record that links to consultants' accounts, providing yet another context for observed contemporary animal-human practices.

Finally, what makes the ethnographic method such a strong approach is its recursiveness, enabled by a researcher's long-term stay in a community. What is meant by recursion is that similar events are witnessed more than once, often over the course of a whole year (i.e., in different seasons) and in different social contexts. As the field-worker takes note of these events in different contexts, ever more nuances emerge. A new detail helps inform future inquiry, while it also enables the observer to recalibrate past recordings. By deliberately working in this recursive manner, the ethnographer is able to work out details that would not become evident during a single short-term visit.

As an anthropologist, my work is not that of a trained ethologist or other animal expert. At no point in this book do I aim to make any claims regarding the intentions of animals. As a student of human culture, I aim to relay the perspectives of the people I worked and lived with in regard to the animals with whom they shared their lives. In some cases, I also convey my own experiences and interpretations of animal behavior. But in no case do I aim to explain animal actions from a scientific perspective.

What has set anthropological work apart from many other disciplines involving fieldwork is participant observation. Anthropologists observe the participation of others in activities, but will also participate in many of these activities themselves. Thus the description of events is informed by a kind of immersive technique, which in some cases can amount to apprenticing. For an ethnography of animal-human relations, this is a very important aspect. Field-workers seek not only to learn about animal-human relations but also to experience these connections through their own bodies by engaging with animals and landscapes.

The fieldwork that informs this book relies on these and other classical anthropological methods. In order to live as closely to my collaborators as possible, I lived in the home of Baianbata at Uro for the majority of my fieldwork. This allowed me to share in his life rhythm as a herder, observing and participating in many of his and his brothers' interactions with the animals of their households. It also gave me a base from where to visit other herders in the valley. After establishing rapport, usually by way of a relative's introduction (which included an explanation of who I was and what I was trying to learn), I would offer to help with household chores such as cleaning out stables. As my relationships grew with neighboring households through repeated daytime visits, I would be able to ask more questions to accompany my observations and experiences of daily activities.

During the later part of my fieldwork, I brought my own family into the field. Together with my spouse and our two sons, we were offered a small cabin at Uro that had belonged to Aunty Vera's late parents. By living in this cabin, we effectively joined her extended household. In the following summer, we migrated with Vera's household to one of her son's family's summer pastures on Tustuk River. These arrangements enabled us to live as a nuclear family unit, while being in daily contact with the larger clan to whom belonged the summer shelter in which we stayed for that season. These arrangements enabled us to keep a few chickens of our own, while exchanging meat and milk for canned foods, which we had brought with us. Primarily, however, we paid for our family's accommodation and our meat and milk share through a monthly fee our families had previously agreed on.

CHAPTER 1

MIRRORED HOMES

A fine blue-grey mist had formed over the grassy hills on both sides of the valley. It was ten thirty at night in mid-May, and the sun had long disappeared beyond the western mountains. I began to wonder where Borzhon was. He had promised to pick me up for his nightly roundup. Another ten minutes passed. The wooden door to my kitchen space opened and into the light from above my table stepped Borzhon. As usual, he greeted me with a quiet smile to which I responded in like manner. I slipped into my black rubber boots, flung on a jacket, and followed him into the dusk. Borzhon had come on his horse. We crossed the Urda-Uro, the stream from where I gathered my water, and headed into the hills. I walked, he rode.

After a short while, we could make out movement on the steep, dark hillside above us. Furry bodies of a large herd were calmly moving in deep grass, their shaggy white tails gently swaying in the cool night. Trying not to startle them, we approached the scattered herd from behind, staying as calm as we could. I had anticipated a much longer search in the darkening hills, but without a horse at my disposal, I was glad to know Burzhon's five dozen yak (*harlag*) and hybrids (*khainak*) had not moved any farther that day. Slowly descending in occasional switchbacks behind the heavy herd, I kept glancing over to Borzhon who was riding back and forth along the slope to collect stragglers. Several of the recently born yak would come up close to inspect me, then leap back and run to rejoin the herd. Fourteen had been born so far that season, but Borzhon had already lost one to the wolves two days earlier.

On our descent to the corrals, I noticed two dams feeding their young—neither of them fazed by our stampede. Coming from behind, Borzhon swiftly galloped past them as if they had escaped his notice. Some time later, with the animals safely corralled for the night, Borzhon invited me in for a late night tea with Ranzhur's meat and noodle soup. I was curious as to how difficult some of the more extensive nightly roundups could be. But Borzhon assured me, "It's not difficult, unless a dam is having a calf. After birth, a dam fiercely defends her young. She won't allow anyone or anything near it. You can't move her then." The dams we had left behind that night clearly fell into this category. Being close enough to the valley, they would be able to descend in their own time if they chose.

In winter, Borzhon's yak would roam as far as Uro's former reindeer camp on the upper reaches of the Urda-Uro—about an hour's ride on horseback. On their own they would roam no farther, unless they had been startled by bears, in which case they might cross the mountains into the faraway Iakhoshop Valley. From here it could take Borzhon and his sons, Regbi and Buinto, several days to locate and return them. In summer, when Borzhon moved his household and all their stock to pasture at higher altitude, his yak would wander as far as the northernmost summer camp on the upper reaches of Sorok River. Here they could climb to an altitude of 2,400 meters, and Borzhon and his sons would ride out to the herd every night to drive them back to their corrals at the summer camp.

According to Borzhon, "Yak never return home on their own at night, unless one keeps their young at camp." As had been the case with reindeer, this practice enabled people to better control lactation and maintain a milking schedule. "But not these days. No one milks them now." Curious as to what might have led to the change, I asked Borzhon about it. He looked at me in amusement and replied, "Haven't you seen their small teats? With Mongolian dairy cows around, it makes no sense to milk yak." Indeed, yak, like reindeer, are relatively cumbersome to milk. They resist the process and produce little more than is required for the growth of their own offspring (see Wiener et al. 2003: 136).

Independently roaming the hills and coming "home" only when necessitated by a herder, I was left wondering how householders like Borzhon positioned their yak on a wild-domestic continuum. Intending to provoke a discussion, I committed the classical interviewer's sin by asking a leading question in Russian: "Are these yak wild (*dikie*) or domestic (*domashnee*) animals?" Bound by the narrowness of our common language, Borzhon replied: "They are domesticates, of course" [Rus. *oni iavliaiutsia domashnymi, konechno*]. Then he justified his categorization using very practical terms: "I feed them supplementary hay every morning all through the winter."

Indeed, not all householders did this. Not even his younger brother Baianbata supplemented his yak with hay, except in catastrophic years when the snow crusted so much that even animals of the forest were dying of starvation. As if dissatisfied with the simplistic notion of domestic, Borzhon later qualified his response. Yes, he drove them home every day. Yes, he fed them regularly and, obliged by the law, he had them vaccinated annually. They were no strangers to the corral, even if yak had historically not been held in corrals (see

Vainshtein 1980a: 78). But, he insisted, "These animals are entirely independent of humans. If I left them to fend for themselves, they would do just fine!" To say the least, a can of worms had been opened for me that night in Borzhon's kitchen: How were ideas of wild, tame, and domestic to be understood in this landscape?

* * *

In this chapter, I will approach this can of worms from two angles. After briefly examining the Western concept of the household, or domus, I will illustrate how the Soiot household positions itself within a wider landscape as it mirrors the work and affairs of local spirit-mastered households. I mention the Western concept here because I believe that it is more nuanced than we often make it out to be. At the heart of this reflective process lies the attribution of sentience to all beings as well as the need to maintain reciprocal balance in all one's relations with them. Second, I examine what happens when members of the spirit household in Oka cross over to the human household and vice versa. Here I draw special attention to some of the differences that exist between these two domains and how moving back and forth between spirit and human households may result in a kind of perceptual expansion. This second part reiterates the root argument of this book, namely, Oka householders rely on their animals' ability to recognize and benefit from resources wild and tame.

PERSPECTIVES ON THE DOMUS

The well-known British philologist Walter W. Skeat tells us in his Concise Dictionary of English Etymology (1993) that the adjective domestic derives from the Latin *domesticus*. The latter refers to "belonging to a household," which comes from the old Greek domus (δόμος) "a house" (1993: 123). Classical scholars Kate Cooper (2007: 4) and Moses Finley (1973: 58) tell us that in the Roman context the idea of the domus included animals and slaves among other property. Becoming the property of such a household is what is meant by domestication, a kind of "accustoming to home," according to Webster's Dictionary (1913). For the philologist (Skeat 1993: 123) this accustoming procedure must logically precede any kind of "belonging," suggesting mere presence within the house does not constitute domesticity. Instead, a kind of habit in relation to place as home must be formed first.

What the English language accomplishes in its suffix -ation—as in domestication—the Russian achieves by way of its prefix o-, as in *o-domashnenie* (domestication). The prefix describes the process of something or someone turning into something—in this case into a domestic entity. But a more commonly used Russian word for domestication is *priruchenie* (taming), which does not mention the domus at all. While taming refers to a change in an animal's behavior, the Russian *priruchenie* emphasizes proximity. Pri- indicates approximation to something, and the root word *ruchenie* comes from *ruka* (hand). Taming in this sense is a matter of bringing something close to the hand and not necessarily to the house, which is precisely what happens when young reindeer are habituated to their human owners' scent by licking salt from their hands.

If domesticity can be expressed through proximity to humans, then how important is the actual house to the household? The Oxford Dictionary (Stevensen, Waite 2011) describes the "household" as a "house and its occupants," both of which are "regarded as a unit." Classicists also confirm (e.g., Saller 1984) the connection between people, animals, and place or buildings in the Roman understanding of the domus. Although based on a transhumant lifestyle, Buriat and Mongolian herding cultures similarly congregate their animals around built structures, even if these are mobile yurts and seasonal stables (see Marchina 2015). In contrast, however, mobile households in this region are not seen as fenced-in units, but as what anthropologist Natasha Fijn calls ecosocial spheres in which encampments serve as focal points dotted throughout a larger landscape (2011: 55). The notion of movable focal points in an open landscape also fits Oka where taiga hunting intersects with herding techniques borrowed from the steppe.

Rather than focusing on the residential structure (i.e., the house) as the center of the household, there are two pivots that form the core from which all domestic activities and relations emanate in Oka. The summer and winter hearths are the domain of the wife in the transhumant home, and the horse hitching posts (Bur. *serge*) outside a family's summer and winter abodes are the symbolic center of male leadership (Galdanova 2009). The *serge* is a highly ritualized site, relating to the male domain of horses and horse training, and it is placed on the south side of the human residence facing the entrance (Zaksheeva 2009: 48). These two locations form the loci from which the household fans in and out of the landscape according to season. Fire and *serge* mark the focal points of a set of stratified relations, headed by the masters of the household. At Uro, Borzhon was such a master, with Ranzhur by his side, together overseeing the relations of their extensive household.

Interestingly, the Russian term for master (*khoziain*) forms the root for the word household (*khoziaistvo*). The suffix *-stvo*, when attached to master, will turn the word into the collective noun masterhood, which is the word used for household. This is not unlike English where the household is literally a house held by a householder. In Buriat, *ezen* or *ezhen* refers to master, owner, or possessor, and it must be connected with the word for house—*ger*—to form house owner, or *gerei ezen*. However, in Oka a master is best known on the basis of his or her herds rather than the ownership of a particular house.

Illustration 1.1. Brick oven and bark floor. Photograph by the author.

In the Roman context, the domus belonged to a master known as the dominus, or proprietor, who assigned members of the household a place within its asymmetrical power structure. Scholars have diverged on whether this power asymmetry of the domus was defined by domination, as suggested by Louis Dumont (1970), or by a more nuanced process in which it relied on a household member's recognition of a specific authority (e.g., Cooper 2007: 7; Gregory 1997: 7–8). Historically, domination in this context has been defined as "the power of the master (dominus) over things (dominium, 'property rights'), and even more, the power of the master over the slave (potestas dominica)" (Vasilu 2004: 227). Such a rigid application of dominance in the household seems to diverge from Soiot conceptions of masterhood.

However, scholars like Kate Cooper (2007: 7) have critically reassessed the application of such dominance even in the classical dominus: "Although a hierarchical relationship was asymmetrical where power was concerned, the ideal of reciprocity required that recognition of both authority and accountability be symmetrical. If symmetrical recognition was withheld by the inferior partner, the superior partner's standing was accordingly undermined."

Here Cooper offers a much more nuanced understanding of power in the hands of the dominus. Although the Roman domus differs from the Soiot household in several regards, Cooper's approach to power does strike a chord with the concept and application of mastery in Oka.

SPIRIT- AND HUMAN-MASTERED HOUSEHOLDS

The Soiot idea of the household head, or *ezhen,* parallels the concept of local master spirits who also are known as *ezhen*. In Russian, these spirits are often referred to as *khoziaeva mestnosti* (masters of a place). Their mastery is expressed in maintaining balance in the social relations of persons within the physical landscape under their auspices. Ethnographic descriptions of people seeing the spirit world as a reflection of the physical world go back to the very annals of anthropological observation (e.g., Tylor 1873). In many societies with relational epistemology, the spirit world constitutes part of the social universe engaged by humans (e.g., Bird-David 1999: 77, Harvey 2006: 9). In the context of such worldviews, we find another widely subscribed understanding, often referred to as relational personhood. In contrast to individual personhood, which is emphasized in Euro-American contexts, relational personhood can emerge from association with humans, objects, locations, animals, and spirits (e.g., Fowler 2016: 398). As such, relational personhood is ever in flux. Objects, such as stones, may temporarily attain the status of a person, enabling others to relate to them. For many indigenous Inner Asian taiga dwellers, personhood is rooted in the ability to respond to spirits, animals, and the forest (e.g., Fraser 2010: 328). This is true also, to varying degrees, for many Soiots and Tofas of the Eastern Saians.

The spirit master governs nonhuman persons living within a territory, thereby forming the equivalent of a human household. Presiding over a specific area, a master spirit may be encountered in any of his or her household members, roaming or standing (as may be the case for a tree) within that territory. In a similar manner, freely wandering yak or reindeer can be traced to their human master. Like the spirit master of the forest, whom one may encounter for example in a bear, a wolf, a deer, or a fish, the human master of a herd is said to be reflected in the demeanor of the animals he or she owns. In other words, the character of the head of the human household is mirrored in the temperament of his or her animals.

The relationship human and spirit masters have with their household members is marked by a sense of autonomous sentience extended to all its members. Masters and household members understand that all sentient beings within their reach possess a degree of volitional freedom on which they may act, no matter their hierarchical position vis-à-vis another. This extension of autonomy secures a degree of unpredictability in all relations, and it resonates with Cooper's "recognition of authority and accountability" (2007: 7) among members of the Roman domus. Rather than ruling household members by domination, the Soiot *ezhen*—as much as the Roman dominus—must hold together the household, trusting that its members will accept his or her authority. In part, this relational trust is earned through the successful balancing work of spirit and human masters.

One way to describe this balancing work is by looking at economic transactions that occur within and between human and spirit households. A local master spirit provides for the members of his or her own household, but he or she can also respond to the needs of human masters and their dependents by sending animal gifts to human hunters. Where this occurs, the spirit household engages in a reciprocal exchange that is answered by gifts coming from the human household. While both human and spirit masters operate in the same landscape, each possesses its own physical and independent locus from which to observe the movements of its own, as well as each others' animals.

Local spirit masters are known by their focal points in the landscape, which are usually prominent land features, such as rocky outcrops, freshwater springs, mountain passes, or ravines. In the human household, these loci find their correspondence in the hearth and horse hitching posts. Neither spirit nor human masters are bound to these points, and both move about freely in their dealings with animal property, often overlapping each other's operational radii.

Although the focal points of spirit masters are positioned toward forested habitats, and the foci of human households stand in relation to pastures, animals of either household are seen as belonging to herds. All herds belong to a master who looks after them. In Buriat *agaha(n)* is used to refer to animals as cattle. The term *adagalkha* means "to put on fetters" and *adaglakha* "to watch over," "track," "follow," or "look after." Both spirit and human masters look after or check in on their animals in similar ways. In spite of these parallels, people differentiate between the herds of spirit and human masters, particularly where the same species is kept in both households.

In Buriat-speaking Oka, this differentiation between human- and spirit-owned animals is perhaps best reflected in an animal's linguistic relation to the forest. Spirit- and human-owned animals may both roam the forest, but both are not "of the forest." In the trans-Himalaya region (e.g., Wilson and Reeder, eds. 2005: 690–91), wild yak (*Bos mutus*) are known to roam and interbreed with domestic yak (*Bos grunniens*). In Oka, by contrast, there were no wild or feral yak during my stay. Similarly, no horses were known to roam entirely free of human claim. Thus people did not differentiate between domestic and wild yak or horses on a daily basis. However, they did make a distinction if a type of animal had a counterpart in the spirit master's household.

As we learn from linguist Valentin Rassadin (1996: 53–55), goats and reindeer are among such animals. In Buriat, wild goats (Siberian ibex) and domestic goats are both known as *iamaan*. To differentiate between the two, *oin* is attached to the wild variant. *Oin* stands for "of the forest," and *mal* refers to "cattle." A wild goat doe is thus known as *oin eme iamaan*, and a domestic doe is known simply as *eme iamaan*. Wild reindeer are *oin sagaan* and domestic reindeer *mal sagaan*. Hence, *mal sagaan* are "cattle reindeer," *oin sagaan* "forest reindeer," and *oin iamaan* "forest goats." The forest-cattle differentiation seems to be a Buriat introduction, as nondomestic reindeer used to be known as *ak-an* in Soiot (Rassadin 2003, Rassadin 2005).

Independent of the diverse linguistic distinctions that have existed between human- and spirit-owned herds in the history of Oka, animals regularly moved back and forth between spirit and human households during my fieldwork. When they did so, however, they were usually dead. Their bodies would be conferred by the spirit master to a hunter in the form of gifted game. Conversely, an animal sacrifice could be made to a spirit master by a herder-hunter. In a less voluntary manner, the spirit master could also claim stock from a human master by way of predators. Somewhat less often, living animals crossed from one household to another. This was usually in the form of domestic reindeer straying from the domestic herd to mate with wild reindeer, thus enlarging the spirit master's herd. Least common were accounts of forest animals joining the herd of a human master. Yet, it is this transition that we have in mind, conventionally, when we speak of initial domestication.

Indeed, the transition of an animal from a wild herd to a domestic herd would seem more straightforward in a setting where wild herds frequently intersect with the animals of free-roaming human households. Reindeer specialist and veterinarian Sergei Kertselli (1925), who spent much of his professional life studying northern Soviet reindeer breeding, argued that the so-called Karagass (Tofa) breed in the Eastern Saians was not only the tallest but also least picky eater, making it the "most domesticated" of all Siberian reindeer breeds. Such domestic features are suggestive of a longstanding heritage of interaction between reindeer and humans in the region, and the fact that domestic animals have bred with wild animals for so long hints at the possibility for a domestic strain, even in wild populations.

PROXIMITY AND NEGOTIATION

The vignette of Burzhon's yak herd points to at least two defining factors in most, if not all, Soiot human-animal relations. First, these relations are defined by fluctuation of proximity between humans and animals (Stépanoff et al. 2017). Second, they are characterized by ongoing negotiation of intentions between species. These two characteristics are indicative of a nuanced approach taken to animals in Oka, an approach that cannot be explained simply by using a wild-tame, either-or dichotomy, even though such a dichotomy was well known to my interlocutors whose languages accommodated such notions.

The view that proximity and negotiation co-produce open and context-related human-animal relations in the Saians pushes back boundaries imposed by language, in this case by Russian and Buriat. It focuses on how often silent herders and hunters interact with animals beneath the terminology that has come to describe their interactions linguistically. Hence, we cannot take for granted that what things are called necessarily corresponds to what things are known to be in practice. Like horses, reindeer, and other species, a yak may be considered domestic, yet spend little time near humans. On the other hand, select animals from a herd may seasonally spend quite a lot of their time near humans for tracking, milking, riding, or transportation purposes.

Recent work on ancient genomes of domestic and "wild" *takhi*, or Przewalski's horses, of Central Asia shows the latter are not actually wild in origin. Instead, *takhi* found roaming in parts of Mongolia are suggested to be feral descendants of horses herded by the Eneolithic Botai culture of northern Kazakhstan, known as the earliest site of horse domestication anywhere (approx. 5,500 years ago) (Gaunitz et al. 2018). These findings suggest not only relatively close proximity between feral and herded animals, but also that crossbreeding would have taken place between populations, further complicating our understanding of the domestication of horses.

In Oka, proximity between humans and animals is crucial in that it perpetually fluctuates, as the result of immediate and unforeseeable circumstances, due to routine seasonal changes or as the result of long-term historical events. Wolf and bear sightings help a herder anticipate possible herd displacement, and they serve as an example of immediate circumstances affecting the distance between householders and animals. Startling followed by displacement not only affects the nature and distance of a herder's routine movements toward the animals, it can also affect the animals' behavior upon their return to the herder's household, as can be seen in horses after they have been attacked by wolves.

By contrast, regular seasonal fluctuations in distance and interactive intensity between animals and householders are more predictable. For instance, in early spring pregnant yak will hide in the hills to give birth in seclusion, avoiding all contact with humans. Riding horses are released for the winter in autumn, marking the end of a season of close collaboration with their owners. During these times people see much less of their animals, but they usually have a good idea of where to find them within their ranges. Conversely, with the opening of the hunting season in autumn, the proximity between humans and dogs, reindeer, game, and even wolves decreases significantly. Such fluctuations of proximity and communicative intensity are part of predictable seasonal changes in the landscape.

Interruptions or changes to these seasonal routines occur when socioeconomic circumstances lead to changes in the economic importance of a particular species. Often such shifts affect long term changes in the relationship people have with a type of animal. The introduction of Mongolian cows is a case in point. Locals referred to their dairy cattle as Mongolian cows, which belong to a hardy, if diverse, species with a long genetic history in Inner Asia and beyond, valued for their ability to live in harsh climatic environments (Mannen et al. 2004). The subsequent emergence of dairy cattle hybrids (yak-cattle mixed offspring), profoundly impacted the amount of physical contact people enjoyed with yaks through their daily milking. Similarly, the collapse of prices for sable and squirrel furs affected human-dog relations to the point of changing emphasis in how dogs were bred and trained. This included *soboliatnitsy* (Rus.), or sable hunting dogs.

The other aspect touched upon here is negotiation. Both humans and animals perpetually negotiate each other's intentions, no matter the seasonal distance. As I will explore below, domination by brute force is not a common way in Oka to relate to animals, whether animals are located far or near the household. Borzhon did not drive his yak as much as he solicited them to move in the direction he intended for them. Such solicitation can amount to outright co-commitment in humans and animals as they jointly engage in tasks that may be perceived as rewarding to both parties (see Stépanoff 2012). Such forms of collaboration are generally negotiated rather than forced, and they are seen to grow in intensity and efficacy over time and with practice.

In either case, communication of intentions always relies on movement, maneuvering, and utilization of various material implements, including environmental and architectural features. These non-verbal, often corporeal negotiations are rarely a one-sided endeavor; both humans and animals make use of modalities in their own communicative styles. Borzhon's yak, much like other species, such as wolves or horses, read and interpreted his maneuvers, responding with their own. The outcome of such negotiations never seems entirely predictable, which lends a degree of openness to all human-animal relations I have observed and recorded in Oka.

MORE THAN LINEAR—MORE THAN HUMAN

It is this openness that lies at the heart of my argument: domestication relationships should be seen not merely as a matter of hereditary and unidirectional morphological adaptation, but also as a matter of ongoing fluctuation in communicative intensity. In the Saians, as perhaps in other mountainous taiga environments, domestication relationships involve the relational potential of a species, which is called upon when an animal's proximity to another species is reduced over time. The wax of communicative intensity that results from close proximity between two entities will wane again as the distance between them increases. Thus, familiarity and communicative intensity must be reestablished periodically in humans and animals. We will witness seasonal reaffirmation in chapter 5 using the example of the annual horse round-up. An example of a more historical re-establishment between species can be seen in the reintroduction of reindeer herding to Oka, described in chapter 3. On both scales—seasonal and historical—we observe the effect of distance on interspecies relations in a particular geographic context.

In a more general sense, Western science has understood plant and animal domestication as processes that revolutionized human social development and enabled the formation of civilizations. We thus speak of a Neolithic Revolution; a term coined by archaeologist Gordon Childe (1892–1957). In his view, "Neolithic societies began deliberately co-operating with nature to increase the productivity of edible plants and to protect and foster the multiplication of animals that yield food as meat, blood, or milk" (Childe 1958: 34). Childe himself was less invested in the revolutionary aspect of his own term than were many subsequent archaeologists (e.g., Lien et al. 2018). Although his idea of "cooperating with nature" does provide some space for the notion of mutuality, or nonsingular intentionality, Childe's emphasis lies largely on human intention. This emphasis has stood at the heart of most official definitions of domestication ever since.

The United Nations Convention on Biological Diversity reads, "'domesticated or cultivated species' means species in which the evolutionary process has been influenced by humans to meet their needs" (1992: 3). This official definition reflects a conventional Western stance toward the role of humans in the world at large. While it is inherently anthropocentric, it does not sum up all of the ways in which human-animal relations and domestication have been understood, even in the West. Certainly in the Saian Mountains, where not only humans are known to run households, domestication relationships do not begin or end with human intentions alone.

Childe chose the term "revolution" to describe a very lengthy and less than well-understood process, which he never intended to describe as abrupt, and neither was he certain at what point one might speak of its zenith (Childe 1958: 39). Childe's cumulative perspective of domestication thus leaves room for a degree of nonlinearity. However, we are reminded by anthropologist Rebecca Cassidy, emphasis in traditional definitions of domestication has been on "distinguishing between discrete states characterized by fixed properties" (2007: 11). In other words, historically it has been assumed that a linear course could be plotted for the morphological transformation in a species from the wild to the domestic stage.

Perhaps one of the earliest manifestations of this linear thinking is found in the three-stage theory of ancient Roman scholar Marcus Terentius Varro (116–27 BCE) and Neoplatonic philosopher Porphyry (234–305 CE), who proposed that hunting and gathering were replaced by pastoralism, which in turn would give way to agriculture, while maintaining elements of both previous models (Kramer 1967: 73). German ethnologist Eduard Hahn (1896) was one of the first outspoken critics of this approach showing how various "stages" could occur at the same time, as well as out of sequence, making them not really stages at all (Isaac 1970: 6). The seeds for rethinking the linearity and anthropocentricity of domestication have thus been with us for a long time.

Historically, in anthropology there have existed rather divergent approaches to domestication. Some—among them the zooarchaeologist Juliet Clutton-Brock (1989: 7)—have framed domestication as a socio-economic and biological event, triggered by human intention, and as a relationship in which the nonhuman animal becomes subject to exploitation through human commodification and ownership. More recently, scholars within and outside of anthropology have been more critical of the either/or quality of such definitions, pointing to the porous nature of domestication, observing interspecies commonalities, reciprocity and coincidence in human-animal and human-plant relations (see Cassidy 2007: 2). Such qualities speak against a linear gradient from wild to domestic, constituting a process that defies clear hierarchies of power, as suggested by Clutton-Brock.

From this newer perspective, domestication relationships represent a non-linear and recursive process as much as they are a balancing act between the roles of benefactor and beneficiary. They are relationships requiring negotiation and continuous mutual adjustment. This need for consensus between sentient beings is indicative of a sociality of exchange in which human participation is not guaranteed to end up on top. Hahn had already blazed this less anthropocentric trail when he suggested that people represented merely one among many species affecting behavioral and physiological adaptations in other animals.

In his seminal work *Die Haustiere und ihre Beziehungen zur Wirtschaft des Menschen* (Domesticates and their relationship to the human economy) Hahn writes, "From the beginning I assumed that any definition [of domestication] had to take for granted conditions evident in the animals, and that any viewpoint that puts man into the foreground had to be abandoned entirely" (1896: 1). Numerous scholars have followed Hahn in this line of thought (e.g., O'Connor 1997; Rindos 1984; Zeuner 1963). Of course, Hahn emphasized evolutionary morphological adaptations as the leading marker of domestication, but domestication itself for him was merely another term to describe environmental alterations that in similar ways could be performed by other species or circumstances.

For Hahn, the human impact of captivity and care of nonhuman animals was evident, of course, but he did not want to dwell on the specificity of the human role in this process. Instead, he saw the biological changes that occurred in domesticated species as natural adaptations to fluctuating circumstances. These adaptations did not, in principle, differ from conditions that could be found in the absence of humans. This is another way of saying that the changes that occur in an animal, which archaeologists generally identify as characteristic of domestication, are the consequences of changes in webs of relations with the environment and its human and other-than-human participants. Yet, even in an archaeology focusing on animal domestication as the product of human intention, the connections between hunting and herding have been quite blurry.

Going back to British archaeologists Eric Higgs and M. Jarman (1969), we encounter the tantalizing argument that archaeological evidence of morphologically unchanged bone concentrations belonging to one or two species may be indicative of a close human-animal relationship, but that there is no saying from such findings whether we are dealing with hunter-gatherers or with early forms of domestication. In fact, the two went so far as to provocatively conclude that there may never have been an age of hunting and gathering as such, but rather that there may have existed symbiotic relationships between humans and other animals dating back as far as the early Pleistocene (Higgs and Jarman 1969: 39).

Archaeological observations like these are among the earlier precursors to current anthropological thinking about the fluctuating distance between species, including humans, which affect biological and behavioral changes in what we conventionally call domesticates. In this process it is not excluded, depending on climatological changes and other environmental factors, that a so-called semi-domesticated species may go feral several times before showing any significant morphological change associated with the domesticated state familiar to us today. The process of domestication may then involve multiple crossings back and forth, a process that is easy to imagine in a place like Oka, where animals live at the intersection of forest (or spirit) and human households.

INTENTIONS IN DIALOGUE

Now that I have discussed some of the shortcomings of the unidirectional linearity in conventional understandings of domestication, let me take a closer look at human and other animals' intentions. The old idea that intention, and especially that of humans, is to be credited as the driving factor for physical changes in animals of the human household has been challenged by scholars in recent years. Archaeologist Helen Leach (2007) argues that our ten-thousand-year history with domestication may be divided into four stages. In the first stage, she identifies nondeliberate human selection. At the second stage people begin to use generic breeding techniques to retain preferred varieties. Then, at the third stage, deliberate crossbreeding and inbreeding sets in. Finally, at the fourth stage, fully intentional genetic manipulation is practiced. Although this is a gradual linear progression, Leach shows that the last two innovations fall only within the past three hundred years of our history (2007: 73). This is to say, human intention has driven domestication only in the past three centuries, while the preceding millennia of domestic prehistory are the product of human-animal coexistence and its largely unintentional outcomes.

Leach's argument echoes Hahn's observations from over a hundred years ago in that it qualifies and limits the significance of human intention in the process of domestication. Some authors will go even further in arguing against the anthropocentric tendency that has been at the heart of the domestication debate. Science writer, Stephen Budiansky (1992), describes animal domestication as a coevolutionary process in which benefit is derived not only by humans, but also by the animals involved. He notes, "A close look at other evolutionary odd couples in nature—species that have gained an advantage in the struggle for survival by flocking with another species in defiance of the norms of defensive behaviour—reveals biological motives that are apparent in all domesticated relationships" (Budiansky 1992: 46).

Drawing on paleontologist Friedrich Zeuner's (1963) examples of the role and function of human urine in domestication, Budiansky points to the coevolution that seems to have occurred between indigenous Sámi hunters and their reindeer. He argues for a "more equal symbiosis" in which reindeer profess a kind of "free will" in adjoining themselves to human encampments, attracted as they are to the salt contained in human urine (1992: 51; see Stépanoff 2012). The author's numerous examples of unsuspected human-other animal relations, in which nonhuman animals often seem to take the lead, are positioned somewhere within the fuzzy zone between our conventional conceptions of wild and tame. They are examples of webs of interaction in which humans are not in control by default. At the same time, such accounts of human-animal "joint-commitment," to use a term coined by anthropologist Charles Stépanoff (2012), question the very foundations of the wild-tame dichotomy.

The culturally relative foundation on which this wild-tame dichotomy is built, and the extent to which colonial ontologies have affected indigenous ways of knowing, are especially well addressed by authors writing from a wildlife management perspective. Social geographer Sandra Suchet-Pearson (Suchet 2002: 146) shows how "linear notions of social evolution, progress and development underlie Eurocentric ways of knowing wildlife." But this social evolutionary perspective is not shared by most traditional indigenous ontologies. She argues that from a European perspective, "the undeveloped existence of hunting and gathering is defined as the absence of civilization, characterized as untamed, uncontrolled, savage and wild" (Suchet 2002: 146). Western wildlife management has taken philosopher René Descartes' (1596–1650) separation between culture and nature for granted, and therefore it further divides the world into human and nonhuman animals and into wild and domestic spheres.

There exist alternative ontologies, some of which reverse this order. To illustrate the reversal, Suchet-Pearson draws on anthropologist Deborah Rose's work. In her book *Nourishing Terrains: Australian Aboriginal Views of*

Landscape and Wilderness, Rose (1996) "turns upside-down the Eurocentric notion of Australia as progressing from a prior, uncontrolled wild towards a present and future domesticated civilization" (Suchet 2002: 147). For Rose, a landscape that has been tamed by clear-cutting, tilling, or the construction of fences is representative of an isolating space in which inhabitants lack relations to the land, and which for that reason has become wild. Wilderness in this context is a state of uninhabitability and unrelatability, and the recognition of such a state is culturally relative.

If we accept that notions such as wild and tame are indeed culturally relative, then it is not so much a question of where we place an animal in terms of the two categories. Rather, it becomes a matter of how the animal relates to members within its environment. What degree of autonomy does a social participant possess as they move within their relations in a shared environment? As mentioned previously, scholars interested in environmental relations stress the mutuality, co-dependence and collaboration that can be observed between species, including humans (e.g., Pollan 2002; Tsing 2011). Their emphasis on openness in these relations is inspired by a close reading of how contact between humans and animals is established in the archaeological and ethnographic records.

A closer look at these records renders an ambiguous picture of the distribution of power among individuals and populations. Rather than allowing us to pinpoint who exactly has the say in animal-human relations, we see the emergence of mutualisms that often remain invisible to participants, resulting in unforeseen consequences for all (e.g., Cassidy 2007; Star 1991; Zeder 2006). Archaeologist Melinda Zeder, an authority in animal and plant domestication, remains somewhat reserved about this ambiguity, identifying a clear power advantage in humans, which she bases on our highly developed ability to transmit cultural knowledge. At the same time, Zeder recognizes that "threshold criteria that require total genetic isolation and emergent speciation or complete dependence on humans for survival set a very high bar that many, if not most, widely accepted domesticates would fail to clear" (2006: 107).

Even if humans have a power advantage in these social relations, it can be said that porous isolation and imperfect dependence on humans maintain a space for animals from which to resist or manipulate human intentions. Thus, domestication relationships in the Saians are not the product of one party's ability to keep the other in check, but they are relationships in which both parties are able to act upon what they identify as valuable in the other. Similarly, Zeder describes domestication relationships as "highly contingent on a wide range of factors, including the ability of the plant or animal to take advantage of the relationship," but also, and especially, "the strategies and accompanying technologies humans develop to manage the resource and its changing value vis-à-vis available alternative resources" (Zeder 2006: 107). It is this "changing value" perceived in the body of the other that can lead to intentional entry or exit from symbiotic interspecies relations.

A number of theorists have sought to decide whether animal domestication is best understood in terms of human domination, interspecies symbiosis or commensality, with cost-benefit calculations as the foundation. This generally leads to arguments either in support of power symmetry or asymmetry. Rather than settling on either one of the two as permanent arrangements, I hope to show in this book how humans and animals move back and forth between symmetric and asymmetric power relations. Similarly, the accounts that follow will help illustrate how fluctuations exist between mutualistic relationships in which each entity benefits from the activity of the other and commensal relationships in which one entity benefits while the other derives neither harm nor benefit.

As we have seen in Zeder, who speaks of the role of "accompanying technologies," physical materials play a pivotal role in the negotiation of power in domestication relationships. This role is not limited to the economic use of technology, it also applies in terms of its communicative potential. A reindeer and a herder, connected to each other with a lasso, experience a number of possible ways in which pressure can be made to travel through the lasso. Depending on their individual intentions, as well as on possible joint commitment, the direction of the pressure traveling through the lasso will be affected. Is the herder tugging on the deer, or is the deer tugging on the herder? Is the herder communicating with the deer through the lasso? Has the herder started out by tugging, encountering initial resistance from the deer, while at a later point the deer comes along without having to be pulled? The archaeological remains of a lasso does not convey to us a clear image of the quality of this interaction with its multiple possible turns. Yet we must assume that the range of possible scenarios is broad.

Accepting that pressure can flow in more than one direction and that the tendency of this direction changes repeatedly over time allows us to study the domus and its implements beyond the handicap of a subjugation-opportunism dichotomy. Such a dichotomy is bound to put the human either in perfect control over the animal or at its mercy to allow its exploitation. In a scenario where technological implements are open to interpretation by humans and animals, objects such as the hobble and lasso are no longer implements of domination alone. Instead they become communicative devices—means for the negotiation of intentions from one species to another and back.

EXPANDING PERCEPTION

In his radically experimental picture book, "*A Foray into the Worlds of Animals and Humans,*" (2010 [1934]) German biologist and semiologist Jakob von

Uexküll (1864–1944) attempts a comparison of human, fly, mollusk, and other animal perceptions of the environment. Von Uexküll bases his comparison on differences in the biology of each species' receptor organs, concluding that while all these animals share a common environment, each of them reside in a separate *Umwelt*, or phenomenal self-world (2010: 5). Yet, none of these animals live in isolation from each other. Because their divergent worlds interact with a common environment, they are bound to intersect with each other at some point—even if the intersection of their worlds is validated in radically different ways.

A related debate has ensued in anthropology as part of the so-called ontological and animal turns (e.g., Ingold 2013; Weil 2010). At the heart of these intellectual movements lies an interest not only in defining what is—and for whom—but also in how communication is facilitated between beings of distinct life-worlds.

One theoretical approach to the intersection of the perceptive worlds of humans and other beings is Eduardo Viveiros de Castro's (1996, 1998) Amerindian perspectivism. Viveiros de Castro's perspective, which is dictated by the shape of a particular body, is similar to von Uexküll's perception that defines an organism's *Umwelt*. Even outside of an Amerindian cosmological context, in which an animal is understood to harbor human likeness at its inner core, the biological uniqueness of an animal's physical constitution is still understood to have perspectival, or in von Uexküll's terms, perceptual uniqueness. The question is, whether an animal's perception of the world is affected by interaction with beings of another perception.

It would seem then that for a perceptual expansion to occur, no reconstitution of one's biology is needed. All that is required is a degree of flexibility in the way one's bodily abilities are put to use. If this is so, we may speak of domesticates as animals whose knowledge or use of their own body in the world has been expanded to include ways contrary or supplementary to their species' "normative" behavior. What is normative depends, of course, on the context in which the animal finds itself. While not obtaining the phenomenal self-world of another species, the domesticate still comes to recognize—consciously, deliberately, willingly, or otherwise—some of the benefits previously harvested by animals of a different *Umwelt*.

In Viveiros de Castro's terms, the above scenario could be described as someone else's perspective seeping through the porous membrane of the "animal mask" (1998: 471). The animal mask being the clothing, fur, skin, eyes, etc. that cloak the human essence of any nonhuman animal, enabling it to be recognized and to function as a particular species. Although this Amazonian view of animals is not shared by Soiots, for whom a collective master spirit often stands behind the movements of animals, undoubtedly an animal's way of being and thus of seeing is affected by the presence and actions of those surrounding it. In tandem with this expanded perspective, the individual in question may begin to draw on hitherto unrealized biological potential.

French philosopher Dominique Lestel (2002: 56) speaks to the same phenomenon, drawing attention to its effects on rationality when he asks, "What changes does the rationality of one agent undergo when it regularly interacts with another agent possessing skills very different from its own?" One way of approaching this change in rationale is to consider the ways in which individuals begin to recognize and respond to aspects of their environment as affordances or as new possibilities available to them. The use of their existing physiological ability (e.g., their digestive capacity) becomes expanded, and new resources begin to lend themselves to their exploitation. What hitherto was outside of their realm of awareness is now gradually being added. Such a change in the reading of the environment inevitably leads to an expansion in the logic used to make connections within one's *Umwelt*.

Elizaveta Shirokogorova (1919), spouse and colleague of famous Russian anthropologist Sergei Shirokogorov, provides us with a fitting example of such an expansion in the awareness of horses encountered during their joint fieldwork with Evenki (Orochens) of northeastern China. She writes:

> These Orochens belong to the third group we have visited; we shall call them the Kamarski Orochens. Being the largest group of Manchuria's Orochen population, they are primarily hunters, much like Amur Orochens, breeding horses on the side. The horse aids them in their migrations, as well as during the hunt, for which reason the most sought after quality in a horse is its endurance. Because hay making is unthinkable under the circumstances of a hunting lifestyle, horses are first being accustomed [Rus. *priuchaiut*] to abstinence [Rus. *vozderzhanie*], after which they can go entirely without food for two to three days, and then they are grown accustomed to eating berries, shrubs, and eventually meat. At first they will feed a horse strongly salted boiled meat, after which they will feed it without the salt, eventually transitioning to raw meat. A marginal portion—served in the morning, once per day—consists of eight pounds of meat per horse. Nonvegetarian horses will survive in the taiga for twenty-five years, highly enduring and strong as they are. The experienced horse will save its energy in the taiga and skillfully adjusts to given circumstances, while an inexperienced horse will last for no longer than two to three weeks. (1919: 30)

Shirokogorova uses the term "accustoming," or literally to re-teach, to teach anew, or to overwrite (Rus. *pereuchit'*) when referring to these hunters who trained their horses to eat in ways similar to their own. Horses fall between ruminant (bacterial digestive action in four stomachs, enzymatic action in small intestines) and non ruminant (enzymatic action, single stomach) digestive systems (Wright 1999), which explains why they can potentially break down meat in much the same way as humans, pigs, and dogs, all of which

MIRRORED HOMES 37

Illustration 1.2. Fishing with Borzhon on the Upper Sorok River. Photograph by the author.

are nonruminants. Their evident ability to become accustomed to a meat diet is exemplary of the biological potential on which horses are able to draw in response to the environmental shift they may experience as part of their collaboration with humans.

Transitions such as these have an effect not only on the daily dietary composition of a horse's feed, but also on the pacing of its normative daily intake, which constitutes an integral part of its *Umwelt*. No longer can the horse rely on an average of twelve to eighteen hours of synchronous grazing, a behavior that is thought to correspond to the nature of its digestive tract (see Boyd et al. 1988; Burla et al. 2016). It must now move according to the pace set by its human companion. The human companion, in turn, is aware of the adjustment required of the horse and works with it in a sensitive and gradual manner, until a single stomach filling of meat becomes the new norm. At this point the horse has learned to recognize eight pounds of raw meat as suitable food, enabling it to walk through challenging terrain for one or more days. Its embodied perspective has expanded, and it now recognizes the resources of a companion species as affordance.

Shirokogorova's Orochen horses illustrate, to an extreme point, the physiological plasticity that can be drawn on in some companion species. I have used this example to better make sense of the perceptive expansion some animals undergo as a result of their extended social relations with beings of another *Umwelt*—in this case, human hunters' households. While not all domestication relationships within the household result in drastic physiological adjustment, the importance of dialogue between holders of divergent perspectives cannot be overstressed. As we will see in the following chapters, objects commonly identified as implements of human domination (corrals, lassos, hobbles, etc.) deserve critical reassessment for their capacity as devices of dialogue between householders and their animals.

Our observations of the type of power held by the Roman *dominus* and its parallels with spirit and human masters in a Soiot context call into question a dominating anthropocentric approach to animal domestication, particularly in less industrial settings where domestication relationships rely on the ability of animals to respond to human impetus. Furthermore, the Soiot understanding of the human household as a mirror image of the spirit household underscores the importance of reciprocity between the qualities of beings associated with forest and pasture. The overlapping and intersecting of these divergent yet similar household models suggests a nonlinear back and forth that defies either/or approaches to domesticity. Instead, it points to a careful balancing of human and animal intentions, as we have seen in Borzhon when he descends with his yak in the evening.

CHAPTER 2

SACRED ENFOLDING

Before his days of working as an animal husbandry specialist (zoo technician) for the collective farm at Sorok, Badma Khorluevich had lived in a little cabin at the center of the Uro Valley. His cabin was gone when I first arrived in 2013. It had been moved to Sorok, much like yurts used to be moved in the more distant past. On a visit to the valley, Badma took me to the location of his former hut. All that was left now was a vague indention in the grass. Nearby a traditional *serge*, or horse hitching post, was slowly rotting away. Although little else was left of Badma's former life at Uro, for him the landscape was teeming with memories. Beyond his former cabin, there had been two other cabins. Both were now gone and so were their *serge*. One of the two cabins had belonged to a powerful Soiot shaman. He had lived here for many years, together with his wife. One day, when this shaman was "rather old" (over sixty), according to Badma, three eagles had appeared in the sky. They soon landed in the grass near the aging man's cabin. When the shaman caught sight of the three visitors, he knew to waste no time. He reached for his rifle, loaded it, and stepped in front of his cabin. Pointing the barrel under his chin, he pulled the trigger. The shot echoed through the valley, and the eagles took flight. With them—Badma claims—they took the shaman's spirit (Rus. *dukh*).

His body, like the bodies of many other elders, was taken up the west-facing hillside behind the three cabins. I had picked berries here on multiple occasions. It is not rare to spot an eagle, or sometimes up to twelve, soaring high above the larches in a deep blue sky. Unlike the present day, when people are increasingly burying their dead on hillsides in the ground, the shaman's body had been placed on a pyre of dry branches. With additional wood piled on top of the corpse, the man's body soon disappeared in a blazing fire. Badma had seen off many of his ancestors in this way. As the eldest son, it had been his responsibility to take them up the hillside, just like the old shaman had been. He assured me, this was how his people had always sent off their loved ones in the past. They had never buried their bodies. Instead, with the corpse resting on a horse-drawn sleigh-like attachment, the rider would drag a dead body over bumps and through the moss into the hills. When a corpse fell from the sleigh, it was to be left there undisturbed. Although much had changed since the death of the shaman, the eagles were still soaring above us. And with them—or in them—the man's spirit looked down upon us.

* * *

My aim in this chapter is to outline the relationship between two cosmological perspectives held in tandem by the householders I lived with at Uro. Combining the hunting practices of their ancestors with the herding tasks of their Buriat neighbours, Soiot men and women deliberately engaged in ritual activities belonging to both domains. Rather than keeping local shamanic traditions and more recent Buddhist practices separate, herder-hunters and ritual specialists often blurred the lines between ancient ancestral and more recent ways of knowing. This suited the mixed subsistence activities of each household: as yak had become part of Soiot households, so had Buddhism. In the previous chapter I discussed how spirit and human households mirrored each other. In this chapter I will look at the differing approaches proponents of Buddhism and shamanism took to domestication in Oka.

After a brief history of both traditions in the Saian Mountains, I will specifically draw on observations in which the traditions overlapped. I argue that where Buddhist practitioners have domesticated shamanic spirit masters in a complete and irreversible way, a living relationship between the two traditions (or households) is no longer sustainable. Conversely, where spirit masters maintain their control, people continue to benefit from the overlap between both ritual traditions. This argument forms a direct parallel to what was discussed in the previous chapter where spirit and human households engaged with each other as long as each recognized the other's autonomy. Put in different terms, all social relations had to be kept open, incomplete, and reversible. This included relations between humans and animals, between spirits and humans, and between ritual traditions. In terms of cosmology, the most beneficial choice then, was not for a person to renounce one faith and convert to the other, but to position themselves flexibly between the two. This strategy is symbolic of herder-hunter approaches to domestication relationships, which are balanced by herders extending autonomy to their stock.

OF PRACTITIONERS AND THEIR ACTIVITIES

Approaching shamanism from a political historical angle, anthropologists Nicholas Thomas and Caroline Humphrey (1995: 5) refer to shamans as "inspirational practitioners," and to their practices as "inspirational activities." They speak here from a context of power negotiation between "inspirational and state cults," or between the officially sanctioned and unsanctioned. At first sight, such an opposition between types of activity may seem straightforward. But, Thomas and Humphrey argue, "what may be significant are precisely the overlapping and mutability of various forms of contested ritual agency, rather than the clarification of what makes them distinct" (Thomas and Humphrey 1996: 3). In other words, what at times is used to stress difference, is at other times presented as something held in common.

I find this approach to shamanism useful. It acknowledges the ambiguity of boundaries between local and introduced activities, between wild and ordered ways of knowing. It lends itself to Oka where a more recently arrived Buddhism has incorporated local ritual concepts, recognizing that the power of local inspirational activities will, from time to time, strike out against more lofty Buddhist narratives. Here Buddhism does not exist as a rigid doctrine but as a dynamic organism that has adapted itself to the landscape, which has formed a regional identity based on the very differences that emerge from the interplay of introduced and encountered traditions. Yet, Buddhism in Oka does not embrace the same indistinctness and ambiguity in the landscape that indigenous residents have lived with since time immemorial.

Although Buddhism did not come to Oka as a state cult, it did gradually assume the position of an official cult, held largely by the Buriat settler majority. Yet, even to these settlers, Buddhism came as a foreign import that never fully replaced older ways of knowing, such as the Oka-Buriat mountain cult (e.g., Batomunkueva 2011). Prior to the arrival of Buddhism, Oka-Buriats had been fervent adherents to the mountain cult, which venerated three main mountain deities for northern (Nukhen Daban), central (Tailgata), and southern (Orkhoboomo) Oka, as well as their many subordinate spirit masters (e.g., Galdanova 2000: 19; Sharastepanov 2008: 33). The cult had existed in Central Asia as an independent manifestation (Gomboev 2002: 69), and together with other elements of shamanism, it was partially incorporated into a Buddhist framework (see Zhukovskaia and Derevianko 1988: 27).

In spite of its local adaptations, Buddhism was seen by some of my Soiot friends as a kind of import. Local historian Dasha Sharastepanov (2008: 33) recalls that even among Buriats a significant Buddhist following came about only by the late nineteenth and early twentieth centuries, following the establishment of the Zhelgenskii university monastery, or *datsan*. The term *datsan* is used to refer to the Buddhist university monasteries of the Tibetan Gelukpa tradition, which are found in Tibet, Mongolia, and southern Siberia (see Terentyev 1996). It is reasonable to assume that Soiot ritual life was affected by the mountain cult, and subsequently by the presence of Buddhism, especially through Soiot-Buriat intermarriages. Conversely, it is evident that Oka Buddhist practice incorporated elements of the mountain cult.

Several of the lamas I interviewed in Oka and Tunka deliberately refrained from offering explanations of anything that might be construed as a representation of Buddhism as a whole, or as representative of an official view of a religion. I believe they were not interested in providing sweeping statements for what Richard Cohen (1989: 361) has referred to as the role of "place" in Buddhism. "In seeking a universally generalizable Buddhism, scholars have ignored 'place.'" Cohen goes on to explain that it is paramount to understand the importance of place to be able to analytically reconstruct Buddhism. "Place sets the idiosyncratic and the indigenous on par with the trans local and universal, the here and there with the everywhere" (Cohen 1989: 361). Perhaps for this reason, the religious specialists I spoke with were much more comfortable relating to their practices and beliefs in terms of specific places—be it the Tunka Valley or various locations throughout Oka.

Although the Russian Orthodox mission played a crucial part in the history of Tofas to the northwest, the presence of Christianity in Oka is treated, at best, as a footnote in local discourse, and it is virtually absent from the literature. In the rest of Buriatia, Orthodox missionary activity was much more pronounced among Buriats and Evenks (e.g., Mitypova 2005: 101–3). According to Buddhist lama Norbu of Orlik, "there once was a mission outpost (Rus. *missionerskii stan*) ... located in the village of Saiany [also called Sharza]. ... [And] later something of a church ... [with a] clergy member (Rus. *sluzhitel'*), although he died suddenly, leaving behind his family of five children who subsequently fell into poverty." Little more seemed to be known about the early inroads of Christianity into Oka.

There was no obvious sign of Russian Orthodoxy in Oka during my fieldwork, yet I did come across a rarely discussed heritage predating the establishment of the first Buddhist *datsan* while reading an archived newspaper article from 1990. In the article Ts. I. Tsybdenov provides some information on the early work of the Orthodox mission in Oka. The missionary priest Mikhail Petrov, a graduate of the Irkutsk Ecclesiastic Seminary, is said to have been the first teacher at an Orthodox elementary school in Oka. Although he had a tolerable command of the Buriat language, school instruction was conducted in Russian. Tsybdenov speaks of only two school terms with an enrollment of eight and five children, respectively.

The Oka mission post was closely related to other mission posts located in the Tunka Valley south of Oka, where the Orthodox Church had established itself in 1871. By 1883, a mission post was added in the village of Mondy on the border to Mongolia. This post was officially consecrated in 1885 (Kalinina 2000: 434), and it soon became known as the "Oka-Mondy post." Its first school opened in Mondy in 1885, and subsequently a school was opened also in Oka in 1895. Five years later, on 13 July 1900, Holy Trinity Church was officially consecrated at Saiany (Kalinina 2000: 434). Most likely it was the priest of this church that Lama Norbu referred to. At the time of my fieldwork, the memory and impact of this missionary activity seemed largely forgotten.

The history of local encounters with early Buddhist itinerant lamas is somewhat better preserved. As I will discuss later, this encounter has often been conflictual, resembling the historical situation of Buddhist encounters with shamanism in Tibet and Nepal. Yet, because of its Tantric subset of practices, the confrontation of Gelug Buddhism with shamanism in Oka has led not only to conflict but also to dialogue and—to use Thomas and Humphrey's (1996: 3) term—to "overlap." Himalayan scholars have studied in detail the classic antagonism between lamaism and shamanism (e.g., Mumford 1989), while also observing "appropriation of shamanic forms" by Buddhist lamas (e.g., Ortner 1978a). Tantric rites, as anthropologist Sherry Ortner (1978b) illustrates in her work on Sherpa people, often mediated between the relational worldview of shamanism held by common householders and the scholastic "inner" path pursued by the monastic elite.

Anthropologist Stan Royal Mumford, who worked with Tibetan lamas and Gurung shamans in Nepal describes how lamas "transmuted" the mundane needs of lay householders and of shamans into the "profound" aspirations of the clergy, relying on the same rituals. The key to this lies in what he identifies as "hybrid meanings" (Mumford 1989: 29): "Lamaist transmutations employ hybrid images in this manner, but they do not have full control of how they will be interpreted by their listeners." Thus, a lama could perform a ritual that carries one meaning at the level of his own perception, while the householder, on whose behalf it is being performed, reads quite another meaning into it. The ambiguity of the ritual then becomes reflexive, because at least the lama is aware of the hybridity of his performance.

Similarly, it was not always clear whether a Soiot herder-hunter was addressing a local spirit master, a major Buriat mountain deity, or a deity in the Buddhist pantheon when using the Turkic-Mongolian term *burkhan* during a ritual offering. In Mongolia and neighboring regions, the term *burkhan* often refers to master spirits of the landscape (also known as *ezen*) who can take the form of Buddhist deities (e.g., Swancutt 2007). But the origins of the term were long contested among scholars (Laufer 1916).

Arguably, this descriptive leeway enabled herder-hunters to continue their ancestral practices in spaces where ritual allegiances were potentially pitted against one another. Such leeway allowed people to move back and forth between diverse ritual practices and between the services of various ritual specialists, depending on availability. For Soiot clients calling on ritual services, the activities of diverse specialists seemed to overlap in purpose, if not

Illustration 2.1. Badma makes an offering at Shaman tree. Photograph by the author.

in detail. When I asked my neighbor, Borzhon, whether calling a shaman to consecrate the household was any different from calling a lama, he responded: "probably not" (Rus. *naverno net*). "Probably," because Borzhon did not identify as a ritual specialist and making a confident statement would have been inappropriate from his point of view. More importantly, "probably" speaks to the very nature of social encounters with sentience in the sacred landscape. Never certain, rigid, or predictable, social encounters had to be experienced, and they could be ascertained only retrospectively (see Hallowell [1960] 2002; Humphrey 1995: 135).

DIVERGENT APPROACHES TO SPIRIT MASTERS

Less concerned over whether a shaman or a lama was invited, what seemed paramount was the efficacy of a specific practitioner. A more powerful lama was likely more helpful than a less powerful shaman in protecting a household against wolves or other misfortunes. But it was also understood that certain tasks could be accomplished only by one or the other, depending on their field of expertise, knowledge of specific family history, or relatedness to a clan.

Baldorzho had been introduced to me as "the lama from Bokson," a small village south of Sorok. The Dondokovy brothers spoke of him as "the only true Soiot lama." He had attended school with Badma Khorluevich, the eldest of the three Dondokovy brothers, before leaving Oka to undergo Buddhist training in St. Petersburg and Mongolia. Like several other lamas, Baldorzho was a Tantric practitioner. What set him apart, in his own words, from other lamas was his knowledge of localized rituals and chants, passed down to him by his forebears. This was knowledge of which he claimed to be the sole surviving initiate. Baldorzho was known as a lama, not as a shaman. Yet his perspective of the landscape in which people hunted took their relations with local spirit masters seriously.

Baldorzho was a man intimately familiar with two distinct perspectives. He never abandoned his role as lama, and yet he was deeply familiar with Soiot shamanist ideas. Seeking to direct his services to the fears of the households at Uro, his familiarity with the needs of hunters as opposed to herders, allowed him to mitigate between Buddhist and shamanist perspectives. To the people of Uro he was a sort of spokesperson who could approach a spirit master from the perspective of the spirit's Buddhist household. This was the household to which the spirit was said to have converted many years earlier. Quite unlike a shaman who would engage in an exchange with a particular local spirit, Baldorzho would secure a spirit's benevolence by reminding it of the allegiance it had formed with the Buddhist household. What mattered to my neighbors at Uro was that the relationship was maintained between them, their stock, and the spirits of the landscape, something that in their minds amounted to a balance achieved in part through the performance of appropriate ritual.

However, it would be naive to assume that herder-hunters at Uro were unaware of the differences that existed between the approaches of a shaman and a lama to sentience in the landscape. As I will explore below, according to the lamas' narrative, the majority of local spirit masters had been persuaded by itinerant lamas of the past to become subservient to the Buddha's teachings. With their successful "domestication" of the most powerful spirit masters, several of them had attained divine status in the Buddhist pantheon. From a Buddhist perspective, their inclusion with other divinities had rendered them not powerless but harmless, predictable, and benevolent to people. But from the perspective of a shaman, conversion had rendered the spirit masters unavailable to regular exchanges with human-mastered households. Such exchanges had always stood at the center of maintaining balance in the relationship between humans, animals, and the landscape. The divergence of these two approaches to spirit masters was expressed most clearly in a Buddhist layperson's offering and a shaman's sacrifice, both enduring, yet opposed ritual actions.

AN UNDERLYING ORDER OF THINGS

In the absence of pre-revolutionary ethnographic materials for Oka, the historical activities of Soiot shamans are perhaps best understood by looking to what is known about their Tofa neighbors to the northwest. Tofa shamanism is thought to have been influenced by Buddhism over a four-hundred-year contact period (fourteenth to eighteenth centuries). Sevian Vainshtein (1968) and others believe this influence came through contact with Tozhu of Eastern Tyva (see Mel'nikova 1994: 135), as well as with Mongolian tribes of the Baikal region. Beginning in the second half of the seventeenth century, elements of Russian Orthodox Christianity also began to influence Tofa rituals, which otherwise remained consistent with shamanist activities known from the Altai, Western Buriatia, and Eastern Tyva (Mel'nikova 1994: 135). Although the highest ranking deities for Tofa were Burkhan (or Kudai) of the upper world, and Erlik-Khan of the lower world, it was Dag-Ezi who is described as the mountain ruler overseeing all other spirit entities within the Tofa pantheon.

Bernhard E. Petri describes these entities as a "special clan [or kind] of mountain spirits—deity owners—with a strict hierarchy" (Petri 1928: 15), which he lays out as follows: "Dag-ezi rules over the owners of separate valleys, to whom in turn spirit owners of individual undrained or marshland mountain valleys (Rus. *pad'*) are subject, and finally there are the spirit owners of glens" (1928: 15). Water bodies, on the other hand, are described as not being subject to Dag-Ezi, but under the authority of Sun-Ezi the water deity. Not unlike the hierarchical organization under Dag-Ezi, water spirits under Sun-Ezi follow a ranking order from rivers to creeks to streams—with the exception of lakes, whose spirits fall under the direct authority of Sun-Ezi (Petri 1928: 16). The local Ezi of each valley was entreated prior the hunt to ensure success, and similarly fisheries depended on supplications to either Sun-Ezi or smaller local water spirit masters. Dag-Ezi was thought to protect not only wild reindeer, but also herded reindeer, securing the reproductive success of human-managed reindeer and maintaining their feed year round (Petri 1928: 15, 16). In this way, Ezi ensured the fattening of both hunted and herded animals of the same species.

BALANCE AND WILLINGNESS IN THE LANDSCAPE

Most of my interlocutors spoke of animals possessing souls. It was less clear whether the animal's soul could be considered separate from the spirit master in whose care the animal moved, or whether the spirit master served as a single collective soul. In either case, people spoke of souls as if each animal had its own. Searching a forest for animals could thus be understood as seeking their spirits or souls. A hunter would conduct a ritual of entreaty prior to his search, after which he would set out on the trails in a given landscape. His hunt could be construed as a soul search that bears resemblance to the solicitation of spirits performed by shamans on journeys undertaken in a state of trance. The hunter could travel through the forest for days before locating an animal willing to render itself to the hunter. Similarly, a shaman often had to invest great effort in searching for a spirit before such would appear in his presence. Both hunter and shaman depended on the good will (Rus. *blagoraspolozhenie*, see Petri 1928: 15) of the spirits or souls they sought and of those that oversaw or owned them.

Willingness of animals to come to the hunter has been described in the literature of the Altai-Saian Region as dependent upon a hunter's maintenance of balance in all things. In the Altai, this has been referred to as *kire*. Anthropologist Ludek Broz (2007: 298) explains:

> kire, in one of its meanings is often translated into Russian as mera— "measure," "level," "degree" (Tybykova 2005: 109). The more appropriate translation for the context in which it was used, however, seems to be "norm," "share," "portion," or "balance." Every hunter has kire—the amount of animals which it is appropriate to shoot within a certain period of time (e.g. hunting expedition) as well as within one's lifetime.

One's effectiveness in soliciting souls or spirits in the landscape is thus also a matter of how many animals one has been ascribed, and how many of their souls one has already solicited.

The principles by which a hunter's balancing efforts are tracked extend well beyond his usual hunting range. I was told by Buriat shaman Buda-Khean Stepanovich, that wherever he goes, the landscape spirit master of that locality will recognize him. While traveling in Tyva one day, Stepanovich was met by birds who flew alongside his vehicle. He recognized the birds as a sign of welcome from the local spirit master:

> one spirit master conveys to another information about you. So, if you have a certain number of days left to live, that information will be relayed, "as if from radio tower to radio tower" (Rus. *kak by s odnoi radio bashni k sleduiushei*). The same is true of the number of animals you were given by Burkhan [i.e., *kire*]. Say, you were given five, but because you did not need that many, you took only one. Burkhan will not forget your humility (Rus. *skromnost'*) and will request the next spirit master to give you something nice.... Say I were to give you five kilograms of fish for the road to Ulan-Ude, but you were to take only two or three single fish, saying that you did not need more for the trip, then I would call my friend in Ulan-Ude and ask him to give you something nice—maybe a book—since you were humble enough to take only as many fish as you actually needed and not as many as I offered.

Spirit masters were encountered not only in the form of landscape features or fire. They flowed through the animals they mastered, such as the birds that flew alongside Stepanovich's vehicle.

SPIRIT MASTERS MANIFESTED IN ANIMALS

Stepanovich recalled incidents in which Burkhan took the shape of a wild animal or in which ancestral spirits entered animals. But he did not have an account of a living shaman or hunter entering the body of a wild animal as we know it from the Russian Far East (e.g., Willerslev 2007). In the 1960s, he recalled, there had been a well-to-do elder who had hidden from the Soviet authorities all his monetary valuables (a sizable amount of silver rubles and gold) in a cave. On his deathbed he told his son about the treasure and its approximate location. He instructed his son that sixty years would have to pass before anyone was to retrieve the treasure. After sixty years a better time would be at hand (the Communists would be gone), and it would be fine to unearth the fortune then.

However, in the mid-1970s, some fifteen years after his father's death, the son was hunting with two other men on a cold October day, when the group came across the cave in which his father was thought to have deposited the fortune. Together they began digging when a bear attacked them. According to Stepanovich, this was a very unusual location for a bear encounter—bears had never been seen here before. In the encounter, the bear killed two of the three hunters, tearing off half of the son's face before leaving him behind. The bodily warmth of his dog and the flames of a fire he was able to make helped the man survive.

From Stepanovich's point of view, the bear had come to attack the men because the father's coins had transferred into the possession of Burkhan, to whom belong all precious metals hidden in the ground. The shaman was convinced that either Burkhan himself had entered the bear's shape to attack the men, or that it had been the deceased father's spirit who had entered the bear to remind his son that the time had not yet come to unearth the fortune. In either case, the bear incident holds several interesting notions about personhood, property, boundaries and embodiment. Although the bear has been understood as a totemic ancestor by Tofas, and thus is subject to a series of special hunting rituals that clearly diverge from regular hunting protocols (Mel'nikova 1994: 171), Oka Buriats and Soiots do not share this ancestral association. In Stepanovich's interpretation of the encounter, the animal's actions were directed by Burkhan, or possibly by the intentions of the father's spirit. In either case, the animal's behavior could not be considered to correspond to a singular autonomous will (i.e., the animal's own soul). Rather, in the bear's volition mingled the intentions of potential others who could utilize the bear's bodily strength for their purposes. The personhood of the bear thus constituted multiple possible intentions, representing several potential spirit persons.

In our conversation, Stepanovich did not elucidate on whether the father's spirit had become the landscape master of this particular locality, nor whether he had initially chosen the cave as a hiding spot for such reasons. To my understanding, neither the father nor the son had been practicing shamans. But the father's fortune, due to its metallic nature, had become enfolded by Burkhan upon reentering the ground. The bear came to defend the property, his actions being directed in protection of the landscape and of the level of balance maintained therein. The son had sought to disrupt this balance in his need, or more likely in his greed. A sort of hierarchy had come to fore: the father's spirit, who remained subordinate to the will of Burkhan, utilized the spirit master's claim over the domain of the ground to protect his fortune for a later time. It could be said then that the human political realm and the realm of the landscape spirits had become interconnected, and property claims were being transferred between the two.

SPEAKING TO ANIMAL SOULS

Anthropologist Brian Donahoe (2012: 106) writes about Tozhu of Tyva:

> it is the cher eezi [Tozhu equivalent of Tofa ezi] who decides whether or not to give an animal to a hunter; it is the cher eezi the hunter fears and respects, petitions for help in the hunt, thanks for success, and with whom he establishes a relationship of trust, as distinct from doing so with the animal directly. Wild animals are the medium that constitutes the social relationship between the hunter and the cher eezi.

Accordingly, when I asked Soiot shaman Dondok whether animals possess their own volition in relation to offering their bodies to a hunter (since they were understood to possess a soul [Petri (1928) 2014: 65]), he replied that they did not really have a will of their own. Their spirit master would decide such things on their behalf. The spirit was in charge of what happened to the animal. According to Dondok, every living being was given a set number of days to live, much like the *kire* described by Broz in Altai. In the words of a Soiot informant, this not only applied to animals. "If your full number of days has not been reached, then nothing can kill you—whether you are in a car accident or in a plane crash." In the same way, an animal's days were numbered, and Burkhan would not allow a predator to take its life until its days had expired. This is an interesting observation since even the predators belonged to the spirit master's household.

In contrast to Dondok, when I asked Stepanovich whether hunters could communicate with their prey directly (i.e., bypassing their spirit masters), he responded in the affirmative. According to Stepanovich, "a hunter will speak to the animal itself, and not only to its spirit master. In so doing, he encourages the animal to render its body for the preservation of the lives in the hunter's family." Such communication could take place audibly, although it was usually done in silence and more intuitively.

My attempts at distinguishing between the volition of an individual animal soul and that of its spirit master must have seemed like splitting hairs to my shaman and hunter consultants alike. It was clear that animals were offered to hunters, but did the individual animal soul have a say in the process? Although pertinent to my mind—and to that of other circumpolar ethnographers (e.g., Ingold 1987, Nadasdy 2007; Willerslev 2004)—the question seemed artificial to my consultants in Oka. My neighbor and teacher, Borzhon, had told me of the moment in which an animal "gives itself" to the hunter. Soiot hunters waited for this moment, he said. It was in this instance that either the spirit master, or the animal itself, or both, turned the animal body over to the hunter. The moment itself lasted only for "a fraction of a second," and it could easily be missed. The animal might look the hunter straight in the eye during this moment, but it did not have to. If Burkhan had allotted the animal to the hunter, there was nothing to dissuade the gift, not the animal's individual will, or even the mention of its name. And yet, this preordination did not seem to affect the reality that some hunters were more skillful than others. Skill, in this context, seemed to have more to do with one's ability to maintain balance than with tracking or aiming well.

Early one October morning, before departing for a day of hunting, Borzhon quietly set out to work at this balance. He scooped off several cups of milky tea from a large pot boiling atop the steel stove in his hunting cabin, pouring them into a separate dish. Only then were the other hunters allowed to drink of what was left on the stove. He heaped a shovel with glowing coals from the hearth and carried it outdoors, where he carefully set them on a wooden pedestal in front of his cabin. While the coal continued to burn outside, his elder son applied butter to several large pieces of freshly cut bread. These he placed in a soup dish next to the dedicated tea. Borzhon produced several dried juniper twigs and placed them on the burning coals, filling the air with thick smoke. Cutting through the smoke, he placed the buttered bread pieces on top of the incense, and finally sprinkled some of the tea on the offering. With a ladle, he dispersed the remaining tea in the air, following all four directions of the compass. He completed the ritual by walking around the pedestal three times. Borzhon had made a hunter's offering to the spirit master. Offering tea, butter, bread, and burning sage—substances unique to the human household—Borzhon had petitioned the spirit household to grant us the moment he had described to me as "a fraction of a second." The taiga had been spoken to and with it the animals roaming it.

RECORDS IN THE TREES

There were other ways of communicating with the spirit household. According to Buriat shaman Stepanovich, a hunter represented the male members of his immediate family—his sons and their dependents. When a hunter entered the forest, he would perform a hunting ritual, like Borzhon's, for the spirit master of that place. Traditionally, he would then attach as many rags of cloth to a tree branch as there were hunters in his group, or as there were sons in his family, even if the latter were not with him on the same day. If the man had three sons, he would hang four rags on a branch next to the tree's trunk. By so doing he communicated to the spirit master that he was hunting not only on his own behalf, but also for the men who "stood behind him" (Rus. *za nim eshche stoiat*). Displaying his intentions in the trees, the hunter was able to avoid potential discrepancy between his taking of animals and his allotted *kire,* or measure. In fact, he would be hunting not only on his own *kire,* but also on that of his sons.

The next hunter who would come this way—by looking at the position and age of the rags on the branch in relation to the trunk—would know approximately how long ago the first hunter had been here and how much he had intended to take. If enough time had lapsed, the next hunter and his sons would place their rags next to the older set. Thus, over time, the branches of a tree filled up with rags, providing a harvest record that could be read by subsequent passersby. The record also indicated how much time had passed for animals of that location to reproduce since the last harvest.

But balance, or right measure, was not only a matter of one's momentary state of *kire*. It was also a matter of delayed reciprocity: sitting at the kitchen table over yet another cup of tea, Uncle Iura explained that "as much as you take from the spirit master in terms of animals hunted during the summer, that many animals he will take from your herds in winter by way of wolves." He added, this was a kind of cycle, a "give-and-take" of sorts. Reminded of Ludek Broz's (2007) account of perspectival reversal of wild and domestic "cattle" among human owners and spirit masters in Altai, I inquired what would happen if every hunting ritual had been kept prior to each hunt. Would the spirit master still take human owned stock in that case? "No," replied Iura. "A respectful hunter who had ensured proper balance in all his affairs would not suffer wolf attacks in winter." But not all had such confidence. Borzhon later told me, "No matter how carefully a hunter performs his rituals, wolves will always befall his herds in winter." It seemed, for Borzhon this was simply part of an ongoing reciprocal relationship between spirit and human households.

Returning from an unsuccessful hunt in autumn, I asked Borzhon how it was that we had offended the spirit master and come home empty-handed. He insisted that we had done nothing wrong, except perhaps that we had had some alcohol before we left. "Of course the spirit master did not like [that]." But the number of possible reasons for an empty return was vast. Shaman Stepanovich had told me Burkhan could withhold prey for several reasons at once. It may have been that one of the hunters in the group had already hunted, and in spite of having exhausted his *kire*, he had continued to hunt with the group, thus angering the spirit and affecting their collective success. Or, a hunter may not have fit with the group astrologically, causing disharmony. Perhaps one of the hunters, or a relative of his, had been ill. Burkhan may not have wanted such a person to consume animals from his household. Alternatively, Burkhan may have allowed the hunted animal to escape, if it or any one of its family members had recently suffered from wolves or other predators. Or, perhaps, Burkhan knew the offspring of the targeted animal was going to be particularly strong, in which case he may have wanted it to reproduce, much like any good householder would.

BLOOD SACRIFICE

Borzhon and his brothers went to great lengths to secure good relations with Burkhan. Every three years, they invited Soiot shaman Dondok, their relative, to perform a ritual sacrifice on behalf of the clan. The sacrifice involved the burning of the head of an animal—usually a cow or a sheep—on a rock pedestal at the base of the "shaman's cliff." The shaman's cliff was one of several sacred cliff sites in Oka, each known to have a specific purpose (Sharastepanov 2008). Every time we drove by the rock, the driver would stop to make an offering beneath a shaman's tree, which was located some two hundred meters away from the rock itself. While visitors recognized the site as a typical sacred site where one would leave a token of respect (e.g., rice, coins, cigarettes, or strips of fabric), for the Dondokovy, this location held much deeper significance. From here they connected with Burkhan, who oversaw not only the taiga and its animals, but also their own households and animals.

I was not able to witness a blood sacrifice in person, as it had already been completed before I arrived in the field, and there would not be another sacrifice until well after I left. Neither was the whole process advertised locally. It remained strictly a family affair. As I found out later, there was good reason for the hushed nature of this ritual performance. Taking an animal's life as a sacrifice to a local spirit master was considered by local lamas a gross violation of Buddhist precepts. It was not a surprise then that the event was conducted under the auspices of Badma, the eldest of the Dondokovy brothers, by their blood relative, Soiot shaman Dondok. Both shared a strong sense of Soiot identity, which they saw as intimately interwoven with shamanist ritual activities. Dondok and Badma had used shamanism as a tool in their stance against Buddhist assertions over Soiot territory. Without seeking open conflict, both men sought to proclaim their allegiance to the landscape, taking a stance in the spirit world as well as in the sphere of local politics. Blood sacrifice at the base of the cliff seemed like the culmination of their collective stance.

UNFOLDING POWER IN AN ENFOLDING LANDSCAPE

Some individuals, among them Badma Khorluevich, felt quite strongly about shamanism as the only appropriate way for Soiots to relate to the landscape. Being a highly respected Soiot elder, Badma had introduced me to several shamans whose practice he personally trusted. Returning together from a séance at Soiot shaman Dondok Dorzheevich's house one day, I asked Badma what distinguished Soiot shamanic practices from those of Buriat shamans. I had expected him to point out some unique Soiot features that contrasted Buriat practices. Instead he related to me his anger over past Buriat attempts to establish a *datsan* at Sorok, the center of Soiot cultural heritage. Each time such plans were discussed, Badma had strongly opposed them. To date, Buddhist *khuraly* (services) had to be held at the local club house. "There has never been a *datsan* at Sorok in hundreds of years," Badma said, and he did not want to see one now. Dondok, in response to the same question, told me of his disapproval of lama Norbu of Puntsognamdolling *datsan* (a Soiot by descent), who in the past had referred to himself as a "Soiot lama." For Badma and Dondok there had never been a Soiot lama, because "Soiots had never had lamas—only shamans." Their resistance to the construction of *datsans* in Soiot territory must be understood as a direct continuation of an age-old struggle on the borderlands of the Mongolian steppe.

The roots of this struggle lie with the ruler of the western tribes of Mongolia, Altan-Khan. His 1578 meeting with Sonam Gyatso (the Third Dalai Lama) of the Tibetan Gelug school resulted in a monumental effort to translate Tibetan and Sanskrit sacred texts into Mongolian, as well as the construction of monasteries and the training of a large number of religious specialists (e.g., Elverskog 2003). Thus Buddhism made its inroads into northern Mongolia by the sixteenth and seventeenth centuries and reached Buriat tribes who had been practicing shamanism much like other Central Asian peoples (Tsybenov 2001: 39; see Khimitdorzhiev and Vanchikova 2011: 176–85). Following the growing number of mobile Buriat clans who practiced Buddhism on the northern side of the newly formed border between Qing China and the Russian Empire, Empress of Russia Elizaveta Petrovna ratified Buddhism as an official religion in 1741 (e.g., Tsyrempilov 2013: 55, 63).

Anthropologist Morten Pedersen (2003) and others (e.g., Even 1991; Heissig 1953; 2004) have described the repercussions of Altan-Khan's initial struggle as a continued Buddhist attempt to "domesticate" shamanist landscapes in northern Mongolia. Very near Badma and Dondok's homeland, where Mongolian highland steppe gives way to mountainous taiga, itinerant Mongolian and Tibetan lamas are said to have struggled with landscape entities, which in the literature are often referred to as demons (see Charleux 2002: 169). In an attempt to expand the reach of Buddhism, powerful lamas were sent out to locate and subdue these deities and establish *datsans*. In Oka, caves containing Buddhist ritual objects can be found to this day (Dashibalov 2000: 5), and local lore explains these shelters as key strongholds used by the earliest lamas who had come to Oka to tame local spirit masters. This lore echoes Mongolian and Tibetan legends of the famous Guru Rinpoche (or Padmasambhava):

> The majority of pilgrimage sites in the Tibetan world include caves where [Rinpoche] is said to have meditated, occasionally with one of his consorts or dakinis [Tantric priestesses]. In each of these places, he subdued local deities, bound them by oath and "opened" up the site. He is reputed to have hidden gter ma ("treasure texts") for subsequent discovery at an appropriate time, and also for making prophecies that led to later temples' foundations. (Charleux 2002:182)

An example of these and other features associated with Tantric Buddhist cave use can be found in a locally revered cave site near the village of Saiany, north of Orlik.

As Marina Sodnompilova (2009) points out, in the traditions of Mongolian peoples, caves have been understood as the womb of the Earth Mother. They are sacred places. This motherly or parental notion also comes to the fore in beliefs about caves as the residence of ancestral spirits (Sodnompilova 2009). Spirits of bygone ancestors can turn into local spirit masters (see Humphrey 1995: 151), as is the case in Khukhein Khada, a sacred site on the Shumak River, north of the village of Shumak in the Tunka region, just south of Oka. Here, according to legend, two Soiot girls were lost, and they became local spirit masters after their deaths (Sodnompilova 2009: 65). Similar accounts exist for Oka, particularly in reference to influential shamans who later became landscape spirit masters.

But yet another Mongolian view of caves associates them with ritual impurity, understood to be rooted in their femininity. An example of this is "the emergence of the phallic cult in the vicinity of the Erdene-Zuu monastery [of central Mongolia], [where a cult intended] to 'neutralize' erotic activities of the earthly goddess—with [a local landscape feature] being externally reminiscent of the bosom of a lying woman" (based on Nekliudov 1984: 105 in

Illustration 2.2. Sacred caves of Oka. Photograph by the author.

Sodnompilova 2009: 66). Whatever the exact motives may have been for the purification of caves in Oka, it is clear that these physical recesses attest to a history of taming and purification as part of the Buddhist project of domesticating landscapes.

SUBJUGATION AND TRANSFERRAL OF SPIRIT MASTERS

According to anthropologist Mona Schrempf (1999), one of the main purposes for ritual dances performed by Tantric and Bon-Po masters of Tibet (and later in exile) has been to control antagonistic agents in the landscape. This is a process involving "mental as well as physical actions of subjugation and expulsion," rendering "purified and protected" spaces for the construction of a temple, stupa, or mandala (Schrempf 1999: 198). These dances were once widespread in Buriatia and conducted annually in Oka at Zheelgenski *datsan*, where people knew them as *tsam* (Sharastepanov 2008: 35). According to Schrempf (1999: 199), these ritual dances "subjugate the earth" (*sa-' dul*)—a means of taking control of and transforming space. Although not all subjugation ritual is dance, it is this kind of confrontation between powers that lies at the heart of Buddhist expansion and territorial maintenance. Perpetual "taming, disciplining or civilizing" of that which is "uncontrolled, including the mind" is, according to religious scholar Geoffrey Samuel, a core duty of Tibetan lamas (Samuel as cited in Schrempf 1999: 199). Body and landscape become one when (sometimes masked) dancers represent protection deities, thereby becoming invocational placeholders. "By creating a ritual space and divine powers inside their bodies and minds, the dancers inscribe and recreate their environment in turn with their body, speech and mind" (Schrempf 1999: 199). In so doing, according to Schrempf (1999: 199), the perceived duality of body and landscape collapses. Mind and space, comprising and being comprised, become one.

In the Tunka Valley, the heritage of initial power encounters between representatives of Buddhism and local deities is best remembered in the arrival of a Tibetan lama, locally known as Buduun Lharampa (the fat Lharampa). This lama is said to have taken up residence in northern Mongolia after a dispute with the Thirteenth Dalai Lama. His Buriat students had invited Buduun Lharampa to the Tunka valley in 1919, where the *datsan* at Kyren had become a sizable center with as many as five hundred lamas serving the region (Nantsov 1998). The officiating lama at Gandan-Darzhalin datsan explained to me the historic visit of this dignitary as follows:

> the *pandit* [Buduun Lharampa] was a great scholar, a realized practicing Buddhist—a yogin . . . When he came to Tunka, he could see and converse with the five deities of Tunka, and by means of laying out to them the Dharma, the Buddhist Path, he led them into Buddhism. It began [near] the village of Khoito-Gol, at the site of Burkhan Baabai—the deity who, according to legend, descended from the upper world . . . of thirty-three celestial residents, headed by Khormus Khan. Burkhan Baabai is considered one of Khormus Khan's sons. He descended to earth in order to overwhelm evil, [and] coming to the Tunka Valley, he settled on Sandy Mountain (Rus. *peschanaia gora*) . . . [from] where he became the patron of Tunka Valley.

Buduun Lharampa is credited with setting up a *rgyal mtshan* (Bur. *zhalsan*), a wooden post topped with a cylinder commemorating his arrangement with the local landscape deity Burkhan Baabai (or Shargai-Noion). Subsequently, the yogin introduced all five Burkhany of Tunka to Buddhist precepts, converting or "transferring" them (Rus. *perevel ikh*) to Buddhism. The potential ill will of these landscape spirit masters is thus understood to have come under the control of Buddhist order, not so much through force as through a gradual perspectival change. It is understood that encounters at this level (i.e., with the most powerful deities of a region) require the efforts of no ordinary lama. And it is also understood that spirit masters who have not yet attained liberation remain volatile, a point to which I shall return.

THE BENEVOLENCE OF BINDING

In the Tunka Valley, at Gandan-Darzhalin *datsan*, an officiating lama explained to me how "powerful and enlightened lamas" of the past had "either convinced, or subjugated" (Rus. *ugovorit' libo pochenit'*) the mighty landscape entities by "binding them by oath" (Rus. *sviazat' ikh kliatvoi*). For the lama the process of "convincing" or "subjugating" and "binding" was an inherently benevolent act that could be extended to all sentient beings—be they animals (human or other) or landscape deities.

> From the perspective of Buddhism, an animal does not have good intellect (Rus. *razum*) or consciousness (Rus. *soznanie*) enabling it to deliberately commit good deeds. It does not understand that "if I do this, then that is going to take place." That is why... prayers and mantras were read into the ears of animals in order to create a connection with the animal. There would be a karmic connection [for the animal] with the teachings of the Buddha. When a karmic connection comes into existence, [the animal] will necessarily meet again [or return].

The connection with the animal takes place at once between the sutra-reciting human and the animal, and between the animal and the teachings of the Buddha. The assumption here is that being a nonhuman animal (i.e., being at the subhuman level) is less desirable than being human, and by making a connection with humans (and therefore with the Buddha's teachings) the animal is set on a trajectory toward higher rebirths.

The lama explained this connection as a kind of benevolent imprint that invariably leads to a repeated encounter between entities.

> A person who has seen the Buddha—having believed in him, [or] even just having seen him—will always remain [with] an imprint [of this encounter] within him. He will necessarily meet [again]... There is a story in which a disciple of the Buddha, Sariputra [ca. 568–ca. 484 BCE], who had also been a hunter—[at a time] when [Shakyamuni] was not in this world yet—had taken shelter in a cave from the rain, where [he saw a] drawing depicting the previous buddha on a wall... He saw it and believed. He began to have very strong faith, and as a result he entered the right path, that is the Buddhist Path.

The conception of Sariputra's faith takes place inside a cave, enfolded in the landscape, and sheltered from the elements. It is fanned into flame by the depiction of another being whose beauty is now imprinted in his consciousness. This imprint creates in him a karmic tie that is prophetic in nature, calling for further encounters with other representatives of the same kind of being.

Struck by [Kassapa Buddha's] beauty, he wished that in future he might meet an equally beautiful person [the coming Buddha, Shakyamuni]. And for the animal there also exists such a thing. When they see it, when something is done for them, when mantras are read [to them], then something like that is created [in them]. And the animal will be more or less good—there is something with which we can help the animal.

In the lama's example, conviction and subjugation (i.e., taming) take place under sheltered conditions. A new perception of self comes to be inside the womb-cave of Mother Earth. A transformation is affected in this space: Sariputra enters the cave with the perspective of a hunter, but he emerges from the cave as a person who no longer purposefully sheds blood. For the lama at Gandan-Darzhalin *datsan*, Buddhist domestication of sentient Others pivots on this kind of encounter, in which landscape spirits (much like animals) are "helped" on their way to higher rebirths and eventually to liberation.

DOMESTICATION AS COMMUNICATIVE LOSS

With deities (*burkhany*) divided into earthly and celestial entities, it is understood that, unlike the celestials, earthly spirit masters do not possess generative power. Yet, earthly deities are to be recognized for their immense power on earth, and because they still generate karma, this power can be dangerous. Speaking of earthly deities, the lama at Gandan-Darzhalin *datsan* explained: "Since these deities have inner emotions . . . such as anger, jealousy, envy . . . if [the deity] gives something to someone, [the gift] will have strings attached. [The deity] has its own motives . . . and when he generates karma . . . he does not create good. As long as karma exists, there exists an end for that being." Bringing the deity in line with Buddhist teachings is thus a form of domestication in that the deity is gradually brought into the household of the Buddhist pantheon.

At the same time, a celestial *burkhan*—that is, a spirit that has attained total enlightenment, a Buddha—cannot be called upon by a hunter to aid in the killing of an animal. Such assistance would violate every tenet of Buddhist liberation. An earthly deity (i.e., an unenlightened landscape spirit master), however, can assist a hunter in the taking of life, even if this calls the spirit to act against its commitment to Buddhist teachings. It could be argued, thus, that it is to the advantage of many residents of Oka that landscape entities not be domesticated, and that spirit masters who have not become celestial, remain earthly, because day-to-day concerns of Soiot herders and hunters fall predominantly into the domain of earthly deities and their ability and willingness to aid in the taking of life.

This conflict, from the perspective of the lama at Gandan-Darzhalin *datsan*, is reflected in the divergent ways of shamans and lamas in approaching an earthly landscape spirit master:

> When a shaman makes offerings, he will sprinkle vodka (and other things) every day, up to the point that the spirit tires of it. [The spirit will say:] "How tired I am of him! Everyone comes and asks for something... O well! Slaughter a lamb, and I will do what you ask." The lama, on the other hand ... will [say to the spirit]: "Take the offering and perform this good deed. By the power of your good action, you will be reborn in higher worlds. You will accrue good deeds." The spirit will then act out of joy and on his own.

From this perspective, it is as if the Buddhist practitioner were whispering in the ear of the spirit, much like he does into the ear of an animal, reminding it of a previous encounter or past commitment.

The shaman, on the other hand, is seen as having to coax the spirit to conform to his wishes, and each of his encounters with the spirit is marked by resistance, often necessitating bloodshed in the form of sacrifices. A lama, instead, can rely on the predictability of a tamed deity, which does not require the shedding of blood. He expects the spirit to exercise benevolence on its own volition, and having attained a new perspective on what is desirable, the spirit is merely reminded of the source of its own good. It would seem then that the oath bound spirit master is a colonized entity. No longer in need of subjugation, it now must be reminded only of its prior commitment for the benefit of its own enlightenment—a task that falls to the lama.

BALANCING RIVAL MEANINGS

Anthropologist Morten A. Pedersen (2003) illustrates how the people of the Darkhad Depression in northwest Mongolia—people to whom several of my Soiot friends were related—perceived themselves as possessing a black side and a yellow side. The black side is that of shamanism, which is associated with the taiga and its many influences and unpredictabilities, moral ambiguities, powers and "unstraightness" (Pedersen 2003: 180), while the yellow side is associated with a Buddhist understanding of peace, domestication, and moral straightness found in the landscape of the steppe. Darkhad people possess both sides, according to Pedersen, but the yellow side in particular remains invisible until it is exposed by an outsider. While Buddhism may be seen to have come as an ideological intrusion to the Darkhad, attempting to exterminate shamanism, a contemporary Darkhad interpretation of their own history paints the Buddhist project in much brighter hues: Pedersen (2003: 193) terms this the Darkhad "subaltern perspective," a view in which Darkhad people have always been "tame" on the inside, but in a way that required an enlightened outsider, such as the Mongolian Gelupga Buddhist church, to bring to light their hidden potential.

Although I did not encounter identical claims in Oka to those put forth by Pedersen for Darkhad, the willingness to entertain both sides—the "wild" side of shamanism and the "tame" side of Buddhism—was ever present in my encounters with people. The best way to explain this situation is perhaps through Stan Mumford's "unbounded and layered" or "interpenetrating" cultures, as he describes them among shamans and Gurung lamas of Nepal (1989: 11–3). Rather than affiliating themselves with a single ideological side, individuals would find themselves at events belonging to different sides, having to interpret the meaning of each event retrospectively. Where this happens, "intentionality is pulled into a process of use over time, as one keeps negotiating 'what is meant,' in light of rival meanings" (Mumford 1989:12). This is not an unusual phenomenon in frontier and syncretic religious environments where proponents of opposing traditions are actively acquiring each other's meaning making processes—the recipients to enrich their tradition; the itinerants to ease their proselytizing (see Snellgrove and Richardson 1968: 108 in Mumford 1989: 12). In Oka, similar dynamics had been taking shape in the highly localized practices of lamas, among whom was my friend Baldorzho (b. 1963) from the village of Bokson.

Baldorzho's grandfather had been a lama from Oka who had suffered Soviet religious repression in the early 1930s. He had been arrested and taken away, and upon his release with advanced tuberculosis he had died an untimely death in his home. Because his name had been changed during the repressions, there were no archival records for him, but local elders remembered him well during my fieldwork. Baldorzho had never met his grandfather. Yet he had covertly nursed an interest in his religious heritage as a teenager attending the Soviet school system. In later years, an elder lama of his grandfather's generation managed to pass his localized Buddhist knowledge to Baldorzho. With the death of Baldorzho's teacher, the last holder of this local knowledge was said to have passed. In Baldorzho's own words, he himself was now the only lama in Oka to possess the oral Tantric sutras that had been composed by the earliest lamas in Oka who had adapted Mongolian and Tibetan Buddhism to accommodate local shamanic sensibilities to the landscape. Given his knowledge, Baldorzho was a particular kind of lama—one who subscribed to Tantric practices adapted to the Eastern Saian mountain environment—not to be confused with a Buriat *khadasha*, or mountain cult specialist.

BUDDHIST HUNTERS AND THE ZAIAN-TENGERI

The crux of Baldorzho's task lay in "[r]econciling Buddhist teaching with a hunting culture," a task he assured me was "a difficult puzzle" (Rus. *trudnyi vopros*). When Buddhism first came to Oka, it was not transferred as a fully functional system. Itinerant lamas tested every sutra and Tantric ritual for their efficacy in the new landscape. As a result, many practices were adjusted, which is particularly evident in the astrological moon calendar, where Tibetan and Mongolian dates have been changed to reflect the geographic context of south Siberia.

To illustrate the importance of bringing Buddhist teachings into a productive dialogue with the reality of local ways of wresting a living from the land, Baldorzho explained:

> In the past, lamas in Oka were very powerful, having undergone fifteen to sixteen years of intensive training. But there were also highly skilled hunters here. Ordained clergy abstained from hunting, but lay persons hunted for a living, and they would prepare for the hunt in accordance with the astrological calendar, which recommended the days that were advantageous for hunting. A hunter would petition Burkhan for a gift of prey, and as he went hunting, he would be ever concerned for the souls of the animals he killed. His goal was for the soul of each animal to leave the body in peace, finding its path to [a higher] rebirth. Some hunters would light a candle, aiding their prey's soul in finding its way. And when a hunter aimed to shoot, he would recite a special mantra on behalf of the rebirth of his prey's soul in another body.

Thus, some hunters had accepted the Buddhist notion of reincarnation, while holding on to older ideas about the soul and spirit masters who had to be petitioned, or bargained with. While I did not encounter any living hunters who still practiced these prayers, other ways of incorporating (Tantric) Buddhist ritual with local ways of addressing animals by way of their spirit masters still existed.

One evening in September, Baldorzho visited my host, Baianbata, at the winter pasture to perform an annual consecration ritual on behalf of the whole household. He had brought a traditional ritual object, hidden in a square sheath and wrapped in a blue silken shawl (Bur. *khadag*) embroidered with Tibetan script. Baldorzho referred to the object as "the worship of the eternal heaven" (Bur. *Zaian-Tengeri*; Rus. *poklonenie vechnemu nebu*). It somewhat resembled a sword in shape, but was made from a gun barrel that had been cut in half along the shaft, maintaining its tubular shape in the handle area. A rubber grip had been affixed to the handle area, and at the end of the grip a brass "diamond" (Rus. *almaz*) had been attached. A row of four holes had been drilled into the blade; one near the tip of the curved blade, and three holes spaced out between handle and tip. Baldorzho removed the Zaian-Tengeri from its sheath and pushed it through the ventilation hole in Baianbata's hearth. When the Zaian-Tengeri had come to a glow from the heat of the coals, Baldorzho asked Baianbata to stand up in the middle of the room, with his arms stretched out on both sides, and with a gap between his legs. Reciting a mantra, Baldorzho penetrated the air with the smoking sword on all sides of Baianbata's body. Then he placed the sword back in the glowing coals of the hearth.

After pouring water into a clean glass jar on the kitchen table, Baianbata took position in the center of the room again. This time he was asked to lift his shirt, exposing the bare skin of his upper body. Again Baldorzho pulled the sword from the coals, and lifting it to his mouth, he repeatedly touched the glowing steel blade with his bare tongue. Taking a sip of water from the jar, he blew it through the holes in the blade, onto Baianbata's chest. He repeated the procedure for his back, before depositing the ritual object in the water jar on the table. The water, now containing gray floating ash particles, was considered sacred and had to be kept overnight. In the morning Baianbata was to take it outside, where each member of the household would wash their hands and faces with it. The remaining water in the jar was then to be drunk by the members of Baianbata's family. Although the sword ritual was intended to affect general well-being for a household, a client had the liberty to silently petition the owner of the fire (a master spirit) for more specific things during the ritual. Such petitions could be as concrete as the withdrawal of wolves from a particular valley, which was an acute need at the time of Baldorzho's visit. This kind of petition would have been directed at a local spirit master, allowing the ritual performance of a Tantric Buddhist lama to coalesce with perceived local shamanic needs.

AMONG SUTRAS A HUNTER'S SUTRA

During another visit with Baldorzho, I learned about a further adaptation made to Buddhist ritual by his ancestors: the composition of a hunter's sutra. Although Baldorzho had promised to eventually show to me the text of the sutra, he never produced it. It seemed his perpetual delay was intentional. He had been highly protective of the text, asking me not to photograph or otherwise copy it when he would bring it to one of our meetings. According to Baldorzho, the sutra had been written down specifically for use in Oka. Written in Buriat, unlike most other sutras (which were written in Tibetan), the elder had entrusted the document to Baldorzho, shortly before the prior had died. Baldorzho described how hunters were coming to see him, asking prayers for their hunting success. When they did, he would recite a number of Tibetan sutras, mixing in the hunter's sutra. Given that it would take Baldorzho about thirty-five minutes to read the sutra out loud, it was a relatively short one. Judging by Baldorzho's upheld fingers, the sutra's pages measured less than a centimeter in thickness. After reading the sutra out loud, he would sprinkle vodka, milk, or milky tea to all four directions of the horizon, following a clockwise pattern.

Given his advanced level of Buddhist training, Baldorzho was no longer permitted to go hunting. Like other young men, he too had been a hunter in his younger years. He could recall how in years past hunters had often brought gifts of game to the *datsan*. They would come to the *datsan* to have their moral burdens alleviated by the lamas' recitation of sutras, and they would bring the skins of their animal prey as offerings. Those who did not hunt would bring a lamb, and people who did not possess even a lamb would bring its monetary equivalent. The kitchen staff at the *datsan* would prepare the meat of these hunted and herded animals for those residing and working at the temple complex. A large ritual drum at a *datsan* in Orlik had been made from the skin of one of these hunted animals that had been brought as an offering. As all lamas in Oka would insist, none of these animal gifts had been sacrifices. Animal sacrifices were forbidden in Buddhism, but animal gifts or offerings to the *datsan* were allowed.

CONCLUSION

At Uro, people lived between two cosmological narratives. On the one side, there was a landscape that had always been indwelled by autonomous and unpredictable, yet potentially caring spirit masters. On the other side, there were enlightened and committed deities whose intentions did not have to be feared, but whose commitment to Buddhist precepts had to be perpetually reiterated. By incorporating the activities of shamans and of lamas in their daily lives, the residents of Uro found ways to benefit from a spectrum of available ritual practitioners. Other times, specific ritual practices—such as the blood sacrifice—were deliberately used to stress the exceptionalism of shamanism as a form of political separatism. Such politicization of shamanism vis-à-vis Buddhism, however, was largely limited to select influential Soiot elders who represented their people as an indigenous minority among a Buriat majority, and less in contrast to tantric localized ritual but more as a sign set against the colonial aims of an official church. On a more practical level, the seemingly peaceful overlap between Buddhist and shamanist perspectives broke down only where a spirit master had become domesticated through Buddhist ritual (i.e., by way of attaining enlightenment), at which point a Soiot hunter would no longer be able to appeal to the spirit's desire to engage in reciprocal exchange. Where spirits had come under this spell of domestication, the shamanic system of balance, which allowed the negotiation of harmony between humans, animals, and the landscape, arguably had lost its efficacy.

For most Soiots, it seemed wiser to position oneself between such cosmological extremities. It was better to remain open to both ways than to renounce the one and embrace the other. People had come to rely on a combination of herding and hunting activities, and their households actively relied on ritual activities belonging to both cosmological perspectives. Although one might guess a lama would be called for concerns relating to yak, cattle, sheep, or horses, and a shaman to matters of the hunt, in actuality this was not always the case. Tantric practitioners, like Baldorzho, were actively blurring narratives by allowing people to incorporate their own view of the landscape during ceremonies. In so doing, Baldorzho kept open the door to a perpetual state of "semi-domestication" in cosmological terms. Arguably, full Buddhist domestication of a powerful spirit master was as undesirable, from the standpoint of a Soiot householder, as the full domestication of any of his freely roaming animals. To maintain balance in one's social relations with all sentient beings, it was essential that mutual exchange continue, and this in turn required that each party maintain some volitional freedom. Where the Buddhist project of domestication had progressed to the point of effectively denying spirits their volitional freedom, there the work of bridging shamanism with Buddhism had become unproductive.

CHAPTER 3

DREAMING OF DEER

A small piece of ice had fallen on my face, waking me. When I opened my eyes it was still dark, but I could make out the frosty green tarp that had sheltered my body for the night in a deep pasture on the Kara-Buren' River. The other members of our research team were still resting in their tents. Light snow had fallen in the night, and the forest encircling us was perfectly still. Only the gentle movement of the Kara-Buren' to my left was audible. Our horses were still roaming in the forest somewhere, their sweaty saddles airing out under a wooden shelter near where I lay in the grass. In a hunter's cabin on the river, our Tofa guides, Denis and Aleksandr, were still asleep. Breathing softly—muzzles to the ground—our two dogs had taken shelter from the snow under the hanging saddles. I decided to get up, gather wood for an early morning tea, and wait for dawn. As the hills above our camp slowly became illuminated, I could hear the faint sound of bells in the distance. What was this sound? Our horses had no bells. The ringing of bells soon was joined by rhythmical breathing. Looking up from the fire, I could see emerging from the trees two hunter-led caravans of thirteen reindeer each. Quietly passing by our camp, without stopping or slowing down, they passed us by in the snowy grass, only to disappear again into the woods on the other side of the clearing. Had it not been for the freshly trampled snow, I would have thought it a dream, an early morning hallucination.

Two days earlier, I had spoken to Vitalii Lomov in the village of Alygdzher from where we had come. Vitka, as he was known locally, had herded reindeer for most of his life. In fact, he had lived in Uro for two years in the mid-1990s to assist several of my Soiot reindeer herding friends after the Sorok administration had purchased a herd from Tofalariia. I had heard so much about Vitka during my fieldwork in Buriatia that, at times, it felt as if I had known him long before we first met in Alygdzher. Vitka's expertise had been pivotal in bringing reindeer herding back to Oka. Together we flipped through entries from a journal describing his days as instructor in Oka (see Oehler 2018b).

After conveying greetings from the herders he had trained twenty years earlier, I updated him on the current state of the Soiot reindeer herd. No one had seen Vitka since his return to Alygdzher in 1996, and my friends in Oka were not certain he was still alive. With a past of heavy drinking, it was a joy to see him sober and building his own house in Alygdzher. Vitka's life had changed since his return to Tofalariia, and the whole of Tofa reindeer herding had undergone significant changes—even over the past ten years.

As I found out later, the caravans that had passed us on the Kara-Buren' River in the morning had been led by two salaried reindeer herders. Several weeks earlier, they had moved to the reindeer camp at Aleksandr Viktorovich Gimadeev's hunting cabin on the upper Dugol'ma River. Here they had prepared for the annual arrival of hunters from Alygdzher. At this time of year, hunters were collecting their riding and transportation reindeer from the collectively held herd as they were preparing to set out for their winter hunting territories, known also as ancestral taigas (Rus. *rodovye taigi*). Many working reindeer had already been collected when we arrived. Herders had been luring reindeer to the campsite daily, scattering coarse salt onto exposed boulders at the center of the clearing by Gimadeev's cabin. During the day the reindeer would come from the forest, vigorously licking the boulders. Their young would nibble with great interest on every human implement they could find.

The velvety antler skin of the does had begun to peel a few weeks earlier, flapping in the wind like rags. The bull's velvet would soon follow, maturing somewhat later in the autumn. Prior to their departure, the herders had already been trimming antler tines. Bulls' fore antlers were shortened to prevent lethal outcomes in mating duels, and the same was done for does to ease their feeding in deep snow. The females developed particularly sharp tines and to prevent injury, these were clipped. The hind antlers were trimmed only on reindeer used for riding to prevent injury to the rider, and wide racks were shortened to allow passage in dense forest (see Grøn 2011). Cut antler pieces were generally thrown into the creek bed running by the encampment. Now that the two herders had left camp with their own reindeer in tow, visiting hunters—like ourselves—would volunteer by attending to herding tasks on a rotational basis.

* * *

It is observations such as these that mark my time spent with Tofa and Soiot reindeer herders in the Eastern Saian Mountains. To better situate these experiences, I will now provide a brief overview of reindeer domestication in south central Siberia, supplemented by further observations of contemporary herding. The main aim of this chapter is to show how proximity between people and reindeer can fluctuate over time, particularly as the result of other species entering the household. The first section outlines what have been the main theories of reindeer domestication in the Saians, so as to lay the groundwork for a vision of human-animal relations that transcends reindeer. My perspective does not ignore or debunk older theories, rather it builds on them, first by describing a recent transition in Tofa reindeer herding practices from a more constrictive method to a more invitational style. Here historical developments—particularly the establishment, collapse, and later privatization of the kolkhoz system—have affected the proximity between humans and reindeer, and therewith the ways in which they relate to each other. Second, I will build on these theories by making visible the impact of other species on human-reindeer relations, revisiting recent attempts to reintroduce reindeer to Soiot households. Both examples emphasize the flux of reindeer as a key species in south Siberian households.

The propensity of animals to move back and forth between the realm of the human household and that of the forest, as described earlier in the book, is particularly evident in reindeer. The concept of animal autonomy resurfaces here, as a large enough reindeer herd will follow its own sense in regard to timing and routing through the landscape, even when under the care of humans (see Grøn 2011). What this chapter adds to these observations is attention to the presence of other species. Mongolian horses traded from Oka-Buriats, for instance, have for a long time played an important role in the lives of Tofa hunter-herders, especially during the summers when reindeer graze at high

Illustration 3.1. Tofa reindeer camp. Photograph by the author.

altitude and cannot be bothered to transport people and objects from place to place (see Petri 1927b: 34; Rassadin 2005: 53). Tofas are said to have begun breeding their own horses around the turn of the century (Melnikova 1994: 52), although a Turkic equine breeding tradition may predate Tofa horse trading with Russians and Buriats, as is suggested by Tofa folklore, cosmology, and lexicon (Rassadin 2005; Rassadin 1996).

The extent to which horses and reindeer have competed for importance in Tofa households goes beyond the scope of this chapter, but I will address in more detail fluctuations in the importance of reindeer and yak in Soiot households. As we have seen previously, for Soiots, not only the Mongolian horse but also yak herds have played a key role, at least since 1829 (Nefedev and Gergesov 1929). In light of these findings it is reasonable to argue that fluctuation in the importance ascribed to particular domestic species may not be a "modern" occurrence, but a characteristic of a much older regional pattern, reflected in the prehistoric movements of people and animals in and out of the Eastern Saian Mountains.

BIRTHPLACE OF DOMESTICATION

The origins of reindeer domestication feature as an early and prominent theme in the ethnographic literature of Southern Siberia. The Altai-Saian Region has been specifically identified as a possible "birth place" for reindeer domestication in Eurasia. While longstanding scholarly debates on the topic have been summarized more than once for an English readership (e.g., Mirov 1945; Whitaker 1981; Zolotarev and Levin 1940), two main theories emerge from the material. The so-called diffusion theory (Aronsson 1991; Hatt 1918; Laufer 1917; Sirelius 1916) proposes that reindeer domestication spread from Southern Siberia into Northern Siberia and on into Scandinavia. The second theory, referred to as the "evolution theory" (Mulk 1994; Storli 1996; Wiklund 1918), advocates multiple and independent points of origin for domestication. More recently, the focus in reindeer domestication studies has shifted to an analysis of genetic material from Russia (e.g., Kol and Lazebny 2006) and Scandinavia (e.g., Røed et al. 2008; Røed et al. 2011), favoring the independent evolution model. Explorers Carruthers and Miller (1914) and Norwegian zoologist Ørjan Olsen (1915a) were among the earliest ethnographers who examined human-reindeer relations in the Saian Region. Carruthers and Olsen independently spent three summer months among the Tozhu of eastern Tyva in 1910 and 1914, respectively (Stépanoff 2012: 288; Whitaker 1981: 342). One of Olsen's goals had been to show similarities between Sámi and Tozhu reindeer herding practices. He went about this by comparing the use of plant and animal products, and various other elements of material culture, leading him to suggest a single origin of domestication in South Siberia. His work opened up further discussion and research for years to come.

Debates on whether reindeer had been domesticated prior to other species in the area, and whether the Saian Region could indeed be identified as the birthplace of reindeer domestication, were carried on by a number of Western and Soviet scholars after Olsen. In 1928, Russian scholar A. M. Maksimov suggested that "some Turkic or Mongol tribe" had been herding deer for some time prior to adopting cattle ([1928] 2019: 33). Russian anthropologists Glafira M. Vasilevich and Maksim G. Levin (1951: 87) took this argument further, proposing that it may have been under these circumstances that Samoyeds had adopted the practice, taking it with them as they migrated further north and east. This led Soviet archaeologist and ethnographer Sevian Vainshtein (1972, 1980b) to develop a three-stage single-origin theory for Eurasian reindeer herding in eastern Tyva. His explanation would account for the domestication of reindeer at large, as well as for the development of the Saian style of reindeer husbandry in particular. Based on his study of cultural transformations in the Saian Region, Vainshtein (1960) concluded the use of reindeer as load carriers had preceded their use as a means for human transportation. This line of reasoning was strengthened by the findings of ethnographers working with other reindeer herders, such as the Tungus (Vasilevich 1964). Studying saddle designs in archaeological and ethnographic records, Vainshtein (1980a: 131) reasoned that reindeer herding had indeed originated in the Saian Region in ancient times, but people had started riding reindeer only during the fourteenth century.

Vainshtein's argument that reindeer herding may first have appeared in the Saian Region is based in part on the presence of an ancient breed of reindeer, not found anywhere outside of the Saian Mountains, and on Mashkovtsev's (1940) and Kertselli's (1925) observations that Saian reindeer are easier to handle than any other known reindeer (Vainshtein 1980a: 132). This ease may, in part, attest to a first stage of reindeer domestication at a time when Samoyeds, who had been familiar with other forms of steppe pastoralism as early as 2000 BCE, were pushed toward taiga regions by Karasuk and Tagar tribes who had moved into the Minusin Hollow of what is Khakassia and Krasnoyarsk Krai today. Located between steppe and taiga, Samoyeds would presumably have herded deer as a source of meat alongside other species (Vainshtein 1980: 133). According to this theory, the second stage occurred before 1000 CE, when Samoyeds began to move deeper into the taiga, equipping their reindeer with pack saddles, separating reindeer herding from other forms of pastoralism. After spreading across the Saian Region, the practice would have come to an end when Samoyeds were pushed north by horse-breeding Turkic groups (Vainshtein 1980a: 134). The final stage would have come with the birth of a distinct Saian style of reindeer herding. This style may have resulted from contact between the now Turkic-speaking tribes of the Saians with their Samoyed neighbors to the north, when the former re-adopted reindeer husbandry. The Turkic-speaking population would have applied their equine-related practices of dairying and saddle-based riding to reindeer (Vainshtein 1980a: 135–36).

Vainshtein's assumptions, speculative as they may seem, take into account the likely role interspecies relations would have played in reindeer domestication. In his perspective, Samoyeds of the Minusin Hollow had been herders long before encountering reindeer. When they eventually began herding deer, they would not likely have given up the herding of other species. Because the Turkic-speaking ancestors of Soiots and Tofas brought with them an ancient horse breeding tradition, it is logical to assume not only that the continued importance of horses alongside reindeer represents a long-standing tradition in the Saians, but also that the extension of equestrian material culture to reindeer would have occurred naturally. The ability to tweak, rather than to reinvent species-specific material culture, further suggests flexibility in the relative importance of particular species at any given time.

The famous Pazyryk burials of Altai Early Nomads contain sacrificed horses wearing rich ornamentation, dating ca. 305–238 BCE (Stepanova 2006: 104). Their decorated head dresses and bridles have been suggested as indicating a symbolism of predation and transformation, possibly linking horses to predator and prey species, including deer (Jacobsen-Tepfer 1993: 62; 2015: 287,). Among these items is a horse mask mounted with leather covered wooden stag antlers (Rudenko 1953: 214, 219, 1970: 179) and a bridle holding a stylized stag head with antlers (Rudenko 1953: 210–212, 1970: 171–174). However, there does not seem to be any clear link between these stylized deer depictions and early forms of reindeer herding, nor do their antlers seem to resemble those of reindeer.

Stylized depictions of what seem to be Siberian red deer (*Cervus sibiricus*) with reindeer brow antlers can be seen, however, on Mongolian deer stones often found adjacent to the ritual horse burials of semi-nomadic herder-hunters from the Late Bronze Age (1300–700 BCE) (Fitzhugh 2017: 160). The Saian-Altai versions of these Mongolian stones contain their own style of deer and other animal imagery, although they have been more difficult to date (Fitzhugh 2017: 167; Jacobsen-Tepfer 2001: 34). Russian archaeologist Dmitri G. Savinov (1994) suggests the deer were sacrificial animals. Given the presence of bows and arrows in many of these pictographs, a hunting context does seem likely. While such sacrifices might harken to the ritual deer sacrifices of Himalayan Gurung shamans (Mumford 1989), the deer stones do not seem to provide direct evidence of early reindeer herding, as "they are never found in the taiga and mountain tundra zones and in this respect have no discernible connection with Dukha or other Siberian peoples and cultures as they are known in the present" (Fitzhugh 2009: 74).

A growing focus on yak herding among Soiots, particularly as the result of assimilative pressures from Buriat settlers peaking around the end of the nineteenth century, hardly comes as a surprise if seen in light of the continuous prehistoric changes that have taken place in regional hunter-herder practices. If the ancestors of Soiots had indeed been steppe pastoralists who had transitioned to hunting in a taiga setting, then adopting Buriat herding practices in taiga pasturelands may have marked little more than yet another shift of focus in a series of fluctuating subsistence and species emphases over time. The shift then, from herding to secure a means of transportation during the hunt, to hunting in order to supplement herding for meat, parallels the general pattern Vainshtein and others have described for the Eastern Saian Mountains.

During my fieldwork in Oka, I searched for a Soiot oral tradition on the domestication of reindeer. Such accounts have been recorded for Dukhas of Mongolia (see Keay 2006: 2; Ragagnin 2011: 256), Tozhus of Tyva (Stépanoff 2012) as well as for Tofas of Tofalariia. Anthropologist B. E. Petri (1927b: 45) collected one such account from Tofa elder A. E. Tulaev in 1926, while visiting with elders on the source of the Biriusa River, northwest of Oka:

> A Karagass [Tofa] was walking and searching for something to ride on the hunt. This was long ago . . . Karagass didn't even have reindeer then. He met a person.
> — What are you looking for?
> — I am looking for something to ride on during the hunt.
> — Go to the green outcrop at the top of the Uda [River], two reindeer walk there. A white one and a black one walk there. The white one I've caught—he's calm, and the black one I haven't caught—he's wild. I let the white one go—didn't need him. Take it, you'll have livestock. The Karagass went and caught it. From that white reindeer all Karagass reindeer descended. From that time on we've had reindeer.

Interestingly, this origin account takes for granted at least two details: first, Tofa reindeer did not require much taming to begin with because all domestic reindeer find their source with a single already tame (Rus. *smirnyi*, i.e., gentle or manageable) individual. Second, the calm original individual had a white coat, a color known scientifically to indicate domestication in reindeer, that is to say, as a genetic mutation facilitated by domestication (see Rødven et al. 2009; Våge et al. 2014). While the domestication of reindeer among Tofalars is thought to have a starting point—namely on the Upper Uda River, possibly in a location known as Wild Ridge (Rus. Dikii Khrebret, elev. 2,070 to 2,094 meters) in eastern Tofalariia, the taming aspect of domestication itself is not thought to have a particular origin point. The latter is seen as an affordance or possibility that was already in place, awaiting merely to be recognized and utilized by Tofa.

Illustration 3.2. Tofa riding bulls near reindeer camp. Photograph by the author.

Sadly, none of the Soiot elders I spoke with could recall an oral account for the origins of reindeer domestication. An anonymous religious Soiot specialist from Bokson (b. 1963) explained the loss of this knowledge as the result of years of Soviet ideological repression. In his opinion, Soiot elders had taken most of this knowledge to their graves.

FROM REINDEER TO YAK

Another explanation for the absence of such an oral account may be the in-migration of Buriats to the southeastern Saians, described in the introduction of this book. The influx of Buriat settlers had been accompanied by a growing Soiot emphasis on yak and cows (e.g., Pavlinskaia 2002; Petri 1927a: 14), long predating Soviet collectivization and industrial intensification in the 1920s. As one might expect, an oral Buriat account for the origin and initial domestication of yak, as well as for crossbred hybrids (Bur. *khainak*) did exist (see chapter 4). Following the introduction of Buriat household animals to Oka, B. E. Petri (1927a: 14) divided Oka-Soiots into five economic groups by the 1920s. All of these groups he had described as transitioning from hunting and reindeer herding to stockbreeding or agricultural practices, the latter specifically in the

Tunka Valley. The collective farms that were set up after the revolution had actively built on this perceived trend, further intensifying existing milk and meat production, while maintaining transportation reindeer only into the early 1960s.

In a summary of his 1926 expedition to Oka, Petri (1927a: 16) reports that only one group of Soiots was still actively engaged in herding reindeer. Among them the Badmaev household was collecting reindeer belonging to neighboring households and taking them to high altitude pastures in the summer. This freed their owners to herd cattle at lower altitude. Cattle owners would still use their reindeer for transportation during autumn and winter hunts, but a division of labor was needed to accommodate the divergent needs of yak and reindeer in summer. According to Petri a shortage of marriageable women among the Irkit clan necessitated intermarriages with Buriats, which also accelerated the transition to cattle breeding (Petri 1927a: 19). By the 1920s, the only group that was predominantly herding reindeer consisted of eight households, numbering twenty-eight individuals, sixty-three reindeer, thirty-seven cattle, twenty-three horses, and nine dogs, all of whom lived around Lake Il'chir (Petri 1927a: 14–15). Further north, on the Khonchon and Khan-Modon Rivers, two other groups were still in possession of reindeer. Here a total of fifty-six individuals were in possession of thirty-two reindeer (Petri 1927a: 14–15). Although avid fur hunters, they were also keeping 203 head of cattle, consisting of yak and Mongolian cows, and seventy-three sheep and goats (Petri 1927a:14). The remaining Soiot groups had given up their reindeer for cattle, although they too continued hunting for furs in autumn and winter (Petri 1927a: 18). Taken together, 250 Soiots owned a total of 124 reindeer, alongside 1,178 head of cattle in eight areas of Oka (Petri 1927a: 15).

Much like reindeer, yak herds roamed over extensive territory in herds of thirty to a hundred during my fieldwork. Unlike yak and hybrids who mingled with Mongolian cows near the household, larger yak herds were not subject to the ways in which domestic cattle were held. They did not, for instance, use winter stables, neither were they accounted for in the summer hay harvest. Instead they grazed freely from valley to valley, taking advantage of the cooling effect of snow patches at higher altitudes in summer, and passing by their owner's household only sporadically. They were driven into corrals only for mandatory inoculations, to have their owner's paint marks renewed or to transition between summer and winter grazing areas. For the remainder of time they roamed freely, often lacking human supervision for extended periods of time. During these times, herders would ride out to them only for rough stock counts or to establish their general location.

Even in winter, yak maintained a high degree of autonomy, procuring their own forage from beneath soft layers of snow. In June, the herders would move their yak to pastures at higher altitudes. While reindeer were kept near camp for their calving period from late April to May, yak at Uro preferred to give birth far away from human settlement. During the calving period, yak were highly protective of their young, often actively hiding their offspring from anyone's sight. According to my interlocutors, it was only when a mother felt her offspring was sufficiently stable that she would come near the human household again, now accompanied by her little one. Much like reindeer, yak had been milked beginning with calving season. Although in many ways yak paralleled the place reindeer had once held in Soiot households, yak never satisfied transportation needs as they have in the Himalayas. Ancient horse breeding tradition, and more recently motorization, had filled this gap when reindeer became less central to Soiot households.

To obtain a better picture of what Soiot life may have looked like prior to the introduction of yak, I visited Tofalariia in the autumn of 2014. Here I was able to see the place of reindeer in contemporary Tofa society, alongside horses and cattle, the latter of which had been introduced by Russian settlers. The majority of contemporary Soiot reindeer, which I will discuss later in this chapter, had been brought to Oka from Tofalariia and were in this sense Tofa reindeer. Tofas who reside in Irkutskaia Oblast are the northern neighbors of Tozhu, Soiots, and Buriats. Many of their communities are connected by an extensive trail system that predates Soviet sedentarization. These cross-border trails are not used on a regular basis now, but stories of historical and more recent visits along these tracks abound. Denis, a Tofa hunter I befriended in Tofalariia recalled that, "a very long time ago, maybe as long as a hundred years ago, Tofa herders were keeping reindeer near the Ia River." Here the grazing range overlapped with that of Soiot reindeer herders from Shasnur in northwest Oka. What follows is a description of my encounters with Tofa reindeer herders and hunters northwest of the Ia River.

THE WORKINGS OF A REINDEER CAMP

Early in the evening when we arrived at Gimadeev's hunting camp, which currently served as a reindeer camp, hunters Nikolai Semenovich Kangaraev (b. ca. 1965) and a younger hunter known as Sania (Aleksandr) welcomed us. Both had come here in search of their transportation deer. Nikolai had been looking above the tree line for several weeks, and he was still short two castrates. In the low brush of a slope near the edge of camp, six of his adult riding deer were calmly resting next to three of Sania's bulls. Each animal was tied down by a rope from its halter to the exposed roots of a tree, or to a loose tree trunk lying on the ground. This method of tethering ensured a grazing radius of three to four meters for each animal, and a distance of at least two meters between each animal. On his morning and afternoon searches, Nikolai would encounter bulls and does belonging to the collective herd, as well as yet-uncaught castrates belonging to other hunters.

Depending on the area and on personal preference, some hunters used horses to catch their deer. Nikolai preferred to walk. The terrain above the tree line could be particularly treacherous for horses, and most hunters gave their horses as much rest at camp as possible. When Nikolai spotted a castrate with his own initials scissored into the pelt, or with one of his ear marks, he would calmly walk up to the animal, salt in hand. According to Vitka, one of the scissored initials stood for the owner's first name, the other for his last name. A patronymic was not required "because all hunters know each other." Only in case of doubles was a third letter added. Gently, but firmly, Nikolai would take hold of one antler once in reach, tying a rope around its joined base with the other hand. Well secured, the bull and his herder would descend into the valley where the animal joined the others beneath the trees. Once Nikolai had found all eight of his working castrates, he would walk them to his home at Alygdzher for proper saddling and packing. From here he would depart with his caravan for three or four months of hunting in his ancestral taiga.

During our visit at Gimadeev's camp, multiple groups of five to ten reindeer would come running into the premises daily. Together they licked salt and human urine from the large boulders in front of Gimadeev's cabin, while large unruly bulls would chase the does around camp. Each time a group came in, the hunters would look up from their tasks, checking for new arrivals. Mother does and their offspring were marked in their fur with numbers to keep track of the size of the reproductive herd. It was immediately clear if deer had arrived at camp for the first time that season, because their antlers had not yet been trimmed.

On several occasions a doe and her two-year-old offspring had shown up lacking any sign of numbers in their coat. These were not "wild" animals, I was informed. They had simply opted not to return to human encampment for one or two years consecutively. Upon return, their numbers were simply trimmed into their coat anew. This observation took me by surprise as it indicated that in current Tofa herding style it was acceptable for animals to skip a roundup cycle or two. This would have applied to does and their offspring in the first place. Skipping a cycle then meant an increase in overall distance between humans and reindeer, something that would particularly affect the habits of yearlings. However, the return of mother-child couples after one or two years is confirmation that prolonged dispersal did not have to result in animals becoming feral.

The autumn reindeer camp served the hunters both as a convenient location from where to collect their means of winter transportation while grooming members of the reproductive herd, but also a place conducive to the animals, not least for their mating rituals. Nikolai explained that when a doe had sufficiently tired of being chased around camp by a number of overly eager bulls, she would settle on a single one of them. Allowing the bull to stay near her, she would benefit from his protection against other pressing male suitors. In the bull's company, and together with her yearling, she would eventually leave camp for the winter. These small family units could then be seen grazing the banks of upper streams. For the remainder of the winter the free herd would roam the forest, staying together loosely.

Two or three years prior to our visit, pregnant does had been making their way to calving camp in late April and throughout May. This site was now in disuse, and come birthing time, the does were on their own. All that remained were a collapsed corral and several stakes for tying down does, located less than a kilometer downstream from the autumn roundup camp. Pregnant does had previously come here in anticipation of bad weather in spring. According to Tofa reindeer herder Vladimirovich, reindeer use the precipitation to help wash away blood that might attract predators. In addition, a careful herder always leaves some of the sharper tines on a doe's antlers in autumn to allow her to defend her offspring immediately after birth. A doe will shed her antlers roughly a week after giving birth.

During the birthing season, herders would tie down the newborn reindeer during the day while allowing their mothers to graze freely. In the evening, the young would be released and their mothers tied down. The does would not venture far from their little ones during the day, and offspring stayed close to their mothers throughout the night. This rhythm of tying and releasing continued at summer camp (see Mel'nikova 1994: 66–72).

In autumn, when new offspring had grown in size, herders would reverse the process. The young would now graze during the day, and with their mothers tied down at camp, they would return for milk in the evening. After allowing a calf to activate its mother's lactation by nudging her teats, the young reindeer was taken aside and herders would milk the doe for their own needs. Up to one and a half glasses (Rus. *stakan*) (200–300 ml) of creamy milk (17 percent fat) could be collected per doe per day, if milked morning and evening. By mid-September production would slow down, and by mid-October it would run dry (see Mel'nikova 1994: 70). Although Nikolai had recently milked a deer, the last time he had seen this done regularly was in 1982.

Chatting with the hunters inside Gimadeev's cabin one early evening, I could see through the open door a number of does descending into camp. Each doe had its full antlers, indicating that this was their first visit to the camp. The men glanced at each other, grabbed their ropes and headed out of the cabin and toward the does. Denis and Sania caught two of them with their bare hands, tying a rope around head and antlers to form a halter that would allow each animal to be tied to a nearby tree. While a third hunter was holding the second doe by the rope, Denis held the first animal tightly against the stem of a tree.

Saw in hand, Sania cut through the bone material, trimming the resisting doe's right and left antlers. To keep the area around the tree uncluttered, the clipped tines were immediately thrown into the stream that ran behind the camp. Here countless antler pieces from previous seasons were piling up under the rushing waters. Unlike the does, who had lost most of their antler velvet already, the working castrates were yet to shed theirs. To prevent infection, the hunters did not trim male antlers until shedding had set in, which would come about with a further drop in temperature.

ON A STROLL WITH THE CASTRATES

Vitka remembered how the kolkhoz had given each working animal its own identification number. Each working castrate retained this number for life. Presently, numbers were given only to animals belonging to the collectively held reproductive herd (Rus. *matochnaia stada*), and hunters like Nikolai identified and named their castrates on the basis of primary coat color, pace, gait, personality or other features unique about the individual. The chief sovkhoz herder (Rus. *glavnyi pastukh*) would lend reindeer to hunters in autumn. Larger animals were allocated to hunters whose taiga was further afield, smaller ones to those with hunting grounds close by, and elders received animals known to be calmer. At present, working animals were owned by families, and they were passed on from one generation to the next. Temporary exchanges of castrates between hunters could also occur from time to time, and different animals were still being used to access different hunting territories. Hunters with access to grounds in less mountainous areas rode their horses, and increasingly snowmobiles, while those hunting in steep terrain continued to rely on reindeer. At the time of my visit only twenty-eight hunters had entered their names in the owner's log at the reindeer camp. Others may still have been on their way to camp, but the majority of the remaining seventy or so hunters from the village were relying on their horses, snowmobiles, or the state-subsidized helicopter service to reach their winter hunting grounds.

At camp, Nikolai and Sania were taking turns locating and pasturing each other's animals. One morning, after Sania had departed into the hills, Nikolai invited a colleague and me to join him on a reindeer grazing walk (Rus. *vypas*). We walked over to the hillside where the caught castrates had been dozing in the morning sun. Nikolai untied a deer from the roots of a nearby tree after which we loosed another one, tying his halter rope to the antler base of the first deer. One by one we released all the remaining deer, tying them to each other in a right-left-right alternating order. This was also the sequence in which the deer would travel together over longer distances in winter. Nikolai would lead the way as he held the halter rope of the lead reindeer (see Pomishin 1971: 129).

According to Soiot hunters, the dual-track trail pattern, which is produced in soft taiga ground from repeated migrations of caravans tied together in this manner, remains visible to this day in historic reindeer grazing areas of alpine and subalpine Oka. After walking the caravan straight uphill for some fifteen minutes, we found an area with good lichen. With the lead deer tied to a tree, Nikolai began untying the caravan. This time he started with the last animal in line. In releasing each animal, Nikolai would raise the left front leg, while lowering the animal's head to wind the halter rope around the leg. The remainder of the rope was then tied around the left rear leg with a Tofa knot. It did not matter to Nikolai which side of the deer was tied, in fact sometimes he switched sides on the animal to prevent chafing, and in winter he did not include the front leg to allow for better scraping. It did not take long before all nine deer were calmly grazing, moving downhill at a relaxed pace for a period of about two and a half hours. As the deer satiated, they lay down in soft moss. Once all deer were lying down below the trees on the hillside, Nikolai began to gather them again. We tied them up in the previous pattern and walked the caravan back to camp.

CHANGING TIMES, CHANGING HERDS

Tofa herding history is marked by many fluctuations in distance between deer and people. If it had been typical for south Siberian hunter-herders to own herds of fifteen to eighty reindeer before the revolution (see Grøn 2011: 79; Turov and Weber 2010), then such relatively small herds would have largely followed their owners' hunting activities. In fact, Denis was of the conviction that his ancestors had never set up camp in the same place. Even their hunting cabins (Rus. *izbushki*) had never been kept for long periods, as they had preferred to build new ones regularly. But with sedentarization at lower altitudes in the late 1920s, and Tofa collectivization in 1930 (Mel'nikova 1994: 222–25), geographic distance between people and reindeer had become inevitable. The small herds of hunting families who had been moved to Alygdzher were now joined into a large state-owned herd. The intention had been to increase their count, albeit at a distance from the settlement. Some of the disenfranchised hunters were later allowed to keep an unknown number of privately held reindeer (Mel'nikova 1994: 232, 233). However, as families were settled at Alygdzher, they lost their relation to the lives of reindeer in the taiga, and herding itself became the task of a small group of specialists, the majority of whom were men. Similar developments took place in Tozhu, Dukha, and Soiot collective farms (Donahoe 2003; Endres 2015; Pavlinskaia 2002). Not only did community-herd relations change, sedentarization and collectivization also led to changes in herd-size and in the methods used to divide herds.

Although the new collective herd had been kept at a distance from the settlement of Alygdzher, castrates had been a common sight in the village during sovkhoz years. This was still the case at the time of my autumn and spring visits. When hunters departed and returned from the taiga, their teams of eight to twelve deer would stand tied down by their owners' houses, waiting to be loaded or unloaded. These points of contact with the settlement were brief and still dominated by men who primarily engaged in hunting and trapping activities. In fact, all reindeer contact with the environment of the settlement was purposefully kept brief. As Vitka recalled, elders had claimed that working reindeer were prone to contract foot rot while in the village.

To prevent the disease from spreading throughout the herd, Tofa reindeer were divided into reproductive (Rus. *matochnaia stada*) and working herds (Rus. *rabochaia stada*), both herds being of near equal size. Another reason for the separation had been that working castrates were known to lack a sense of protection for new offspring. This was particularly counterproductive when the herd was attempting to flee wolf attacks. When in panic, full grown castrates were quick to trample the younger members of the herd. But, added Vitka, "This is what the elders thought. Now they all mingle."

According to Denis and Vitka, reindeer presently moved back and forth between winter and summer camps, following memorized routes. By late June, and all throughout July, they were "moving themselves," or "following the herder with their young ones," as they ventured to feeding grounds at higher altitude. The routes by which the herd frequented between winter and summer grounds had been altered periodically over the years to ensure the regrowth of lichen and adjacent foliage. These planned route moves had left a series of abandoned winter, spring, and summer camp sites in the landscape. A few hundred meters upstream from the autumn round-up camp were located the overgrown remains of a former camp. What was left consisted of a collapsed corral that, according to the hunters, had been used around the time of World War II or earlier. The summer camp that was in use at the time of our visit had not changed its location in several years. Russian ethnographer L. V. Mel'nikova (1994: 66) describes summer pasture fence and corral structures that had been in use at various locations throughout the 1980s. None of these were used at summer or winter camps now. Only the use of salt and urine was still common to attract reindeer to the campsite for protection from lynx, wolves, and other predators, and to keep them attuned to human presence.

Although Denis believed that the reproductive rate of the herd had gone down since working and reproductive animals had been re-amalgamated, he also thought that the herd's poor growth was in part due to an increase in wolf predation. Many hunters had noticed a rise in the wolf population as the wolf poison reserves of the sovkhoz had become depleted. Although wolves were occasionally trapped in wire snares set up for musk deer, Nikolai pointed out the lack of a systematic hunting strategy to control wolf populations, as there once had been. Reflecting on Alygdzher's and Gutara's herd sizes in the 1990s, Vitka spoke of the current size as reflecting a long-time low. He recalled how the herd had dwindled to five hundred head as the result of a hoof disease epidemic in the 1970s. By 1980, the herd had recovered, and herders were counting a thousand head again. Only a decade later, in the early 1990s, numbers had dropped once again, this time due to the herd having been privatized. The resulting lack of care was amended when the herd came under new collective management, allowing it to regain its original size by the late 1990s.

For Denis, the current count of about three hundred animals, which lay far below the average count of the past forty years, was so embarrassing that he thought it unfit for Tofas to claim they were herding reindeer at all. With his many years of herding experience, Vitka was of a different mind. From his point of view the herd was not significantly in decline. In not growing much, it had merely reached a kind of natural balance. The maintenance of a quasi-Soviet model of reindeer herding, coupled with the chronic lack of funds to make it work well, had resulted in a herd mingling and roaming more liberally than ever previously. This state of reduced control was reflected by a recent illness that had swept the herd, but which no one was qualified enough to identify. After all, even "the local veterinarian couldn't care less, (Rus. *emu vse ravno*) he is not paid for reindeer inspections."

This laissez-faire approach was also characterized by a present lack in architectural constrictions, such as corrals, fences, and tie-downs. All of these structures had been built and maintained in the past, but without a dedicated workforce most of these structures had gradually rotted away. Their absence naturally led to an emphasis on what I will call invitational measures in herding practice. With the disappearance of corrals and migratory fences positioned throughout the landscape, contemporary Tofa hunters and herders increasingly relied on flexible and portable measures. Among such measures were salt feedings and smudge fires, which helped draw animals into camp. Sun shelters were still used above the tree line at summer camp, and summer smudge fires were still set in relation to changing wind patterns as they had been in the past.

Vitka explained how summer morning winds rise from the bottom of the valleys to the top of mountains, continuing this for most of the day. By evening the wind direction usually reverses, blowing from the top of mountains into valleys. Whenever the weather changes, the wind direction fluctuates continuously. To make a good reindeer smudge, Vitka would set alight a pile of dry wood, upon which he tossed moss, fresh cedar, or rotten wood. Thick smoke would then billow into the prevailing wind, protecting the reindeer from insects, such as the much dreaded reindeer warble fly (Rus. *paut*, or *olenii slepen'*). At summer camp, herders would pet the newborn reindeer to accustom them to human scent, and by mid-August, the entire herd would begin to descend in the direction of the autumn camp.

Until ten years ago, Vitka recalled, the reindeer had been kept at the autumn camp until later in the season. Depending on snow fall, the deer had been released to graze freely beginning only in October or November. In order to track them more easily throughout the winter, it was necessary to have snow on the ground. At present no one tracked herd animals over the winter. Now and then, the herd would move between the upper reaches of two or three creeks during the early winter, and it was best to leave them to themselves, abstaining from any kind of intensive herding during this time. If they were moved around too much they would become nervous.

At the same time, there were always some animals who preferred close proximity to human campsites, even during the winter. "We call them *tabornye*" (camp buddies), said Vitka. Usually these were animals who had lost their mothers early on, or young ones who had grown up alongside orphaned mothers. Such animals remained closely attuned to the rhythm of a camp by way of their mothers' ties. In the past, deer had been lured or driven to the herders' camp throughout the free grazing period that followed their October release, while the *tabornye* animals would just stay nearby. During these regular drives, salaried winter herders would perform head counts of reproductive family units (Rus. *tabuny*) using the corrals at the autumn camp. At present no one was available to do this job in winter, and the reindeer were effectively left to themselves from September to May, or later.

Returning to my discussion of Soiot reindeer in Oka, visiting with Tofa hunters and their herds was immensely insightful. It allowed me to see how the herding practice in Tofalariia had changed even since the late 1990s when herders like Vitka had been invited to visit Oka to help Soiot yak herders revive their ancestral skill of reindeer herding. In what follows, we will see how present-day Soiot reindeer breeding is as much a testament to recent Tofa practices as it is a continuing experimentation in the juggling of species in changing households.

STRANGERS AT HOME

One afternoon, not too long after my arrival in the field, I was sitting in the kitchen of Borzhon's winter home at Uro. His daughter-in-law, Norzhima, had handed me a family photo album. Leafing through pictures of past hay harvests, I noticed a photograph depicting reindeer grazing among Mongolian cows and yak. I had to look twice to make sure it really was the Uro Valley I was seeing. Indeed, a large number of reindeer had spread out among the winter residences of the valley. In another picture, a young deer was vigorously licking the glass of the kitchen window behind which I was sitting. Its bulging eyes were staring at the old wooden table on which lay the photographs I was perusing. I turned my head to look out the window—there were no reindeer now. Where had they gone?

Many more pictures followed. In one of them, the members of a household at Uro were saddling a deer in preparation for a multiday hunt. Each image, as I held it in my hands, triggered cherished memories for Borzhon's adoptive son, Regbi, his wife, Norzhima, and their son, Buian—all of whom were now gathered around me, commenting on the photographs. It had been a joyful time when reindeer had shared these winter grounds, or at least it was remembered that way. Yet, during my time at Uro, I had never seen a single live reindeer.

Rumors of a journal written by reindeer herders had reached me early on in my fieldwork. The jottings were said to have been made by a group of herders, charged with the care of a newly introduced domestic herd. In 1994, the Soiot Village Advisory (Rus. *Soiotskii sel'sovet*) and its kolkhoz, Fifty Years of October, had purchased sixty reindeer from the Buriat District Directory "Baikal," who represented the Tofa cooperative for animal products and husbandry (Rus. *koopzverpromkhoz*) at Nizhniudinsk (AAMO 38-1-176: 2). The transaction occurred as part of the "Oka project for the protection of the genetic base of disappearing animals," and it involved the movement of forty-five does, seven males, and eight trained riding reindeer (AAMO 38-1-176: 5). No one had herded reindeer in thirty years, and the sight of domestic reindeer in Oka had been a cause for celebration. After searching for several months, a tattered notebook of handwritten notes emerged from the home of an elder in the village of Sorok. It turned out to be the reindeer herders' journal. At this point I had been working through reams of Oka kolkhoz records in the archives at Orlik, hoping to learn about the people and their reindeer after 1920. After the bureaucratic language of Soviet bookkeeping, it was refreshing to read the deeply personal and often humorous notes composed by a group of young herders in the 1990s. Although written in Russian rather than in Buriat, these notes had clearly been composed for their personal recollection and not as a formal report of their activities.

Although buried under piles of other papers in a private home, these handwritten pages are a rare testimony to the laborious process of a people having to relearn the perspective of a species long lost to their households. In spite of having grown up under the guidance of experienced yak herders and horse breeders, these young men describe their frustrations with reindeer whose preferences in feed and movement often differed sharply from more familiar yak and other cattle. The root of their frustration, however, may have stemmed from more than the common stress experienced by being confronted with something new. Reindeer were supposed to have been in the very blood of these young men, according to some elders. Even if they had never seen the species as children, their grandparents had grown up with reindeer. It could not possibly be so difficult to reintroduce the animals.

Following the collectivization of households in the 1930s, the new kolkhoz system of Oka had maintained several reindeer herds as a means of transportation for autumn and winter hunting brigades, much like the sovkhoz of Alygdzher in Tofalariia. Archival records show that only sixteen years after B. E. Petri's expedition, nine kolkhozes in Oka were herding as many as 543 reindeer (AAMO 11-1-149: 1–3; AAMO 11-1-305: 1), a number that far exceeds the 124 reindeer Petri had recorded during his initial expedition of 1926. Collectivization thus had led to a substantial increase in reindeer. However, after a final peak in 1952, these herds had been in gradual decline, and following an official directive from Ulan-Ude, the last two surviving herds were slaughtered for meat in 1963 (see Pavlinskaia 2002: 98; I. V. Rassadin 1999: 17–19).

Volodia, an elder and distant relative of Iumzhap, who himself was an accomplished Soiot reindeer herder, had acquired his own herding skills from the chief herder at kolkhoz KIM (Rus. *Kommunisticheskii Internatsional Molodezhi*) of Shasnur. He recalled seeing some of the earlier mass killings as a teenager at Shasnur. He could vividly recall standing by the side of the gunmen when a vast array of antlers came rushing towards him. Moments later firing commenced, and it did not cease until every last animal had been brought down. Although he had not personally seen it, Volodia, like many of his contemporaries, remembered how "later, in 1963 or so, helicopters were used to hunt wild reindeer." A great number of wild reindeer had been afoot in those days, and the body responsible for their management—the cooperative for animal products and husbandry—had decided to slaughter them also, resulting in two largely contemporaneous, yet distinct efforts to eliminate reindeer from Oka. Although none of my interlocutors were old enough to have participated in the slaughter, several of them recalled the day on which their elders had been called on to assist in the liquidation. All looked back to these events with great disapproval.

A RECURRING SOIOT SYMBOL

The reintroduction of domestic reindeer to Oka in 1994 must be understood in the wider context of a movement toward national revitalization among Soiot descendants, which was gaining momentum toward the turn of the millennium (see Pavlinskaia 2002: 65, 98). In 1993, a group of Soiots had formed their own national association, numbering 812 members. During the following year the village of Sorok was made the official regional center of the newly recognized

Soiot National Somon—a Soiot traditional land-use area within the larger district of Oka. By 1995, census data showed that 1,973 individuals had chosen to identify as Soiots, and by the year 2000 Soiots collectively obtained status as a Small Numbered People of the Russian Federation (Pavlinskaia 2002: 65). These developments were paralleled by a shared desire to reestablish two of the most enduring symbols of the Soiot way of life. One was hunting and reindeer herding as a core mode of subsistence, and the other was the ability to speak in the ancestral Soiot language, a language that would have been heard in all Soiot households of Oka prior to Buriat becoming dominant (Rassadin 2010: 9). The language was not offered in primary school until 2005, but the 1994 purchase of the Tofa herd played an important symbolic role in the self-assertion of Soiots as a distinct people.

The desire for official recognition as a distinct indigenous people has long stood in connection with attempts to maintain reindeer herding as a subsistence practice. Records attest to an Oka-Soiot delegation being sent to Irkutsk in 1930 to formally complain about being prevented from purchasing and transferring a herd of reindeer from eastern Tyva to Oka (Pavlinskaia 2002: 61–62). This purchase had likely been intended to relieve a drastic decrease in Soiot herds (Petri 1927a: 16–17). Judging from archival materials, Soiots had considered it a basic right to decide about their own economic future, all the more so after receiving initial recognition as a Small Numbered People of the North from the Northern Committee (Pavlinskaia 2002: 61–62). The 1994 purchase of reindeer from Tofalariia may therefore be understood as having been of utmost symbolic importance. Arrival of the Tofa herd not only strengthened a newfound sense of Soiot identity; it also marked the triumph of a long-sought affirmation of economic self-reliance.

The primary purpose of the attempted purchase of 1930 may well have been an attempt to stabilize a regional subsistence strategy. However, the fact that it had been prevented by the local administration suggests that it may also have been understood, at the time, as strengthening unwanted pan-Turkic relations among indigenous minorities. Tozhu-Soiot relations had already been weakened by the border dividing eastern Tyva (then part of sovereign and independent Tannu Tuva) from Oka. Further disempowerment of Soiot land-based identity was accomplished by forcing herders to relocate to form centralized kolkhozes. The 1994 purchase can thus be seen as a late but symbolic statement in response to this history. For Soiot beneficiaries the arrival of the animals signaled a newfound independence; a material confirmation that the time of cultural repression had officially ended—independent of whether reindeer herding as a way of life was to be revived or not.

ACCLIMATIZATION

Grandfather Dondokov Tsyren-Dorzho (b. 1947), one of my key interlocutors, was one of the men who had travelled to Tofalariia by horseback to bring back the new reindeer herd. In October of 1994, the men had driven the acquired herd from Alygdzher (and initially from Alkhadyr Mountain) to Oka's northerly settlement of Saiany. After their arrival on the first of November, they loaded the animals onto two large trucks and transported them to the village of Sorok. Once unloaded, the herd was driven on foot to the winter pastures at Uro. Here the recipient herders quickly established a herding camp on the Iakhoshop River, which would serve as their base for the following three years.

In the first summer, the herd moved to a camp on the Khonchon River, but the reindeer refused to stay. On their own, they soon returned to the winter camp on the Iakhoshop River. For the next two years, the herders decided to keep the animals at their Iakhoshop camp in winter and in summer. My friend Iumzhap (b. 1974), who had been among the first herders, recalled how in spite of losses to wolves during these first years, the herd had grown from sixty to over eighty head. According to Iumzhap's elder brother, Baatar (b. 1970), in those days the herd was the property of a stock company newly formed at Orlik. Archival documents attest to the early brigade's expenses, including salt, hay, fuel, and building supplies for the hut on the Iakhoshop, all of which were billed to the company (AAMO 1995 38-1-183: 1–9).

In spite of the herders' intimate knowledge of the terrain—places they had hunted and herded in since their youth—it was imperative for the men to acquire a new point of view: that of their reindeer. To explain the importance of this viewpoint, we must return to the work of Jakob von Uexküll, for whom the Cartesian approach to animals as machines was less than satisfying. His argument is that each creature resides within its own *Umwelt*, sharing a common physical environment with other organisms, while each species possesses its own perceptual lifeworld. Relating to the discussion of human herders and their reindeer, von Uexküll's idea does not end with the observation that divergent perceptual lifeworlds are being lived side by side in the same physical world without ever colliding. Instead, his work is that of a semiotician, investigating signs being sent and received, not only between organisms and the environment, but also between organisms of divergent perceptual lifeworlds.

To make use of the *Umwelt* concept, it could be said that the arrival of Tofa reindeer in Oka introduced another perceptual lifeworld to the region. Even if herders are unable to truly enter the perceptual worlds of the species they herd, in Oka there certainly existed a well-honed body of knowledge and skill in assessing the preferences of animals. As hunters and as herders, people relied on careful attention to animal movement. Learning how each of the species with which they had grown up perceived the land was part and parcel of any local upbringing. Part of this sensibility was directed to the kinds of opportunities different species were known to recognize in the physical world. Soiot herders were deeply familiar, for instance, with the preferences of domestic livestock in every season and at each altitude.

With the arrival of reindeer, men like Iumzhap and Baatar were reminded that this herd possessed its own way of moving about the landscape. Their behavior was much closer to the reindeer the men had been hunting in higher hill country. Describing a particularly frustrating time during the first summer, one entry in the herders' journal reads: "It took three days to drive the herd from the peaks.... In hot weather reindeer turn out to be restless animals. They need to go to the very peak." "Restlessness" and needing to "go to the very peak" were evidence of their Otherness, characteristics that set these animals apart from more familiar livestock. Yak, I was assured by the herders, also sought the cool of higher altitude in summer, but they rarely insisted on climbing to the very peaks of mountains. Reindeer, by contrast, were straining upward for grassless lichen-covered rocky patches.

Perhaps the most significant difference between reindeer and more familiar domestic animals was the herd's habit of straying much farther from human encampment than did cattle. Iumzhap, who had been among the first caretakers of the reindeer from Uro, recalled: "It's not like keeping cows. [Reindeer] are quite the animals after all. You had to get them back from the mountains, and often you'd spend the whole day walking after them." In terms of their straying quality, Iumzhap would refer to the herd as "semi-wild" (Rus. *polu-dikie*). While many Soiot households drove their livestock from winter to summer camps in early June, and back again in late August, reindeer would decide for themselves when, where, and for how long to be in any place. This unpredictability clearly upset the migratory plans set up by Iumzhap and other herders, who had tried unsuccessfully to align the seasonal movements of the reindeer with established seasonal patterns for their yak, horses, and sheep.

Much of the trouble experienced in the early days of the brigade would also have had to do with the fact that the herd had not been able to work out their own annual migrations. The lead animals of the herd had no memory of past routes to draw on in Oka, and under the auspices of largely inexperienced herders, the animals needed all the more time to ground themselves in the landscape. Moreover, the herders themselves had to learn how to read the hills for vegetation that was naturally inviting to reindeer.

Entries in the herders' journal illustrate the early challenges of acclimatization, not only to the land, but also of people to animals, and vice versa: in an attempt to draw the herd back to camp on the night of 11 March 1995, the men had lit fires in the darkening forest. They were attempting to lure the deer back by providing a haven safe from wolves spotted around camp. In spite of the flickering fires, none of the animals returned that night or the next.

Two days passed before their bells could be heard again. When the deer were finally approaching, the ringing of their bells was drowned out by the persistent barking of the camp dogs signaling the presence of wolves. The men fired shots to scare off the wolves, which seemed to work for a while. When the herd had finally come in, the crew decided to move camp to Doshpok River. But upon arrival at Doshpok the next day, the brigade and herd found poor feeding conditions. Under cover of night, the herd abandoned camp again, returning to the previous location.

Not only was it difficult for the herders to anticipate how the herd would decide to move, but their own knowledge of the landscape was not based on the feeding patterns or preferences of reindeer. Knowing a place well did not mean that one knew how reindeer would respond to it. A related challenge was the growing size of the herd. With an increase of at least seventeen head since their arrival to Oka, the herd had reached the limit of what Tozhu herders would traditionally have considered manageable (see Stépanoff 2012: 306).

By early September 1995, on the anniversary of the herd's arrival to Oka, the brigade attempted to move winter camp to a spot near the Belaia River to the northeast of Sorok. By 4 October, roughly a month later, so many of the reindeer had abandoned camp at Belaia and moved in the direction of the previous year's winter camp that the herders decided to pack up and follow their herd. They drove them into the upper reaches of the Iakhoshop River and set up winter camp in the previous year's location. It seemed the herd was establishing its own familiarity with the land, basing its movements on the previous year's movements rather than adhering to their herders' discernment.

The struggle of intentions between reindeer and herders recorded in the journal speaks not only to the learning curve of becoming attuned to the *Umwelt* of reindeer, but also to the ability of reindeer to actively resist human herders and follow their own leaders instead. In retrospect, one may reason that the herders had not yet developed the skill of working with lead animals. On the other hand, even a seasoned Tofa hunter once told me, "Reindeer are the dumbest animals I have ever seen. They get it into their heads to feed in a particular place, and that is where they will go, no matter what." This statement suggests that even a skillful herder may not always be successful in swaying his reindeer away from wolves and other dangers.

OF LOSS AND NEW BEGINNINGS

The brigade did not mind keeping their herd on the upper Iakhoshop River for the first few winters. The location was within riding distance to Uro, and the young men were able to check in on their families every so often. Yet, there were a number of problems with the site. Representatives of the stock company owning the herd had concerns about its slow growth rate. On the Iakhoshop River, the animals had frequently been ill, and wolves consistently took weaker animals. Finally, it was decided for the herd to be transferred to the care of Dasha Dorzhievich Dambaev (b. 1952) near the settlement of Saiany, in the hope that the animals would fare better.

In 1999, Russian ethnographer Larissa Pavlinskaia visited the herd at their new home in Saiany. Looking back over the first five years of herding in Oka, Pavlinskaia offers several critiques of Soiot herding in light of what she sees as a general loss of reindeer herding knowledge (2002: 98–99). During her visit, the herd was counting only sixteen head more than it had on its first arrival to Oka. This was stunning, given the herd had produced thirty to forty offspring every spring (Pavlinskaia 2002: 98–99). For Pavlinskaia, it was clear that the herders had been ill-equipped in dealing with predators and disease, and she found better care was taken of other livestock. It seemed to her people did not understand reindeer had to be tamed and attuned to their owners and winter camps. In her writing she laments herders were not providing protective structures, such as sunroofs, fences, and smudges.

Although these criticisms may have rung true for the state of affairs at Saiany, the journal, which describes only the first half decade in the area around Uro, contains evidence to the contrary. While Pavlinskaia expresses hope for the herd to finally flourish at Saiany, my interlocutors at Uro recalled that by 2001—two years after her visit—the herd had shrunk from over seventy to twelve animals. Some of the former herders from Uro reasoned that the wolves had likely not been better at Saiany. But more importantly, they suspected a lack of management, which had resulted in extensive mingling with wild reindeer. Additionally, the men suspected that several animals had been sold for meat, even at a time when the herd was clearly not growing.

The following year, what was left of the herd, including a single bull, were transported back to Uro in the hope that under new stewardship it would be possible to rebuild a herd once more in the Sorok area. My friend Iumzhap and his wife Tserigma took the deer to their summer pasture on the upper Sorok River in the first year. Then, from 2002 to 2003, brothers Baatar, Iumzhap, and Tsydyp, together with their families began rotating herding responsibilities at a dedicated summer camp they had built specifically for the herd on the upper Urda-Uro, a two-hour hike east of Uro. Every night the deer would return from their daily foraging excursions high upon the Iakhoshop Ridge—where the herd had spent much time during the mid-1990s. Upon their evening descent, they would spend the night inside the families' fenced encampment at the bottom of the valley.

In spite of these precautions and a steady birthrate, cattle-borne disease contracted from dairy cows at Uro and persistent wolf attacks continued to ravage the herd, reducing it to a meager twenty head once more. In 2004,

Iumzhap's elder brother, Baatar, decided he would try something new. He would drive the now thirty-two head strong herd back and forth between their family's summer reindeer camp at Urda-Uro and a new winter hunting camp on the distant Onot River. This movement would require a bi-annual 180 kilometer trek through difficult mountainous terrain, but it would also pass through important hunting grounds on the way. Finally, winters would be spent in a range where the snow was too deep for wolves to pass.

Thinking back to the decade of herding that followed the demise at Saiany, Iumzhap took stock of their collective experience in 2013. He observed how herders and reindeer had lacked a dedicated winter camp. For several years he and his elder brother had followed the herd through the taiga each winter. On occasion, the brothers would pass by their winter residences at Uro, and the herd would head into the steep hills east of the Sorokskii Range. The brothers had to hunt on foot and sometimes on horseback, because all their trained riding deer had died at Saiany. In 2004, Baatar and his helpers were finally ready to break in the first three-year-old castrates, which had been born at his family's camp on Urda-Uro in the first year of the herd's return from Saiany. The newly trained deer made it possible for Baatar to realize his plans to migrate the herd between Urda-Uro and Onot rivers annually, during which time he would take the castrates on regular hunting excursions. By the following year the herd had grown to forty-one animals, and its owners decided to sell nineteen of the animals for meat. Once again, Baatar and Iumzhap were left with a mere twenty-two reindeer.

As if this recent setback had not been enough, two of the most devastating years in recent Soiot herding were soon to follow. In the springs of 2007 and 2008, newborn and mature reindeer had contracted what seemed to be Bacilær hemoglobinuri, an infectious disease common in cattle and sheep, and likely contracted during their summer stays near Uro. Weakened as they were, many fell prey to wolves. In an attempt to avoid further summer contact with cattle, Baatar moved the herd to his own summer pasture on the Tustuk River, and after the herd was transferred to the ownership of the Sorok village council the following year, he decided to keep it on the Onot River year-round. Since 2010 there have been no illnesses, and thanks to the high alpine environment on the Onot River, the reindeer continue to benefit from deeper snow levels, greatly reducing predation.

OLD OR NEW KNOWLEDGE?

The argument of some anthropologists (e.g., Pavlinskaia 2002) that Soiots had lost their ancestral knowledge of reindeer breeding by the 1990s, much like they had lost their Turkic language several decades earlier, remains arguable but not incontestable. In 1926, B. E. Petri encountered elders with a living knowledge of the Soiot language (1927a: 19), and as late as 1953, reports of passive knowledge in several elders were still circulating (Rassadin 2012: 3). Gathering data in the 1970s for his dictionary (2003) and grammar book (2012), linguist Valentin Rassadin collected material from elders born prior to 1917 (2012: 9). His aim was to record linguistic terms relating to a past way of life, one in which reindeer breeding had played a more essential role.

The Soiot language has been taught in school since 2005 (Rassadin 2010: 9), but it is no longer spoken in homes today. With its disappearance a whole lexicon of herding-related terms can be assumed to have vanished as well. Followed by a thirty-year absence of reindeer from Oka (1963–1994) the break in an intergenerational transfer of herding knowledge would seem complete (e.g., Pavlinskaia 2002: 98). Yet, historian and ethnographer Igor V. Rassadin (2012: 217)—son of linguist Valentin I. Rassadin—was able to reconstruct traditional Soiot herding practices from interviews with former reindeer herders and their descendants. What he found was a close resemblance with well-documented Tozhu, Tofa, Dukha, and Darkhad practices.

In spite of the language shift from Soiot to Buriat, and the lengthy absence of reindeer in Soiot households, not all herding knowledge of reindeer was lost, even when I lived with the community in 2013. Several elders vividly recalled reindeer dairying practices from when they were children. In the mid-1990s, Maria Manzaraksheevna Sharaeva (b. 1937) drew on her own memory of reindeer herding, as she instructed her adult sons, Baatar, Iumzhap, and Tsydyp in the skills she had learned from her father who had herded kolkhoz-owned reindeer near Saiany.

If knowledge of reindeer herding had not completely died out, then why had there been so little interest in pursuing this ancestral lifestyle? One possible reason Soiots did not re-integrate reindeer into their households after 1995 may have been the difficulty of meeting the needs of rangifer alongside those of other established species. The challenge of accommodating the divergent transhumance patterns of each species, seasonal elevation preferences, and speed of movement across the landscape would have played a role not only in the 1990s, but also around the turn of the century when Soiot households began their final shift from reindeer to yak breeding (Petri 1927a). It had become too cumbersome to divide the limited workforce of the household between two or more migratory rhythms, particularly when the number of yak and horses was on the rise and the economic role of hunting in decline.

With special herding brigades formed under kolkhoz management two decades later, it was possible to perpetuate—even intensify—a simplified form of reindeer herding that would accommodate hunting. While it may have looked remotely traditional, this new form of herding (not least for the annual transportation of geological expeditions) only furthered the chasm between herd life and the life of households. In remodeling family-oriented small-scale herds to become highly efficient transportation units, the once multifunctional role of brood-stock herds was lost also. Inevitably this was paralleled by a long-term decline in family-driven reindeer meat and milk production.

Following post-Soviet privatization, former kolkhoz stock became the property of individual households again. However, this time there were no reindeer to be privatized in Oka. Even if there had been reindeer, reintroducing the animals to households whose work force was now invested in privately held yak and other livestock, would inevitably have called for the redistribution of an already thinly stretched private labor force. This shortage of working hands in a non-collective work environment became especially evident in the 1990s, when newly trained reindeer herders could not be present during important cattle migrations and hay harvesting times while looking after a remote herd.

A final argument for apparent differences between the commitment to yak, dairy cattle, horses, and sheep as opposed to reindeer, may be that since the 1990s, no one has held reindeer privately. The notion that poor animal care may result from a lack of private ownership has especially been discussed in Soviet Tozhu and Tofa contexts (e.g., Donahoe 2003). But, for herders Iumzhap and Baatar, commitment to a herd did not rely on ownership so much as on the ability to make sovereign decisions on its immediate management. In 2018, Bataar explained that the main problem of not owning the herd lay in his inability to avert mismanagement resulting from turnover in caretakers. For him, the only way forward lay in finding the resources to start up an independent founder group of at least ten animals. Twenty-three years of herding, he assured me, had taught him a thing or two about what to do, where to go, and how to involve his own family in the care of Soiot reindeer.

CONCLUSION

The previous chapter served as an inroad to Soiot ways of reconciling indigenous and settler sacred traditions. In this chapter, we added a layer to this discussion by looking at the practical implications of settler dynamics on reindeer breeding in a place famous for being the birthplace of reindeer domestication in Eurasia. Although reindeer have been of undeniable importance to Eastern Saian households for a long time, it is difficult to say with any precision when this came to be the case. I have tried to show that Tofa and Soiot reindeer relations may always have been co-defined by the presence of other species in human and spirit households. For Tofa, horses may have played a much more important role historically (e.g., Rassadin 2005) than many ethnographers have observed or cared to admit. Similarly, yak and later Mongolian dairy cattle have played an increasingly important part in Soiot households, particularly as a result of intermarriage with Buriat settlers. Rather than seeing the ebb and flow in the relative importance of various species, including reindeer, as a threat to the integrity of Saian households, I have suggested that such a flux may fit well with the prehistory of the region.

If shamanic sacrifices, as mentioned in the previous chapter, could serve as symbolic counterpoint to Buddhist settler offerings—without expelling a Buddhist presence from the region—then breeding reindeer amid a plentitude of other adopted species could be said to fulfill a similar dialogic purpose. Perhaps Soiot and Tofa identities do not stand or fall with the prosperity of any one iconic species, but with an ability to maintain a living dialogue between multiple species and multiple cosmologies. The key to such dialogue, it would seem, is the ability to see from the viewpoint of the Other, or to sync one's own *Umwelt* with that of another. How easy it is to lose that viewpoint, and how difficult it can be to regain it under politically disadvantageous circumstances, is evident in the twenty-five years it took Bataar and his family to regain a feeling for optimal herd size, seasonal movement, herd dynamics and proximity to other species.

CHAPTER 4

KHAINAK BETWEEN WORLDS

According to one source (Nefedev and Gerasov 1929), Soiots are said to have retreated from northwestern Mongolia (Uriankhai) following political unrest. They first settled in Selenge Aimag of northern Mongolia. Because they had lost all their stock during the uprisings, they had to transition from animal husbandry to hunting. In search of prey, they wound up in the Oka Valley as early as 1729 where they continued to hunt until 1829 (Nefedev and Gerasov 1929: 36–37). This account argues that over time, the game in Oka had become scarce and many Soiots had become impoverished. The collective plight, it is thought, encouraged a gradual transition back to their ancestors' practice of animal husbandry. Surrounded by Buriat settler cattle herders, with whom many had already intermarried, the transition to the ancestral pastoral way of life would not have been too difficult, especially where hunting remained an integral part of subsistence.

If luck in hunting had come from appealing to the spirit master Khan-Shargai-Noen-Babai, ensuring that pastures and hillsides were lush and green for yak and other cattle to thrive depended on securing the good will of the landscape entity Daidyn-Ezhin-Daiban-Sagan-Babai (Nefedev and Gerasov 1929: 47). Hunting and herding took place in the same region, even if they depended on different patterns of movement and focused on different zones in the landscape. The ambiguity of the hunt was not replaced by the certainty sometimes associated with the tameness of domesticated stock. As much as fur-bearing animals could reveal themselves abundantly one season and conceal themselves the next, so the lush hillsides of one summer could give way to minimal growth the following year. Stock exchanged with other herders—like game belonging to a master spirit—could be unpredictable, reflecting the capricious spirit of its former owners. And, finally, wherever one moved, animals of the human household remained subject to taiga master spirits in multiple ways.

Marina, the middle-aged wife of Bulad from Khuzhirtai-Gorkhon, was the irreplaceable hand that ran the entire household, not only when her husband was away. Situated in a small valley adjacent to Uro, she often had her younger brother Aleksei come to help her. To illustrate the ambiguity of herding, she explained: "There are some domestic animals that walk about and disappear, but after a while they return. Khangai does not take them away." Marina, Aleksei, and I had been sitting in their kitchen after working in the family's cow stable.

She continued:

> When you were here last time, we slaughtered a sheep, right? A week earlier [this sheep] had followed the calves, and there it was abandoned—left to spend the night on its own. Down there lives Erdem, right? He went out to get a horse when he [saw his pup standing near] it. [The sheep] was walking to meet him, and so he took it home. When we saw a wolf coming over from the side of Sorok [that night], we thought, "that's it, he ate it." But it turns out Erdem had taken [the sheep] home for the night. If Khangai wants to take an animal, he will do it no matter what. But if he doesn't want to, then no matter how much [an animal] walks about, it will always return. So that it wouldn't get lost again, we slaughtered it ourselves.

Although Marina's example of Khangai's supreme will concerned a sheep in this instance, his sway did not stop short of larger animals within the household. Khangai's power affected all living beings, including those under the care of human masters.

It was almost time to put away the tea and get back to work. As if not quite ready to take up the manure shovel again, Aleksei reminisced, "they say that animals always take on the character of their owner." Nodding, Marina added:

> I may be exchanging a cow with someone. When I get [the cow], she [may be] obstinate. "Aha," they say, "she resembles her [female] owner." "That's it, you're mine now!" And then [the exchanged animal] calms down. And if someone receives [an animal] from us . . . it will be calm. And why wouldn't it be calm? Bulad is calm, I am calm, Aleksei is calm. Why should there be reason for the animal to be rebellious?

As much as hunters had to take into account the character of their prey, and by extension the spirit of their prey's master, so human masters had to pay attention to the character of animals they exchanged with other human masters. In both cases an exchange took place, but only in the latter did the reflection of the former owner's spirit have to give way to that of the new owner's personality or spirit. The newly arrived animal's ties with its former herd and owner had to be ritually severed before it could take on the spirit of its new owner, to which Marina referred as "that's it, you're mine now!"

The submissive calmness Marina spoke of did not apply in equal measure to all species. Aleksei, explained that yak and hybrid cattle had "a mind of their own" (Rus. *oni s kharakterom*):

> Yak and hybrid cattle have a hard time adapting, [especially] if you take them somewhere else, [or] when you pass them on to someone else. Take for instance, Khusurdy [name of cow]—a blue-shaded yak that is the aunt of [a neighbor's] hybrid. Two or three times they tried to keep her at Sorok. But, no, she ran back every time, all by herself. This spring Uncle Slavic said, "Let's take her calf." There was no snow on the ground. Yet, [within days] the calf had jumped the fence, making its way back to our valley all the way from Sorok!

Marina clarified, "They took it out by [jeep], and so the calf knew how to go [back]." The animal had needed no tracks in the snow to retrace its path from what it had observed through the windows of the vehicle. Neither had it submitted to the decision of its master to transfer it to a new owner. This kind of obstinance was what Aleksei had referred to as "a mind of their own."

* * *

In this chapter I will outline the pivotal role of yak and hybrid cattle in the lives of my friends at Uro. While reindeer continued to play a symbolic role in terms of Soiot's ethnic identity, the living pride of contemporary residence was found not in their agile and enduring horses, which will be discussed in the next chapter, but in their highly self-willed and independent yak and hybrid cattle. The chapter examines the growing inclusion of Mongolian dairy cattle, and how this aspect of Buriat settler culture impacted local land management, resulting in an increasing sedentary lifestyle that would eventually become inextricable from the maintenance of hereditary pasturelands. The chapter also traces Oka yak herding to Mongolia and further into Tibet, where the species has long held a sacred status. Given its growing marketability, the chapter examines contemporary breeding efforts before it delves into locally recognized advantages of hybridization. It explores key breeding and herding techniques, including dairying, before concluding with a note on the pressing challenges posed by the activity of bears and wolves.

A WONDROUS CREATURE

In chapter 3 I mentioned the existence of a local legend regarding the origin of yak. Unlike neighboring areas, where various origin accounts existed for reindeer, Oka residents took pride in knowing the story of their yak, having adopted Buriat author F. Baldaev's retelling. The account had been widely reprinted, most prominently in a Russian translation by K. D. Tuluev for local newspaper *Akha* in 2001:

> In ancient times, when there was no god and no devil, when all beings lived in harmony—it was then that these animals appeared on earth. They were grazing on vast expanses, among tall grasses and rolling shrubs. Wondrous creatures they were; cows, yet not cows—void of horns; donkeys, yet not donkeys. Pitiful hoofed ones they were; cloven hooves—void of tail and in shabby coat. Predators began to hunt these helpless animals, feeding on them easily. Their numbers were melting before our eyes.
>
> One day the thinned herd huddled on a small hill, their council in session. How were they to survive? Their chief said: "Our breed is melting before our eyes. It has become dangerous for us to live in this land, we must run from these predators. Think and tell us—how are we to find a way out of this predicament?" "I soon will give birth to twins and, probably, it is my turn to become the victim of these predators," said a pregnant mother with sadness. Suddenly a young, quick-witted male emerged from the center of the herd, offering to seek help from the strong steppe animals. "For example," he said, "Buur lives in the neighborhood—a powerful male camel. Next to him resides a rich bull with a thick neck, [and] I saw a fast stallion with a pale red coat. They protect their herds from predators. Maybe they will advise us on how to survive?" When they came to Buur, [the camel] said: "You need to move into the high mountains, onto rocky ridges difficult for predators to access. But it is very cold there. In order for you not to be cold, I give you warm hair."
>
> Arching his powerful neck, the bull said: "Black animals roam in the mountains where you seek to move. These are bears—the masters of that land. They love to mess about, and they may attack you. But they fear the fanged wild boar, whose voice you may call upon. When the bears hear his grunt, they will take you for a boar, and they will walk away. But just in case, I give you my big horns." The pale red stallion, having listened to their petition, added: "I will have to give you the strength and dexterity of my legs so that you can easily climb steep rocks. [Where you are going,] there are many cobwebs and mosquitoes. I will give you my ponytail so that you can brush them off." And they not only gained a ponytail, but horsehair covered their abdomen and legs. On the advice of the bull they learned from the boar to grunt.
>
> And these helpless animals became unrecognizable. They had a ponytail, warm camel hair, their heads were adorned with sharp horns and grunting like boars, they went to the mountains where they multiplied quickly. People, having seen these strange animals, were surprised: "What eccentric created them?" And they called them "Sarlyki Saridak—Yaks." Some time later, people caught several Sarlyks, allowing cows into their herd. After a year, new animals appeared—they were the size of cows, giving the same kind of milk, except that it was fattier. [These animals] were stronger and more enduring than their parents. People called them Khainak—the omnipotent. Delighted [as they were], people desired even better offspring. But the descendants of

Illustration 4.1. Yak grazing at winter pasture. Photograph by the author.

these were born worse than their parents. And they called them "Ortoom"—"not this nor that."

But inquisitive folk continued to experiment: Ortooms were born weak animals, much like their great-grandparents. They called them "Uhan guzeen," or more commonly, those "divorced by water." And since then, people have been breeding yak and khainaks. And if suddenly a shaggy animal comes at you from out of the bushes somewhere in the Saians—with hair inherited from a camel, waving a ponytail and threatening with its sharp donated horns, giving off a boar's grunt—be aware, for this is our "Sarlyk Saridak."

ON THE DOMESTICITY OF YAK

The Oka region is unique in that out of the four mountainous taiga areas shared by the peoples of the Eastern Saian Mountains, it is the only one that adopted yak herding. Tozhus, Tofas, and Dukhas seem never to have kept yak in their territories, although it is not for lack of interest in cattle and other stock. Wealthier Tozhu herder-hunters of Eastern Tyva have had sheep, goats, cows, and horses (e.g., Zhigunov 1961: 69n). In fact, by 1915 there were two-thousand head of cattle, one-thousand sheep and goats, and one-thousand horses in Eastern Tyva alone. Goats and sheep were being milked three times a day, and a few decades earlier there had been some camel keeping (Ermalova in Vainshtein 1961: 69). It follows that yak, which have been kept in the western and south central mountain regions of Tyva and in Altai, were never established in the eastern part of the republic.

In archived Soviet registers, yak often remain invisible, because they were counted along with regular domesticated cattle (Rus. *krupnyi rogatyi skot*). Although yak belong to the biological family of *Bovidae*, as do other types of domesticated cattle, they are in many ways a highly specialized species, sharing certain qualities with bison, sheep, goats, and muskoxen. Its wild and domesticated variants are known as distinctive subspecies—*Bos mutus* and *Bos grunniens*—although this subdivision has been controversial. While there are some genetic differences between the two, which are expressed in differences in appearance and behavior, both produce fertile offspring with each other. Yet, the consequences of domestication in yak are said to be less prominent in yak than in other species (see Leslie and Schaller 2009). Today, domesticated yak of Siberia no longer have a wild counterpart in the mountainous taiga. Some sources argue (e.g., Shi et al. 2016) that wild yak roamed South Siberian mountains as late as the thirteenth to eighteenth centuries.

It has been suggested that wild yak were first domesticated on the Tibetan plateau some 7,300 years ago (Wiener et al. 2003; Guo et al 2006; Qiu et al. 2015). After the domestication of the yak in the East Qinghai-Tibet plateau, the animals would have migrated, along with their herders, to the west through the Himalayas and the Kunlun Mountains, and to the north through the mountains of the Southern Gobi and Altai Gobi to Mongolia and Siberia. However, it remains unclear exactly how and when domesticated yak first became established in south Siberian households. My consultants in Oka would often speak of yak as animals that have been with their people since time immemorial. As such, reindeer and yak are together considered species of the ancestors—emblematic of Soiot heritage in every way.

FROM YAK TO DAIRY CATTLE AND HEREDITARY PASTURES

Soiot elders told Russian anthropologist Larissa Pavlinskaia that Mongolian cattle—specifically dairy cows—had come to Oka as a result of the spread of Buriat settler culture in the early nineteenth century (2002: 89). Prior to this, Soiot cattle had consisted almost entirely of yak. There were good reasons for the firm establishment of yak in Soiot households. Yak live between eighteen and twenty years, even under harsh conditions, providing milk and fur. After their slaughter they are an abundant source of high quality meat and leather.

Between one and two kilograms of wool and nearly half a kilogram of hair could be harvested from live animals each year, with shearing taking place during the molting period in the spring (Rassadin 2017: 193). Tail hair was used to make rope, and wool was turned into felt (Rassadin 2017: 193). While their milk yield was comparatively low at three to five liters per day, its 8 percent fat content lent itself to butter production. Supplementing the lower milk yield in yak, and providing more frequent access to leather used for clothing, many Soiots also raised goats (Pavlinskaia 2002: 89).

According to local Buriat historian D. Ts.-B. Sharastepanov, all cattle held in Oka today, including yak, originally came from Mongolia (2008: 18). Genetically speaking, there are no significant differences between Russian and Mongolian yak populations (Oyun et al. 2018: 1219). In fact, yak populations from the Gobi in southern Mongolia and the Russian Altai region have been found "relatively genetically distant from all other yak populations," while yak from the Altai, Gobi, and Khubsugul areas "appeared to be related to each other more closely than to the yaks from Tuva" (Oyun et al. 2018: 1,219). Sharastepanov points out that Mongolian cattle were lighter and smaller, but able to withstand harsh climates and frequent food shortages. Where Mongolian cattle interbred with yak, hybrids were produced. These larger animals could be found roaming among yak herds. They had an increased milk yield, amounting to between five and seven liters per day (Rassadin 2017: 193). Known for their fast maneuverability and long sharp horns, hybrid cattle were able to fight off wolves (Sharastepanov 2008: 18), and their male offspring were strong enough to draw sleds year-round (Rassadin 2017: 192).

For a long time Oka herders had been able to move their herds through a vast array of commonly held pastures and grazable forests, preventing overgrazing during years of drought. However, as the settler population began to grow in the eighteenth century, stream-irrigated pastures became the fenced property of individual households, leading not only to annual hay harvests, but also to greater reliance on Mongolian dairy cattle. By the second half of the nineteenth century, these fenced pastures were regularly fertilized with cattle dung to increase the growth of grasses (Sharastepanov 2008: 20). This practice was still in use at the time of my fieldwork.

In the fall, shortly after the first significant freeze, but well ahead of the first snow, people would go out to collect manure from the entire valley. Hardened cow pies were detached from the frozen ground using picks and iron rods. These were piled into wheelbarrows and transported to covered manure piles for winter storage. The following spring the piles were loaded onto large tractor or bull-drawn wooden sleighs. Medium sized piles of the manure were then unloaded from the sleds at even distances throughout the pasture. The piles were scattered with shovels and rakes, spreading the manure evenly. Here the manure would dry in the sun for a day or two. A tractor or yak-drawn wooden scraper would then be driven over the dried manure, gathering it up into conical piles that were covered with wooden slats to protect the dry mass against the weather. The fine manure dust that had been produced by the scraper fertilized the pasture, while the gathered conical piles were used as footing for dairy cattle in barns during winter. For my friends at Uro, the preparation of pastures for the winter was a major work effort undertaken prior to their departure for the summer pastures in May. The winter pasture hay harvest would occur in August.

Because grass grown in the winter valley was insufficient for feeding the cattle stock of some households, their members also harvested grass above the summer pastures in autumn. Many of these locations were not accessible in summer because of treacherous bogs. The cut autumn grass would be gathered into corralled hay piles, and someone would come back in winter to transport the feed over the frozen bogs to replenish the waning hay at the winter pastures. In some cases, these auxiliary hay harvesting lots were a household's former spring or autumn pastures. They had been in use when households were less sedentary, annually moving their stock between four instead of two pastures.

In contrast to pasture dependent dairy cattle, yak graze on steep mountain slopes that are inaccessible to regular cattle. Not only does this aptitude shelter them from predators and domestic competitors (Rassadin 2017: 192), it frees up scarce pasture lands for less agile domesticates. By keeping primarily yak, Soiot households were able to maintain a sustainable balance between species

Illustration 4.2. Yak herd at summer pasture. Photograph by the author.

in relation to the region's carrying capacity. This self-regulated trend lasted until the 1940s when the expansion of Soviet collective farming caused a shift from extensive yak and reindeer herding to intensive use of dairy cattle and sheep breeding. Cattle and sheep heavily relied on the limited hay production of the valleys. By 1958, the combination of a demanding planned economy and limited local hay production had landed cattle breeding in a crisis. Gradual expansion of sheep breeding had caused food shortages for dairy cattle, and in an attempt to meet growing milk quotas, three thousand sheep were culled. While this freed up some of the hay base, the kolkhoz soon imported Kalmyk and Simmental dairy cows, which in no way relieved the stress on hay production (e.g., Pavlinskaia 2002: 90).

WILD YAK POPULATIONS

In spite of the hardy qualities of Kalmyk cattle, the breed is known to thrive primarily in dry steppe and semi-arid and arid regions (Dimitriev and Ernst 1989: 82). In Oka, the Kalmyk breed would have depended largely on valley floor forage, along with other Mongolian cattle. The large European Simmental breed, which had successfully been crossed with many other types of cattle across the USSR (e.g., Frolov et al. 2018), would have been introduced to increase the milk yield of Oka herds. However, it too was ill-adapted to the harsh conditions of the mountainous region and required even greater hay feed. All of these introduced cattle were a far cry from the yak that had been herded by Soiots in pre-revolutionary times.

One of the most evident advantages of Soiot reindeer breeding had been the close phenotypic resemblance between animals of the forest and animals of the household. If the domestic strand could survive on its own as well as its wild counterpart, and if it were given a similar range, then the future of reindeer herding would be as sustainable as that of the wild population. Yak herding had presumably thrived on a similar parallelism. It is possible that wild yak were still roaming the area at the time of the introduction of domestic yak to Oka. There is no definitive evidence of when domestic yak were first introduced to Oka, neither is it clear when exactly wild yak became extinct in southern Siberia (A. T. Smith et al. 2010: 473). It is difficult, therefore, to know about the possible resemblances between wild and domestic yak in Oka.

Today there are approximately twenty-two thousand wild yak in northwestern and southwestern China (Shi et al. 2016: 38). However, even here the distance between domestic and wild herds has increased. According to some sources, even by the 1940s there were no longer any large herds of wild yak in Tibet, and smaller herds could be found only away from caravan trails (Phillips et al. 1946: 213). At the time, these wild yak were reported as significantly bigger than their domestic cousins. Unlike yak belonging to domestic herds, the wild population had a very pronounced sexual dimorphism with males weighing around one thousand kilograms and females only reaching on average of three hundred kilograms (Phillips et al. 1946: 213–14). In spite of these differences, Phillips et al. (1946: 214) report, "Some Tibetans claim that wild and domestic yaks cross occasionally. The crossbreeds are said to be larger and more difficult to handle, but can do more work and are hardier that the domestic type."

In Tibet, the occasional crossbreeding of wild with domestic yak was practiced to obtain animals that could accomplish more work in the household and because hybrid yak were more resilient. Another reason was that they were better at defending their herds than domestic bulls (Wiener et al. 2003: 11, 44). These advantages closely resemble those obtained by the crossing of yak with Mongolian cattle in Oka, as described below. The ability of domestic and wild herd animals to move back and forth between human and wild domains is further confirmed in Tibet by reported cases of domestic yak having gone feral (Wiener et al. 2003: 11–12). Thus, wild animals would cross over into domestic herds to reproduce, and domestic animals would venture to join wild herds.

While we cannot know for certain at this point whether a similar scenario once existed in Oka, the discovery of butchered yak bones at Gorome Cave (Tashak and Kobylkin 2015) at least hint in the direction of a contemporaneous overlap of wild and domestic yak populations in Oka. Two other archaeological sites south of Lake Baikal contain wild yak evidence from the Pleistocene. These sites fall inside the larger area of contemporary domesticated yak populations of Southcentral Siberia (S. J. Olsen 1990: 73). If the found yak remains from Gorome indeed are of wild origin, and if the authors of the paper are correct in their assumption that its butchers were Evenki hunters of the mid-nineteenth century (Tashak and Kobylkin 2015: 18), then the specimen may have belonged to a herd roaming the mountains of Oka at the same time as Soiot herder-hunters were tending to their domestic yak and reindeer only a few valleys over.

ON THE SACRED NATURE OF YAK

Across Inner Asia, herders recognize the sacred nature of select herd animals. In some cases this is based on the presence of particular attributes in an animal. In other cases a herd animal may be selected and sanctified in a ritual performed by a shaman. Anthropologist Selcen Küçüküstel recounts an instance among Dukhas of northern Mongolia in which a shaman was called upon to consecrate a single reindeer belonging to a larger herd. The herd had been subject to unusual and recurring wolf predation affecting exclusively the female deer of that herd. Following the shaman's ritual, the selected reindeer was given a blue collar to identify its new role as protector of the herd. The herding couple confirmed the ritual's efficacy in that there had been no further issues (Küçüküstel 2018: 166).

At Uro I did not witness such rituals for any of the animals in the various herds. However, my friend Erdem, whose household held yak, hybrids, and Mongolian cattle, once told me:

> There are sacred animals among yak. But they are born rarely. They can be of either sex. They have more fur [than the other animals], especially on their heads. You can't see their eyes for the fur! . . . They can be very shaggy. I once had such a yak calf born. It grew to be two and a half years of age. But alas! A wolf came and ate it. It was a pity!

It is unclear from conversations with herders of Uro how these sacred notions relating to yak arrived in Oka, and there seems to be little literature illuminating the question. It would not be difficult to imagine that a reindeer sanctification ritual, similar to that found among Dukhas, was carried over to yak. After all, a number of practices, ideas, and material implements have been adapted from one species to another, the cross-application of reindeer saddles to horses being one case in point.

The symbolic meaning of yak as bearers of the sacred, however, goes back to ancient times, long preceding the arrival of domesticated yak in South Siberia. Rock art from Upper Tibet depicts prehistoric religious symbols, among which are found the images of yak. Some scholars suggest that pre-eleventh century CE Bon (i.e., pre-Buddhist) religion ascribed sacred qualities to wild yak (Bellezza 2017: 6; S. J. Olsen 1990: 84). In these petroglyphs, male and female wild yak—the largest endemic mammal of the Tibetan plateau—are seen carrying protective deities. The scared nature of their riders is in part surmised from the fact that they ride wild yak bulls, something ordinary humans are not likely to do. Furthermore, the white wild yak celestial spirit is considered numinous of many different divinities (Bellezza 2017: 30–31). These "bull-headed" images seem to depict two distinct deities: Yama, the god of death, and Yamantaka, slayer of the god of death (S. J. Olsen 1990: 84). I encountered neither of these meanings in Soiot yak contexts.

On a more mundane level, people were secretive about how many yak they owned. Several reasons may have accounted for this, one of them being the common idea that speaking about herd size may bring bad luck upon a herd. Shortly after arriving in the field, still unaware of the taboo, I set about recording people's private stock. My host, like most other people in the valley, was hesitant to respond to my inquiries. People did not ask each other's stock count. It is not customary to do so, I was politely told (Rus. *eto ne priniato*). However, upon seeing the anonymity of the stock table, most people graciously allowed their data to be entered. Some were curious about what their neighbors had reported. My host quickly identified the yak column, and seeing that someone had listed a hundred head, he inquired whether these were not so-and-so's. Of course he was right. Speaking about herd size and knowing about a herd were clearly not the same.

As was the case with a number of other rituals, people were not always confident about the deeper meaning of a practice or where exactly it had come from. Yet, many of these rites continued to be practiced, and people generally subscribed to them as efficacious. Stock transactions were a site in which a number of different rites could be observed. Before a yak or other stock animal was sold, slaughtered, or traded, my hosts would smear the animal's forehead with melted butter. Similarly, when an animal was transferred from the domain of one household to that of another, the first owner would sometimes sprinkle milk down the animal's spine from its head to its tail. My friend Erdem and a few others still practiced this ritual, although they did not elaborate on its meaning. While yak maintained a very special place in the households of my Soiot friends, ideas about their purity were forming also in places far away from Oka's secluded valleys.

CONTEMPORARY BREEDING

In the Russian Federation there exists a growing interest in the marketability of high quality meat from unique local yak varieties to consumers in urban centers. This growing interest has been mirrored by an increase in research conducted on these varieties, their preservation, and the possibility of patenting especially marketable varieties. Efforts have been made to establish a cryobank of yak sperm for varieties belonging to minority breeds from Tajikistan, the Republic of Altai, and North Caucasus (Bagirov et al. 2009). In Tyva, research has been conducted on selective breeding to increase yak meat yield without losing overall resilience (Chysyma and Kan-ool 2016). Studies have also been conducted on exporting yak from Oka to other regions of Buriatia, where the animals were found to do well even at low altitudes (Nasatuev et al. 2015).

In response to the growing demand for alpine and "ecologically clean" yak meat, the Oka variety of yak have been patented in the Russian Federation on the basis of distinctness, uniformity, and stability (Taishin 2015: 85). Much of the research leading up to the patent was concerned with distinct coat color. Apparently, the diversity of yak coat color in Oka exceeds that of other neighboring populations. Yak in Mongolia are known for four distinct color patterns, while those kept in the Baikal region have three types, and those found in Tyva represent five types. In Oka, a total of nine different color patterns are common, the majority of which are dark (Taishin 2015: 85). These differences are currently being accentuated through selective breeding aimed at solidifying the so-called *Poephagus grunniens L. Okinsky* breed of dark and polled (hornless) animals (Taishin and Anganov 2014: 83).

Not all Oka yak herders are equally committed to securing a regionally unique and marketable breed. Especially for Soiot subsistence herders, there was little incentive in raising herds for mass meat production, as such herds would exceed sustainable herd size and average household capacity to track and secure grazing. The households at Uro would slaughter between one and three mature yak for meat for retail and personal consumption each autumn. Such meat was either sold to middlemen from Irkutsk who would come to buy meat in Orlik, or people would transport the meat in their own vehicles to resell in Irkutsk with the help of relatives who lived in the city. The latter type of small-scale retail did not require certified slaughtering houses, official meat inspections, or certificates of vaccination, and it relied primarily on a network of acquaintances in the city.

ADVANTAGES OF HYBRID BREEDING

Of greater importance to my friends at Uro were the previously mentioned hybrid cattle. Khainaks were the pride of every household. In a way, they were the best of both worlds: strong, resilient, and independent as yak, yet nearly as productive as common dairy cattle. They stood tall and were as strong as cattle bull. They were also divided into two types: ones grazing with dairy cattle near the home and ones considered wild (Rus. *dikie khainaki*). Wild khainaks were the offspring of a yak mother and a Mongolian cattle bull. Their calf would join its mother's herd in the backcountry rather than the cattle herd near the homestead. Where the parentage was reversed, the calf would grow up near other dairy cattle. In either case, male crossbred offspring were always born sterile preventing further crossbreeding.

Although crossbreeding would have emerged in Oka only with the arrival of Mongolian cattle, the practice itself is quite old and shared by most yak breeding societies. In northern Nepal, for instance, the yak hybrid is referred to as *chauri*, and both female yaks (*nak*) and chauri are milked (Dong and Pariya 2009: 957–58). Nepalese herders will cross their yak with Tibetan and Zebu cattle to strengthen their herds as they engage in seasonal transhumance (Dong and Pariya 2009: 961), much in the manner of Soiots. In eastern Bhutan, crossbreeding has been linked to optimizing the use of grazing spaces at different altitudes. While regular cattle will graze at lower altitudes, hybrid cattle are best adapted to feeding at one thousand meters above sea level, and yak are most comfortable at altitudes above one thousand meters (Winter and Tshewang

1989). Hybridization thus makes use of a resource neither yak or regular cattle would otherwise exploit.

Mobile herders from Tyva (also referred to as Uriankhaians) residing in the Altai were known to hold Oirat Mongolian cattle along with domestic yak, horses, and camels (Lkhagvasuren 2012). In contrast to herders of Bhutan, these Altai-Uriankhaians divided their grazing ranges primarily in terms of distance from the yurt. While horse and camel grazing grounds were located the farthest from the yurt, cattle were kept nearby. Bringing their mixed cattle into closer proximity of the yurt every night allowed for the milking of female cows, hybrids, and yak twice per day. After milking, the animals rejoined their herd (Lkhagvasuren 2012: 145). While yak are no longer kept in the Tunka Valley south of Oka, yak and khainaks were a common sight there, particularly in the Turan and Khoitogol basins, as late as the early twentieth century (Mansheev 2005: 76). Here one of the known advantages of yak and hybrids over horses was their gentle grazing, allowing for a quicker regeneration of grasses (Mansheev 2005: 76).

THE KHAINAK

When anthropologist Larissa Pavlinskaia (2002: 90) spoke with head zoo technician Boris D. Tsyrenov of the Sorok kolkhoz in 1988, he insisted that the best dairy breed for Oka were khainaks. Their resilience and high yield of 6 percent milk represented an ideal middle ground between imported cattle and indigenous yak in terms of resilience and productivity. Tsyrenov was convinced then that the kolkhoz could maintain two herds of one hundred khainaks each, without depleting their territory's resources. Instead, twenty-nine head of Simmental cows were consuming the majority of the kolkoz's annual winter hay at the time. Tsyrenov reckoned it would take between four and five years to grow a herd of dairy khainaks.

A yak cow carries her calf for nine months, and a Mongolian cow for eight. The longer gestation period results in a greater survival rate in calves. However, due to the relatively small size of yak cows, and the large size of their hybrid calves, mothers would often die while giving birth to their hybrid offspring. Indeed, a newborn yak weighs on average eleven kilograms, while a newborn hybrid weighs between seventeen and eighteen kilograms (Badmaev 2007: 14). As a result, there is a greater likelihood for hybrid fetuses not to survive. It was possible to receive hybrid calves from Mongolian cows instead, which would ease the birthing process thanks to the mother's larger size. However, here the problem was that their afterbirth expelled so poorly that further births could be complicated. According to Tsyrenov it was therefore better to receive calves from yaks.

Another challenge in breeding a new khainak dairy herd was the fact that hybrid cattle had to be habituated to regular human handling. Taming hybrid offspring generally occurred as calves attended during the milking of their mothers. This method was also practiced with crossbred reindeer. However, the yak herds from which would come the maternal parents of these crossbreeds had not been milked since the early 1960s. In Tsyrenov's terms, "they [had] all become wild" (Pavlinskaia 2002: 90). Of course, this was only a problem where the bull parent was of a domestic breed and the cow mother of a wild herd, but for the purpose of forming a hybrid dairy herd in which cows could give birth repeatedly, this combination was necessary.

Tsyrenov's hopes for the creation of a hybrid dairy cattle herd falls in line with a long history of breeding experiments in Oka. The origin account at the beginning of this chapter already alluded to some of these. In Oka, both artificial and natural hybridization processes are known to exist, but it is relatively uncommon for cattle and yak to breed together under natural circumstances (Badmaev 2007: 12). Only 7 to 8 percent of reproductive cases seem to fall into this category, and yak bulls are generally more common than cattle bulls to pursue females of the opposite species, which may have to do with the fact that after female yak cease to be receptive (i.e., after the mating season is over), yak bulls continue to have a drive, resulting in their participation in the longer-lasting mating season of regular cattle (Badmaev 2007: 12).

There are two observed scenarios in hybridization: either a female yak comes together with a cattle bull, or a Mongolian cow mates with a yak bull. In either case, their crossbred male offspring in the first generation is always sterile, while crossbred female offspring remain fertile (Badmaev 2007: 12). Hybrids of the second generation are referred to as *ortoms* (*ortooms*). These are the result of a reversed crossing of a khainak female with a cattle bull. Where this takes place, the crossbred offspring most resembles the cattle parent, and when a female khainak is crossed with a yak bull, the calf will look more like the yak parent. Second generation crossing is not desired because of the low productivity of the resulting offspring (Badmaev 2007: 13).

A number of hurdles must be overcome for yak and regular cattle to crossbreed. The mating seasons of cattle and yak do not perfectly coincide in Oka, and there exists only a brief overlap occurring at the tail end of the cattle mating period, marking the beginning of yak receptivity. At this time most cattle cows have already been impregnated by conspecific bulls (Badmaev 2007: 14). Second, yak and cattle graze in different locations and at different altitudes, further reducing the likelihood of natural crossbreeding. Finally, yak and cattle that were not raised together will generally not pay attention to each other. In fact, it is believed that yak and cattle who were raised together as calves will imprint upon each other. Only animals with this experience may later mate (Badmaev 2007: 14).

Since the dissolution and privatization of the kolkhoz system in the 1990s, the residents of Sorok were no longer subject to imposed milk and meat production quotas. Consequently, I did not encounter any pure crossbred dairy herds as described by Tsyrenov. Instead, people had long returned to a more balanced breeding regime in which a small number of dairy khainaks would graze alongside other Mongolian dairy cattle near the household. They would migrate to their summer pastures along with other stock of the household in May. Wild khainak would join their yak mothers, roaming the hillsides of the backcountry as part of larger yak herds consisting of fifty to sixty animals. In summer they were taken to higher altitudes above the summer pastures.

Given the birthing difficulties described by the kolkhoz zoo technician, I had expected the birthing season to be an exceedingly busy time for the household. It turned out however, most yak births did not require any human intervention, and during my stay at Uro, I did not witness any khainak births. Baldorzho explained that in most cases births went quite easily, as calves were born head first. That year, all his yak calves had been born in this manner. On rare occasions, a calf would come out with its hind quarters or rear first. This could cause problems, and usually required a herder's help. But such births occurred less often. A greater danger were the wolves. Yak cows preferred to give birth to their young in isolation and far from the homestead. Often they would return to the winter pasture without their calves, having lost them to a wolf pack.

HERDING TECHNIQUES

At Uro, two yak herding techniques were used. Most households designated someone to ride out to the herd each evening. This would either be the father of the household or one of the sons. Upon finding the herd, they would drive the yak either into the corrals near their home or into the fenced pastures surrounding the winter residences. In summer, the same would be done at higher elevation. The other approach was not to drive the herd back to the valley at night, but to ride or walk out to them every few days for a brief stock count. This technique had been more common in past years. Because of the growing wolf population, ever fewer herders would allow their herds to stay in the hills for the night. By late April and into early May, when the cows were having their young, the herders ensured all their yak were corralled by eleven o'clock at night.

Driving home a herd of yak could be challenging. In Oka, herds could consist of up to 120 mature females, plus five to six reproductive bulls (Badmaev 2007: 8). At Uro, the herds were smaller, with one or two reproductive bulls. According to Sergei Badmaev (2007: 8–9), Oka herds were often headed by several older khainaks, or by one or two dominant yak cows. The bulls would mingle with the reproductive herd only during the rut, and for the rest of the year they stayed together as a smaller independent group. The sterile khainak males, castrated on their first birthday to suppress their sexual drive, would form yet another group. Because these males were larger than the yak breeding bulls, they could repel yak bulls from cows that were in heat from June to September. The herders at Uro were well aware of these internal dynamics, and also carefully observed as herd members were in constant communication with each other about potential threats approaching them.

On a day in late April, as households were preparing to leave the winter valley for their summer migration, I was sitting near the center of the valley from where I could observe various sheep and goat flocks as they were moving about freely. None of the flocks seemed to mingle with each other. The yak herds on the hillsides also did not seem to mingle with each other. Instead, each herd stayed together, mirroring the distinct households to which they belonged. Using binoculars, it was easy to follow Uncle Burzhon's yak herd as they were peacefully grazing on the same hill as Tseden's yak. I could see how the two herds of approximately fifty to sixty head each were slowly approaching each other. The proximity between them gradually decreased, and eventually they had passed each other. Throughout the process, each yak had maintained a distance of no less than fifty meters from the members of the other herd.

My neighbor Tseden explained to me later that afternoon that herds of different species did not mix unless they belonged to the same household. But, he noted, all of this was a recent phenomenon. When the collective farm had been active, workers constantly had to separate animals into reproductive units. When the farm closed, all the stock were divided among local households. The new owners continued having to separate animals into herds for a long time. As the years passed, herds began to form in relation to the households that bred them. At present, the herds of one household no longer grazed with those of another. Animal herds and households were thus deeply intertwined. To further illustrate this point, Tseden recalled the summer his yak had been taken to the same pastures as Uncle Borzhon's. Both herds had grazed together all season, being treated as one large herd. In August, when the animals were driven back to Uro, both herds immediately separated again.

Interestingly, this is not where the story of herd mixing ended—at least not for dairy cattle. When I arrived at the summer pasture on the Tustuk River the following month, I noticed how the Mongolian cow herd of my host mother was freely mingling with the cow herd of her mother's household. Both households spent the summers sharing common pastures on the Tustuk. In Uro, the cows of our household had refused to mingle with cows from other households. Here on the Tustuk they did not seem to mind mixing with other animals. It took me a while before I noticed that my host mother and her sister had been milking cows from both herds in the same corral. Each milker belonged to one of the two households that owned the herds. Perhaps the two herds had merged because they were milked together. In the case of yak and sheep, this reasoning did not apply, as neither were involved in any dairy routine.

Although summer pastures were not harvested for winter hay and often remained unfenced, they too were considered hereditary. It was therefore the responsibility of the owning household to look after the grazing patterns of their stock and to ensure one's own herds were not consistently grazing in the pastures of other households. One morning in early June, approximately one hundred yak belonging to our neighbor Ilia had crossed the rushing waters of the Tustuk only to emerge on our side of the river. A few minutes later, I could see Amagalan, my eleven-year-old host brother, mounting one of the horses hitched by our cabin. He swiftly rode out to Ilia's herd, skillfully weaving back and forth, as he drove the herd back to the water's edge. From here he encouraged the herd back into the cold waters and into their own pastures.

DAIRYING

Nestled on the confluence of the Iakhashop and Tustuk Rivers, our summer pasture was located at a crossroads. Anyone whose pastures were located upstream on either river had to come through our pastures. As people were going back and forth between their summer residences and the village of Sorok, many would stop by our cabin for a cup of tea and a chat. One evening my friend Uncle Aiusha (b. 1958) came to visit our house. After we had shared some tea, we sat outside for a while. Looking down to where the two rivers merged, Aiusha recalled how during the earlier years of the kolkhoz ten women milkers (Rus. *doiarki*) and their families had resided here. Each of them had maintained a little cabin on the river bank, which had always been a strategic location connecting two valleys. Now there was no trace left of the cabins. But Aiusha recalled that each of the women had milked twenty five of the 250 or so yaks that had been in the area.

Their husbands would likely have been employed as wranglers (Rus. *tabunchiki*) looking after kolkhoz-owned horses. The *tabunchiki* had kept several summer camps, some of which survive to this day, and one of which was located upstream on Iakhoshop River. A shift work schedule allowed the wranglers to see their families regularly. The women not only milked the yak, they also separated the milk every night, churning extracted cream into fresh butter. Before sunrise each morning, they would transport the butter on horseback to Sorok. These memories of Uncle Aiusha's must have been of stories he had been told as a child, since he would have been only about two years old when the kolkhoz stopped milking yak.

The loss of yak dairying in Oka may be argued to have had significant consequences on the relationship between humans and their herds. The main method of establishing approachability or habituation to human presence in yak calves was to have them present while their mothers were milked. Not only would the presence of the calf stimulate the mother's expression of milk (e.g., V. I. Rassadin 2017: 193), it would also allow the calf to be near the milker while in its mother's presence. The calf would be allowed to stimulate its mother by suckling and consuming some of the milk. This would get the milk flowing for the milker who would allow the calf to consume what was left in the udder after the milking was complete. As yak milking was no longer practiced during my field stay, yak calves had become quite skittish and practically impossible to approach.

YAK IN THE KOLKHOZ

Following Larissa Pavlinskaia's 1988 conversation with Boris D. Tsyrenov, the zoo technician of the Sorok kolkhoz, I had the opportunity to meet his colleague Vladimir Chemitevich, some twenty-five years later. Chemitevich had been chairman of the kolkhoz association for six or seven years of his career, and he was considered a knowledgeable elder by my friends at Uro. Like many other retired kolkhoz workers, he maintained a house in the village of Sorok where his wife spent the winters. Meanwhile, Chemitevich spent his winters herding their own yak at winter pastures in a remote valley.

Recalling his work for the kolkhoz, Chemitevich's main complaint was that the system had never seriously taken into account the limited capacity for hay production in Oka. Archival sources from as early as 1931 indicate that the administration was well aware of the number of pounds of hay required to feed the stock held by each kolkhoz, and how many pounds of hay were actually being produced by each kolkhoz on how many hectares of pastureland (AAMO 1931 1-1-11: 21). However, these numbers were not seen as static. These were values that could be increased to match the growing demands on milk, leather, and fur in a planned economy.

Each kolkhoz would receive minimum performance benchmarks (Rus. *udarnye zadachi*) to which the collective had to produce. These expectations often did not correspond with what was physically achievable or advisable in the eyes of locals. In 1962, an order was issued for the local newspaper to publish monthly production results for each kolkhoz (AAMO 1962 2-1-165: 1). Presumably, this was to inspire workers of different kolkhozes to compete with each other and thereby to increase their collective production. But when the local hay base failed to support the growing cattle count, Chemitevich recalled the farm having to truck in large amounts of hay and compound feed, which cost a lot of money.

Reindeer and yak, on the other hand, had been nearly cost-free sources of meat and fur. Neither had required hay or compound feed, as they were self-procuring year-round. The administration had argued it did not need "semi-wild" (Rus. *polu-dikie*) animals, whose meat yield did not meet quota. In a last effort to increase the meat production of these semi-wild animals, the district imported yak bulls from Altai. In comparison to Oka yak, Chemitevich found these bulls to be "almost wild." Significantly larger than the local breed, they had been transported by train from Altai to the station at Sliudianka on the western shores of Lake Baikal. From here they had been trucked to Sorok. Although their offspring had indeed been markedly larger, the kolkhoz association eventually decided to cull all yak in Oka. The last remaining reindeer had already been eliminated; yak were to follow.

Chemitevich recalled one elder who had refused to abide by the order to cull yak. The man had hidden a herd of yak in the mountains, while all the other yak of Oka were being slaughtered. "Today we have this stubborn elder to thank for the survival of yaks in Oka!" Chemitevich exclaimed. I had come across this phrase multiple times in Oka. People were generally aware of this heroic man, who had not only allowed for a more sustainable way of herding to survive but also presumably risked much in order to retain one of the last markers of Soiot cultural identity.

BEARS, WOLVES, AND YAK

One early afternoon in mid July, Iuri Viktorevich (b. ca. 1980), a middle-aged herder-hunter who lived in the historic Khan-Modon Valley, came to pay us a visit on the Tustuk River. He had ridden his horse down along the Iakhoshop River on his way to Sorok. After pouring him a cup of milky tea, my host mother hinted at a promise he had made about bringing back some yak meat the week before. Catching a ride in a demilitarized tank with a group of drunk hunters from the city, he had been traveling upriver to check on his herd. Apparently he was not in the mood to be reminded of a promise made under such circumstances; he retorted that the wolves had been a catastrophe. Apparently his herds had taken major damage over the last few years.

Viktorevich spoke excellent Russian. He belonged to a generation that had grown up in the residential school at Sorok. As a young adult he had moved to Khan-Modon, where his wife's parents had moved twenty-five years ago. The valley had been one of the last locations where their Soiot ancestors had been in possession of transportation reindeer when anthropologist B. E. Petri visited them in 1920. No one was keeping reindeer there now, but as an avid yak herder, Viktorevich was genuinely concerned about the predators he shared the valley with. Since the outlawing of wolf poison, the region had not been doing too well in his opinion. Jokingly he suggested I write about the Russian Federation's neglect of Soiot herders: the government were clearly not taking care of Oka's wolf problem.

At Khan-Modon, Viktorevich had always kept around seventy head of yak. This year his stock count had dropped to thirty-four animals. Viktorevich seemed desperate enough not to mind mentioning how many animals he still owned. In total, half of his herd had been killed by wolves. The reason for this, he explained, was that he lived in a location where four river valleys met. It was extremely difficult to look out for wolves in such a landscape. Unlike other locations, where wolves usually descended one mountain, or at least came from a single direction, Viktorevich had wolves coming and going in all directions. It was his assessment that these wolves were regularly passing through on their travels, feeding on his stock each time. But wolves were not his only trouble.

Due to its remoteness, there were few neighbors at Khan-Modon. The upside of this isolation was that Viktorevich could keep both summer and winter pastures in the same valley. This required minimal movement of stock between the two. The downside was the high level of exposure to predators. Two years earlier, a large bear had ventured into his summer pasture. It had entered a corral and attacked the yak standing inside it. The ground had been covered in snow already, allowing the bear to sneak up on his prey without even alarming Viktorevich's dogs. When he went outside, he found two dead yak in the corral. Bear tracks were going in the direction of his summer pasture where another man was staying at the time. The man had been on his way to the outhouse when he saw the bear nearing. On his way, the bear had overtaken several yak marching toward the pasture.

Attacking the yak from behind, the bear had ripped at the base of their tails. Several of the animals were immediately paralyzed. Frightened by the sight, Viktorevich followed the bear tracks on his horse toward his summer camp, a distance of approximately seven kilometers. Halfway between camps, the bear had left behind a total of eight yak, which were either killed or maimed. The muzzle of one yak had been severely damaged. The bear had struck it with such force that its broken facial bone was hanging loose. Clearly the animal had no chance of survival. A little way further, a grown bull was lying on its side, unable to stand up. One of its horns was bored into the ground. Viktorevich wiggled it loose.

He pursued the bear on horseback for a long time. Whenever it came into sight, Viktorevich would aim his rifle. Several times he fired, only to miss. Finally, when the bear had arrived at the base of yet another hill, he saw it run up the slope and disappear. Viktorevich carefully approached the hill. As he was climbing, he noticed a faint brown patch among the snowy bushes on his left. It was the bear. Viktorevich had only barely escaped what he considered shrewd trickery. Having left the line of sight, the bear had turned into the bushes, where it was hiding for a surprise attack. At least this was what Viktorevich surmised the bear's intentions had been. He had read of similar tactics in a book. Viktorevich's account was detailed, passionate, and peppered with a mix of awe and hatred. But his was only one among many.

Before we had moved households to the summer pastures, I had visited Uncle Aiusha's house with my host's elder brother, Uncle Borzhon. Aiusha and his wife lived alone in a cabin tucked away on the lower Sorok River. He had told us of his more distant neighbors who had recently caught eight wolf cubs. Spring was the time to hunt them. By Aiusha's account the wolf population was higher now than it had been in years, and the loss of livestock to wolves was unprecedented. Uncle Borzhon recalled that in Soviet times, when wolves were still being poisoned, a herd of one hundred yak could have as many as eighty-five or even ninety calves, all of which survived the spring. Nowadays a comparable herd might have six surviving calves. Two percent of the total loss might be from sickness, he estimated, wolves accounting for the remainder.

Some of these deaths occurred not at a distance, but very close to home. On the morning of 10 May, as Borzhon was counting his yak before releasing them from the corral where they had spent the night, he noticed that one of the newborn calves was missing. He searched all around the outside of the corral looking for tracks in the snow. Indeed, wolf tracks were found leading to the backside of the corral. The calf had been dragged from the corral, across the frozen river, and into the woods. Such accounts had become quite frequent. Wolves were increasingly coming to be a threat to yak and other stock not only in the remote backcountry, but even at the center of the valley, a location that had long been considered a safe haven.

CONCLUSION

In chapter 3 I discussed the heritage of reindeer breeding in Soiot and Tofa contexts. This background is pivotal to an understanding of the place yak and hybrid cattle have taken in contemporary Soiot society. While reindeer have increasingly acquired a symbolic status, pointing to Soiot indigeneity and rootedness in the mountainous taiga of the Eastern Saian Mountains, yak continue to represent a living cultural heritage. While this sense of cultural identity may not set Soiots apart from Buriats as a recognizable ethnos, the animal and its hybrid offspring have been adopted as markers of an equally genuine Soiot household in many ways rivalling that of reindeer.

From an anthropological point of view, it could be argued that the much-treasured hybrid yak—perhaps more even than reindeer—can serve as a metaphor for a Soiot sense of identity. While reindeer of the human household continue to move back and forth between the domains of forest and encampment, hybrid yak physically embody aspects of both worlds. In so doing, they undermine the very divide we like to construct between wild and tame. Considered part of the human household, and in no way to be confused with prey of the forest, the khainak maintains a mind of its own much like prey. It thereby perpetuates in a pastoral economy the ambiguity of the Soiot hunt. While meeting the demands of a more settled life through its high milk production, the khainak also maintains its wildness, thriving under the rigors of a vertical life. Highly autonomous in its movement, self-willed and better able to defend itself against predators than any other species of cattle in the region, the khainak truly conflates the polar notions of wild and tame.

CHAPTER 5

IN THE SOCIETY OF HORSES

Our group of five researchers packed their large duffle bags early on the morning of 17 September, balancing them on two pack horses. Two palynologists, an archaeologist, and a geographer had joined me on this autumn trip to Tofalariia. Denis and Alesha, our local guides, saddled our six riding horses, and after each of us mounted our own horse, we quietly rode off into the taiga. Denis was leading the caravan with Alesha riding at the back. The sun was rising bright and clear, its warm rays sparkling through a thick canopy of golden leaves lining the winding shores of the Uda River. Riding behind Denis, I could hear the even pace of our horses. Their hooves were treading sandy forest floor, loose rocks, swamp, rushing waters, and then sandy floor again. Every now and then, I had to glance over my shoulder to check on our caravan, making sure all were there, our chainsaw was still in place, and no bags had come loose.

Unlike any hunter I had hitherto met, Denis talked ceaselessly all day long. Only when the wind and rushing waters were drowning out his speech, would he switch to singing. Singing and riding in the taiga went hand in hand for him. His uncle had forced him to sing as a child. This was a traumatic memory for Denis. As a child he had tired of singing for long periods of time. But he had to thank his uncle for teaching him to be a hunter, and now that he was an adult with his own wife and children, Denis could sing for as long as he could talk. Knowing that I had lived with Soiots in Oka, he would ask about their horses. How did they compare to Tofa horses? Did they handle as well as his in this mountainous terrain? And how many horses did they keep on hand in summer? Denis had many questions. But as time passed, I realized that most of his inquiries were merely rhetorical. His mind was made up on horses: no horse came close in skill or build to a Tofa horse.

Not surprisingly, Denis frowned when I told him my Soiot friends were equally convinced their horses were superior to those of their Tofa neighbors in the north. How could I have been misled to believe these Soiots? Compelled to convert me, Denis took every opportunity to point out how well his equines were handling the sometimes steep terrain. Each time we tackled a river crossing, a steep wooded incline, or a deep frost-covered bog, he would ask me to compare his horses with the ones I had ridden in Oka.

There was little use in trying to explain to him that I had not meant to offend him, and that I was not trying to establish who had the better horses. In Oka, most horses had already been let go for the winter. Denis had kept his horses near the house for our visit, and for a final move of cargo to his hunting camp later in the month. Once these tasks were accomplished, he would release his horses too. I told Denis how in summer Soiot herders used their horses to wrangle yak and cows, and how in autumn they would take them hunting in less demanding terrain, only to release them later for the winter.

In Tofalariia, he told me, people still relied on a good winter's hunt in steep terrain. Only reindeer could navigate these locations. Now was the time people were transitioning from their horses to their reindeer. I was here to witness this seasonal switch, described in chapter 3. But with near equal periods of time left to themselves, how distinct were human-horse relations from human-reindeer relations? And did their interchangeability lead to any conclusions regarding their wildness or their tameness? Whatever the case, Denis felt strongly about his horses. They were not an afterthought introduced merely to bridge the time while reindeer were unavailable.

* * *

In previous chapters I have focused primarily on human-animal and human-spirit relations in a direct sort of way. This chapter continues with a relational outlook, but it does so by focusing on material implements as communicative devices between horses and humans. It illustrates how the meaning of lassos, ropes, and hobbles can change over the course of a horse's life. This becomes especially evident in the description of the annual roundup, horse roping techniques, and the re-shoeing of a mature gelding. Through these descriptions, the chapter touches on the role of the horse in the Eastern Saian domus, particularly in terms of its shared history with hunting and reindeer herding. While horses and reindeer were recognized for their divergent qualities, they had both been used extensively for transportation purposes, albeit at different times of the year and for different kinds of terrain. In the Saians, where the Karagas breed of reindeer reaches exceptional shoulder height, horse and reindeer saddles were somewhat interchangeable.

This sharing of material implements between species was indicative of an overlap in cultural traditions that had increased hunters' flexibility in the landscape. The chapter thus argues that features associated with wildness in animals—features conventionally sought to be bred out of domesticates—can also be seen as desirable features. In the case of stallions, for instance, this occurrence inverts the notion of tameness as a foundational feature for domestication. Consequently, domestic traits were often not a matter of a wild-tame dichotomy. Instead, domestication had to be understood in terms of negotiation or management of human and animal intentions, some of which were meant to remain unruly. As familiarity grew between householders and their horses, the implements that brought them together would become ever more nuanced communicative devices.

THE WILDNESS OF DOMESTICATED HORSES

As described in chapter 3, reindeer of the spirit-mastered household and reindeer of human-mastered households inhabit the same landscape. The same may once have been true also of yak, as discussed in the previous chapter. Although no longer the case, horses of Central and Northern Mongolia, and possibly Southern Siberia, are known to once have shared a common range with their non-domesticated relatives. Natasha Fijn (2015) has written about the reintroduced *takhi*, or Przewalski wild horse, seen roaming Khustai Nuruu National Park in Mongolia.

Fijn contrasts the *takhi* with contemporary Mongolian domesticated horses, citing research (Myka et al. 2003; Vilà et al. 2001) that suggests "substantial overlap in terms of their mitochondrial DNA, or the maternal line" between the two populations (Fijn 2015: 292). This overlap suggests ancestors of Mongolian domestic horses interbred with *takhi* roaming the same area. As mentioned in chapter 1, more recent work on ancient genomes reveals that *takhi* themselves are not "true" wild horses, but rather the feral ancestors of horses that had already been herded by the Eneolithic Botai culture as early as approximately 5,500 years ago (Gaunitz et al. 2018). Consequently, we are observing yet another example of multiple waves of domestication.

Although we cannot be certain to what extent householders encouraged or discouraged interbreeding between herded and feral populations, it can be assumed that the consequences of such crossbreeding were evident in the physical composition and demeanor of domestic horses. Tofa and Soiot reindeer herders, like all reindeer herders, were apprehensive about domestic reindeer mingling and interbreeding with their cousins in the wild. If such mingling did not result in the loss of mature does to wild herds, then at least it resulted in unruly offspring. It remains open to what extent the same would have been true of horses and their human households of the past.

In Oka and Tofalariia, people were keenly aware of the established hierarchies within horse groups. Rank was expected to play on an animals' demeanor, and a good householder knew to accommodate it. Although groups of horses could be seen grazing near the homes of people, they were expected to move freely and on their own volition. In contrast to animals of the forest, horses formed part of the human-mastered household, even if only a small number of them were ever bound to a *serge*, the traditional tethering post that symbolized the center of the household. The behavior of horses in the household therefore stood in relation to their extensive periods spent at a distance. During the short summer months, when horses were drawn to be with or near humans, their interactions were still marked by experiences outside the human compound. Such experiences could range from recent predator interactions leaving deep bite marks on their bodies and affecting their social behavior, to changes in intra-group relations staked out in the taiga.

Many of these dynamics that would take place away from the realm of human settlement resemble the descriptions of ethologists studying free-roaming wild and feral equids (e.g., Ransom and Cade 2009; St-Louis and Côté 2012). For this reason, it may be suggested that horses in Oka are best understood in terms of an intersection of the ways of the taiga with the ways of the household. For the horses at Uro, time spent away from direct human influence seemed to bestow them with many of the features commonly associated with wild or feral horses. Highly independent in their search for forage, they would fight off predators. In winter they endured extreme cold, scraping for forage in much the same way as yak. The hierarchies they established during their long absences from the winter pastures in the valleys affected how their groups navigated the landscape. All of these features influenced the ways these graceful animals interacted with the household.

Yet, these horses differed clearly from wild horses in that their sociality had been co-shaped by deliberate household intervention. No matter how far horses were ranging from human householders' residences, their sociality in the taiga was always co-shaped by their relationship to the human household. This relationship was expressed in different ways for different members of a group of horses, but it could entail one or more of the seasonal practices upheld by horse-owning households, including rounding up, corralling, inoculating, hobbling, shoeing, grooming, castrating, training, and slaughtering. Nonetheless, several of these aspects of close physical contact with human members of the household, affected only a small number of horses. Usually these were the ones selected for riding. The remainder of the herd would have much less contact with people, which inevitably resulted in a broad spectrum of tameness for these domesticated horses.

My Soiot friends often referred to their reindeer as semi-wild or semi-domestic animals—beings with a high degree of human-independent willpower. Although people did not generally refer to their horses as wild or even semi-domestic, horses too were considered to have a strong sense of independence. It was understood that human care was not essential to their survival, which in this sense put horses in the same category as yak and reindeer. Much like feral horses of North America, who "because of their highly adaptive nature were able to thrive in a multitude of environments" (Ransom and Cade 2009: 1), Soiot horses were understood to be utterly self-reliant. At the same time, they were known to possess a profound level of familiarity with their human collaborators. Over the course of twenty-five to thirty years of a horse's lifespan, human and horse intentions could come to align in remarkable ways.

Perhaps the strongest confrontation of opposed human and horse intentions was displayed every spring when householders rounded up their horse groups for the first time after a long winter marked by utterly independent movement. My Soiot friends referred to this process simply as catching horses (Rus. *lovit'*, Bur. *barikha*). But the views differed broadly on how easy or difficult this simple catching was. Everyone seemed to agree that initial contact with a horse in spring required actions and materials that would draw the animal into a space from where horses and humans had the opportunity to reestablish their relations for the following season.

OF TIE AND RANGE

The main reason for letting horses go for the winter was the limited availability of harvestable fodder discussed in the previous chapter. Residents of Uro maximized their hay harvesting surfaces, and the carrying capacity of their hereditary hay patches was directly expressed in the number of cows and sheep each household could hold in a given year. In fact, people would adjust the number of stock they kept in relation to fluctuations in annual hay harvests. Thus, a poor hay harvest could call for greater stock slaughter in autumn and winter. Yak, reindeer, and horses, on the other hand, were able to forage for themselves in winter because they grazed over larger distances and far beyond human harvesting ranges. The fact that yak and khainaks fended for themselves contributed to their semi-domestic status. Surprisingly, I have never overheard similar reference to horses, although they spent a near equal amount of time fending for themselves.

The ability to locate fodder away from human settlement was highly valued, because it diversified the use of the landscape and maximized natural meat and milk yields without the need for outside fodder supplementation, as was the case with such domestic breeds as sheep, goats, and cows. In this sense, horses were affordable and sustainable means of transportation, and a highly valued asset. Much like reindeer, their existence was entirely secured through year-round underfoot forage (Rus. *kruglogodnyi podnozhnyi korm*), a fact that further informed how human and horse autonomy were played out in and around Uro.

It was mid-October, and the temperature was dropping quickly. All my neighbors' horses had long left the valley for the winter, and it was good to visit with Borzhon and Ranzhur in their warm kitchen. Flickering warm light was thrown from Ranzhur's hearth against the kitchen wall, and the large tea kettle on top of the cast iron plate was soon to boil. I used the opportunity to ask Borzhon about his horses. Were they wild or were they domestic animals? Beligte, Baianbata's wife, had told me earlier that in Buriat these terms were not generally used. *Emnig* referred to a non-domestic horse, but wild animals in general were known as *zerlig anguud*. The home or house was the *ger*, and domestic animals were those which lived near the home or house: *gerei* (domestic), *gerei takhianuud* (domestic chickens).

Instead of speaking of an animal as either domestic or wild, people would refer to a particular species, the status of which was well known to all. But in Russian, Borzhon referred to his horses as domestic (Rus. *domashnye*). I countered, noting that for the larger part of the year his horses, like all other horses in the valley, were out on their own. Why did he consider them domestic? He agreed, but then pointed out that even in winter, when he did not bring in any of his horses for riding, they would periodically come back to the house in their groups to lick the salt he would set out for them. In this sense, he suggested, they were very domestic indeed. However, as he went on to explain, while he would leave his horses to themselves in winter, they were really more or less on their own all year round.

Even in summer, he would keep only three or four riding horses near the cabin. At night, he would hobble their legs to prevent them from wandering off, and during the day they would stand fully tacked and hitched to one of his *serge*. The remainder of his herd of fifty head would wander freely within their individual family groups. Together they could be found grazing anywhere within the wider vicinity of his summer pastures. The key to Borzhon's conception of domesticity seemed to lie in how he thought about nearness and accessibility. Borzhon was generally able to locate his horses within the course of a single day. In summer, he or one of his sons would saddle a riding horse and head out into the hills to perform routine counts. Because the men knew where their horses' favorite grazing areas were, finding them was relatively easy. But there were exceptions to these predictable grazing ranges.

During an autumn hunt with Borzhon and another hunter, our group once noticed a man riding at a distance in the hills. A large group of horses had gathered behind him. As we approached the rider, Borzhon recognized him as Munko of Sorok. Munko had come to check on his horses, and he had found them in the sand dunes north of Grandfather Tseren-Dorzho's summer camp. While the other hunter and I waited at a distance, Borzhon and Munko stood in the wind, smoking cigarettes, exchanging news. Munko had a group of horses who were roaming west of the Oka river, and among them he had recently found a horse that did not belong to him. Judging from Munko's description, Borzhon figured this was a horse he had lost almost two years ago. Borzhon was glad of the news, and I was glad that now I had a better sense of Borzhon's concept of the home range. The lost horse had left Borzhon's home range when it joined Munko's herd. Several days later, I saw Munko walking the lost horse to Borzhon's home at Uro.

It did happen that horses would not return to their households at all. They could slip on ice in winter or fall prey to wolves. They perished while out on their own. And in some cases they did not return because of age. One year, an old horse of Borzhon's appeared at his residence to lick salt in the depth of winter. It had come alone, which was unusual. Normally horses came to lick salt in large groups over a period of one or more days. After the single horse had paid its visit, it slowly walked back into the hills, never to be seen again. Not even its bones were ever located. Borzhon was quite touched by this final appearance: "It almost seemed like it had come to say goodbye one last time." It seemed Borzhon had told me this story for two reasons. First, it illustrated how strong the tie between him and his horses was, and second, it showed that his horses were domestic. A wild horse would never have come to bid him farewell at his winter residence. While there could be long weeks during which there was no sign of a horse anywhere near Uro, Borzhon always had a rough idea of the whereabouts of his equines. They held a bond with him and with his *ger*. Even if they could not be seen, they were within accessible range—they were domestic. But horses were not always described to me on such clear terms.

On another visit to Borzhon's winter residence, his daughter-in-law Norzhima (b. ca. 1986) recalled a trip she had taken to the city around New Year's Eve the previous year. She had been traveling with other passengers on a minibus through snow-covered Tunka Valley, when suddenly a group of wild horses (Rus. *dikie loshadi*) came running into the road. The driver barely avoided a collision. Confused by her choice of words, I asked Norzhima what she had meant by wild horses. She explained that she had meant a group of horses, a *tabun* that had belonged to someone, but which had been running free all winter. These horses had not been wild in the *takhi* sense of the word. At this time of year, Norzhima had chosen to describe them as wild. Of course, these horses were no different from her father-in-law's, although he had described his horses to me as domestic. Norzhima knew that these wild horses belonged to someone who would come looking for them in spring. They were not wild in their genetic makeup. Rather, she had referred to them as wild in terms of their winterly disposition, manner, and placement within the landscape. Rounding up this domestic herd would pose an encounter with a seasonal state of wildness.

SPRING TIME ROUNDUP

My friend Erdem, who was at the time looking after his parents' stock, told me one day how their horses were quite difficult to round up in spring. Having spent all winter on their own, they preferred to be left alone. "They have their places ... come spring they will run and hide from humans." Often it was impossible to catch them on foot. In winter, Erdem and his parents would keep one horse near the cabin, or they would share the cost of keeping a horse through the winter with a neighboring household. A winter horse would be fed daily. Come spring, it was ridden in pursuit of free-ranging horses. Erdem's neighbors, Marina and Bulad also kept a horse over the winter months. In lieu of a motorized vehicle, they had called their black winter steed "Taxi." According to Erdem, horses preferred to be left alone in their own habitat, but over the course of the summer months they would become re-accustomed to their household duties. Following the initial spring roundup, subsequent rounding up of steeds became easier as summer approached.

Marina's younger brother Aleksei, who stayed upstream from Erdem's place, liked to compare horses to yak. For him there was a great resemblance between the challenges of catching either. Bringing in lean yaks was easier than rounding up well-fattened ones, and the same could be said of horses. Like horses, yaks were on their own throughout the winter. Having to scrape snow and ice with their hooves to reach the sparse edible foliage beneath led to yak losing much of their weight over the cold season. In spring, when they were driven back to the general area of their human household's winter residence, a single person could direct the massive body of a yak by holding on to its fur with his or her bare hands. But as soon as a yak had regained its strength from eating fresh grass, single-person maneuvering became unthinkable. If horses or yak were worked too hard in autumn, they would enter winter with insufficient fat. This could lead to their death in the cold.

Aleksei thought it advisable to pace the exertion of horses and yak prior to the winter season. Horses should not be too lean entering winter. Preferably, they were also not too strong come spring. While Erdem and Aleksei had their tricks for tackling the challenges they found with rounding up horses and yak in spring, others in the valley did not regard rounding up their animals challenging. Several herders argued it was not a difficult task. It seemed to me that they either preferred not to come across as inexperienced, or that they wanted to emphasize how domestic their animals were. In either case, locating and bringing in one's free-roaming animals after the winter was a subjective experience. As such it was described in different ways by different people.

On a visit to Aunty Vera's house in late April, I spent some time talking to her son Tseden (b. 1986), a good friend of mine, who was resting on the couch. He had just come in from several hours of chopping firewood. As soon as he would be done splitting the new batch of wood later that week, he was planning on taking his older brother Dagba (b. 1984– †2014) to try and catch their horses for the summer. According to Tseden, Aunty Vera's horses did not wander far over the winter. In fact, they would be grazing somewhere on the east side of the valley. Somewhere in the upper reaches of the Urda-Uro—a day's walk from Vera's cabin at the most. When I asked Tseden about some of the challenges involved with rounding up horses, Tseden smiled. For him there was no difficulty in catching horses. Given their close range, it was no major task to bring them in.

Listening in on our conversation, Aunty Vera interjected: "Horses always need time to get used to people—year after year." By the end of our conversation, it seemed there were multiple ways in which the coming and going of horses was experienced by people. Some emphasized the struggle involved with rounding up horses for the first time each year, while others preferred to stress the fact that their horses' range was predictable, and that therefore it was easy to bring them in. When Tseden and his brother finally found the time to ride out in search of their horses, it took both of them several attempts to locate and then round them up that spring.

During a visit in mid-May, Tseden and I sat at his mother's kitchen window, sipping her milky tea, quietly watching the hills. Aunty Vera was bending over a bucket on the kitchen floor, making cottage cheese for her chickens. She had promised to give some to me for my chickens, when Tseden suddenly motioned to look out the window. He had spotted some movement on the far side of the valley, and quickly reached for his binoculars. Scanning the bare hillsides of Urda Uro, several persons on horseback had come into sight. They were trying to cajole a group of horses to turn in the direction of our valley. It looked like the horses were making every effort to stay away from the valley.

Moving with utter care, the riders were halting regularly, observing the group's responses to their approaches. Some nineteen untacked horses were in the group, and to keep them calm and moving in one direction the riders were cradling them by riding loop formations, drawing in stragglers and those attempting to sway the group another way. Whenever the riders halted, the group would stand still. As they resumed, the riders would move in such a way as to cut off the group's path back into the hills. From where I was standing by the window, these interactions between the riders and the group resembled a kind of choreography of resistance. The horses and their wranglers were clearly in negotiation with each other. Both parties were actively attempting to avoid direct physical confrontation.

After many looping maneuvers, the riders finally succeeded in driving the whole group into our valley. On their way down, the riders had split ways, dividing the winter horses into two groups. The two riders I had been following most closely through Tseden's binoculars turned out to be Borzhon and his wife Ranzhur. They had separated nine of their geldings from the larger group, so as to arrive in the valley with them ahead of the rest. Tseden had run outside to prepare one of Aunty Vera's corrals for their arrival. Her corrals were better positioned to receive horses coming in from the east, and thus both groups were going to use them. When I joined Tseden outside, he had already opened the gate of the closest corral, fervently knocking on an empty metal bucket to invite the approaching horses with the promise of salt.

By now, other household members had come out to position themselves in a funnel, leaving the corral gate as the only possible route for incoming horses. Walking very slowly, and stopping periodically, the group of rounded-up horses seemed reluctant in every way. From the front they were lured with salt, on their sides they were being prevented from veering by household members, and from the rear they were driven by the riders. Thus the first group eventually trotted into the corral.

Minutes later, Iumzhap showed up on his horse. He had been among the other riders on the hillside, and taking advantage of Aunty Vera's extensive corral structures, he proceeded to drive his bachelor band of geldings and colts into Tseden's second corral. One of the horses had a piece of rope, some five meters in length, loosely tied around his neck. Apparently the men had tried to separate him from the rest of the herd by lassoing him. Now the horse was trailing the rope behind, and every time another horse stepped on the rope, he bucked furiously. Once the second group was enclosed, Borzhon and Tseden climbed into the corral and positioned themselves at the center. Jointly, they were holding on to the rope of the bucking horse, which was now wildly running in a counterclockwise manner along with all the other horses. With every circle, the men would shorten the length of the rope, drawing the bucking horse to the center of the corral and preventing him from running with his companions. Flinging his head up in the air, the bucking horse was now lacking space to rebound, and so he fell and rolled on his back. Jumping into the turbulent corral, two other men cautiously held his head to the ground, while a fifth person released the aggravated horses from the corral. I was later told that this was the only effective way of isolating a horse from the remainder of its group.

What I had observed from the comfort of Tseden's kitchen window, and later from the side of one of Aunty Vera's corrals, had been the gradual transition of a group of freely roaming horses from the domain of their autonomous winterly movement to that of their summerly duties under human care. In this transition, the proximity between humans and horses gradually decreased to the point of using ropes and applying physical pressure. Yet, all of this happened one step at a time and with great caution. While displaying every sign of reluctance, these horses had walked themselves into the corral, if guided ever so closely by the riders and other household members. No physical pressure had been applied with the exception of the young colt, who had resisted being separated from his group.

The visible tension between the horses and their wranglers had been managed well enough to prevent them from breaking out. The most difficult part of the spring roundup had been overcome, and subsequent encounters between horses and people would be increasingly less tense. The bachelor group and the family group had been familiar with the corrals, with the sound of the bucket's clanging and even with the lasso used up on the hill. They were returning to an aspect of their lives, the familiarity of which they had not lost during their wanderings in the taiga. Although it had not been their choice to descend into the valley, they had refrained from striking out against their wranglers. In a way, their allegiance to the household was being re-solicited by the people of the valley.

TABUN DYNAMICS

As a novice to equestrian practice, I was repeatedly struck by the remarkable memory each of my neighbors had of their various roaming horse groups. Even individuals who owned fifty or more horses seemed to remember which ones had been gelded or broken to ride, at what time this had been accomplished, by whom and what each of their horses' character qualities were. In like manner, there seemed to be little confusion in identifying belonging. Even from a distance, when branding was not visible, people identified individuals by their gait and group. No records were kept of horses, other than the mental notes taken by householders throughout the year and particularly during the summer.

By springtime a household's horse groups generally consisted of several mixed-sex herds, or harems comprising mares, their one- and two-year-old colts and fillies, foals and one senior stallion (Rus. *proizvoditel'*). When colts and fillies were driven out from the herd by the senior stallion, they would adjoin themselves to bachelor bands (Rus. *kassaki*) or other groups generally referred to as *tabuny* (herds). Bachelor herds consisted of not yet broken to ride geldings, trained riding horses, and colts awaiting either castration, or formation into a new family group.

A *tabun* usually consisted of ten to fifteen mares, but it could consist of as many as twenty or twenty-five. At the age of two or three, male offspring underwent castration. Select males, usually no more than one, could be retained as future stallions to form new harems. Upon maturation, such a reproductive male would impregnate all the mares of his harem for a period of up to ten years. During this time, a good stallion would aggressively fend off any male competitors. In order to keep the blood of one's herds "fresh" (Rus. *svezho*)—that is, to maintain genetic diversity and prevent inbreeding—every so often several mares from a harem were taken to be paired with stallions brought in from afar. Such a male would usually be traded in kind, or it could be purchased on occasion. The invited stallion would then stay with his new mares, creating a new *tabun* for his new human household.

With limited grazing, and numerous horse-owning households spread throughout the hills, herders maintained no more than one or two harems, including several riding horses. Borzhon and Ranzhur owned ten riding horses at the time, three or four of which they were keeping near the house in summer. The remaining six or seven riding horses were left grazing freely in the hills. Borzhon would switch out the riding contingent on a monthly basis to ensure that no steed was ridden for longer than a month at a time. For this rotation to be feasible, bachelor groups had to stay within an accessible range, especially during the summer.

Unlike riding horses, harems did not usually have to be driven back to the winter residence in spring. Over the month of May, these *tabuny* usually came on their own to the pastures surrounding their human householders' cabins. By this time in the year, several of the mares would already have given birth, arriving in the valley together with their foals, while others were only about to give birth. For the latter, birthing would take place in close proximity to human residence, just prior to the households' departure for their summer pastures. Giving birth near human residence warranted greater protection from predators, but it could also mean more frequent encounters between the stallions of diverse family groups and other incoming males.

Broken to ride, not yet broken geldings and colts would on occasion collide with breeding stallions at these intersection points, which could lead to serious injury. Damage was usually inflicted by highly protective stallions on curious or impulsive outside males. One morning, as I was watching Borzhon's ten-year-old nephew and fourteen-year-old niece driving a *tabun* on horseback in the direction of their uncle's stables, the stallion of the *tabun* was agitated at the sight of a colt emerging from a corral on the other side of the house. Each time the colt would approach his harem, the stallion forcefully chased it back in the direction of the corral. Both horses repeatedly galloped by us at full speed, with the stallion attempting to strike the colt with his front hooves.

Several days before our departure to a reindeer camp in Tofalariia, one of our riding horses at Alygdzher had come too close to the stallion of a harem. The stallion had struck our horse just above his left eye. Splitting the brow, the stallion had left our horse with a cut so deep, that it led to an inflammation affecting his vision and jeopardizing his transporting and navigating capacity. At Uro, Borzhon and other herders made every effort to nurse their animals back to health upon injuries inflicted by predators or between rival males of household herds, but they were even more careful to prevent such encounters around the winter pastures in the first place.

Geldings did not usually mix with any of the other horses. Instead, many of the riding horses stayed together in the taiga, even if they belonged to different households. They would pool together during winters and summers, roaming the landscape together. In this way, geldings contradicted the pattern of herd segregation described for other species in chapter 4. Harems, in contrast, did not mix across households, unless they had been moved for the summer to the wranglers' collective camp (Rus. *tabor tabunchikov*). Located approximately halfway up the Iakhoshop River, this camp—much like a reindeer camp—was seasonally maintained by designated *tabunchiki* (horse wranglers). The camp had been established during the Soviet period as a remote seasonal outpost of the Sorok kolkhoz.

My friend Ilia, who knew a lot about horses and had experimented extensively with breeding techniques, spent most of his summers out here as a younger man looking after the kolkhoz's horse herds. During my stay, several wranglers would periodically check on a large number of harems belonging to households who had migrated to their summer pastures along the Tustuk River. By sending their harems to the wranglers' camp, herders were able to secure feed for their stock at the summer pasture while preventing undue encounters between their geldings and harem stallions. In a way, the wranglers' camp also resembled earlier Soiot reindeer camps, which had freed herders to look after their cattle as had been the case during B. E. Petri's expedition of 1926.

SELECTING HORSES

One of the tasks of the male head of household was the reproductive management of horse herds. The whole point of large herds was to maintain a pool of strong and healthy animals from which to select the best for riding and the least suitable for meat. This selection could involve several members of an extended family, as relatives from the village would adjoin their horses to larger herds in the backcountry. In April, Borzhon was waiting to hear back from his brother Badma who was to come and castrate the family's colts. Badma had been a veterinary worker at the Sorok kolkhoz for fifteen years of his career, and although he now lived between homes in Sorok and Orlik, he still conducted a good number of veterinary chores for his own relatives at Uro.

In most cases colts were castrated to become geldings, except where a reproductive male was required by a distant relation, or if a herder desired to start a new harem. A herder would select animals either for training, for further breeding, or for food. Borzhon and Badma had selected six of their colts for castration that spring.

Castration did not mean that a horse would not end up being selected for meat at a later time. It merely reduced the level of tension in a group, and it allowed householders to observe an animal's character before deciding whether or not it might be suitable for training. In either case, the colts Borzhon and Badma had selected for castration that spring would not father families. In seven months any one of them could be chosen to provide food for the winter. At the end of November—a month before the annual yak winter slaughter—one horse would be selected for slaughter from the bachelor group. Usually this would mean one horse per extended family. In the case of my host's household, two families came together to share a horse each year. Because their families were too small to consume a whole horse, they took turns in providing a bachelor each year.

During my stay, it was Baianbata's turn to provide a young male. Candidates for meat production were selected based on their behavior. An unsettled gelding (Rus. *nespokoinyi*), or one refusing to enter a fenced area or a corral, would be singled out for slaughter. Led to the side, such a horse was killed and dissected in much the same way as stock or game. But unlike sheep, cows, or yak, a horse's head was first covered with a jute sack or similar item to cover its sight. Because of its comparatively thin skull, it took merely a well balanced strike of a hammer to the forehead to kill the gelding, as opposed to the blunt side of an ax used on cattle or yak foreheads.

Spring was also the time when Borzhon selected training candidates from his bachelor band. Geldings chosen to be trained for riding were evaluated on their character, which he grouped into categories ranging from "race-worthy bloodstock" (Rus. *rysaki*) to "pacers" (Rus. *inokhody*), or "big ones" (Rus. *zdorovye*) and from "strong ones" (Rus. *moshnye*) to "solid ones" (Rus. *plotnye*). "Such ones [can] be chosen" for training, according to Borzhon. His younger brother, Baianbata, who was always on the lookout for horses suitable for yak herding, put particular emphasis on gait. Theoretically, gait was best determined in pasture. But practically, according to Regbi, Borzhon's eldest son, it was quite difficult to make detailed observations of one's horses in the hills. He knew this well, as he had trained many horses.

Regbi had made it a practice to unhesitatingly castrate any male that kicked, or that showed any sign of the habit of "biting like a dog." Such unmannered traits were unacceptable in horses, especially riding horses. If such unruly qualities were found in the right combination with other features, however, they could become desirable. Especially for a stallion who was to defend a harem, aggression in combination with desirable size, gait, and solidity was worth looking for. In cases where aggression, defensiveness and self-will were selected for, tameness could hardly account for the leading characteristic of what it meant to have a domesticated horse. A good stallion could be unruly in some ways, while optimally shaped in others, only to produce offspring from which self-reliant and enduring horses could further be selected. If self-initiative and fearlessness made a dog a better hunter for the household (Oehler 2018a), then behavior such as "biting like a dog," which for a gelding was considered unmannerly, could in the case of a stallion secure cohesion for a harem.

In the past, coat color had played an important role in the selective breeding of horses. But for herders like Regbi, the color of a horse was no longer a primary concern. Likely for this reason, he could no longer recall the varied terms that existed in Buriat for each hue. For Regbi it was sufficient that a horse be good for maneuvering stock and for longer excursions into the hill country. But coat color had once been of importance. Borzhon recalled how Soiots of the past had strategically used their horses' coat color in the hunt: "They would hunt reindeer during the rut by hiding behind a white horse." The reindeer, "whose eyesight is poor," will mistake the white horse for its own kind. When this happened, the hunter would shoot from behind his horse. The horse thus served the hunter as a lure while at a distance, and once he had come into close range of the deer, the horse would serve as a mask. In this way a hunter did not have to dress in reindeer skins, hold on to antlers, or mimic a reindeer in other ways, which better enabled spontaneous hunting. Although the practice was still known at Uro, neither Burzhon nor any of the other hunters I came to know still practiced this method.

FROM COLT TO GELDING

On a wet and cold morning in May, Borzhon, and his youngest son Bator (b. 1990), walked over to their corrals to collect a young colt. Bator led the horse by his halter to the front of his father's house where he maneuvered him to an open space of well-packed sandy soil with patches of short grass. Five meters away, three other horses stood hitched to the family's *serge*. Bator calmly positioned the colt to face the house in preparation of a technique used in laying down horses for hoof work. This morning it was not shoes that had to be attached or removed. Badma had arrived two days earlier to castrate the colts. This colt was the last one awaiting the procedure.

With Bator's every attempt to wind a rope around his front legs, the colt would shake it loose again. What set out as a delicate dance, in which Bator and the horse slowly went round and round—the one to bind, the other to remain free—eventually grew into a dense encounter more resembling a controlled wrestling match. I will describe this match with the aid of a series of photographs (from a to t Illustration 5.1). Standing face to face with the horse, Bator was now holding on to a rope, one end of which was connected to the colt's halter (a). The animal's left front and rear legs had already been hobbled by a rope contraption with toggle fasteners (Rus. *trenog*). The hobble ensured that the horse did not gallop away. Then Baianbata, Bator's uncle, handed Bator a second rope.

Holding the halter rope and one end of the second rope in his left hand, and standing on the left side of the horse, Bator carefully ran the other end of the second rope across the horse's back (b). When the rope touched the ground, he reached between the horse's legs for its end. Now holding both ends of the second rope in his right hand, and the halter rope in his left, the horse was tethered to Bator, both at its muzzle and from withers to brisket (c). Tying one end of the second rope to itself, forming a large noose with a flexible knot, Bator skillfully pulled the noose over the horse's head, gradually tightening it at the colt's upper forearms (d). Holding halter and the rope end of the tightened noose in his left hand, just below the horse's muzzle, Bator now carefully lowered to his own feet (e). From here he secured the hobble to include both front pasterns with the rear left pastern, after which he released the noose from the forearms. The colt was now fully hobbled.

Now tying the middle of the second rope to the halter, Bator ran one end of it under the hobble, around the left rear pastern, and from there back through the halter tie ring, forming a triangle that could be tightened, and which brought the cannon of the rear towards the forearm (f). At the same time, this mechanism also lowered the head, preparing the animal for a smooth rolling transition to the ground. But when the horse still refused to lay down, Bator released the lasso, and Borzhon entered the picture.

Tying a wider piece of webbing around the horse's neck, Borzhon now took the lasso from Bator and quickly formed a self-tightening loop, which he ran under the neck's webbing. With the horse's left rear leg raised to the forearm once more, the animal was now standing on three legs (g). Borzhon's involvement had signaled a transition in this horse-human contact: Bator's earlier dance-like motions were now being replaced by a tactile assertiveness more akin to wrestling (h). Not only was Borzhon getting tired of the game, he did not want the other horses to be alarmed by the tenseness of the situation. They were, in fact, already beginning to move back and forth nervously. Still moving in circles, but ever more abruptly, Borzhon finally gave the colt's tail a powerful jerk (i). With his hooves in the air, the colt had finally been sent onto his left side, in which position Borzhon drew his tail through the groin to keep him on the ground, as Bator prepared to hold down the head (j).

Bator and Borzhon were gradually introducing the colt to a procedure that in future would require less time, involve little resistance and require fewer implements. This being the colt's first time to be laid down, he could not know what was expected of him in this communicative encounter. The gentle tugging of Bator's ropes did not yet resonate with the animal, as there had not yet been established any memories of similar encounters. And given his agitated state, which might upset nearby horses, Borzhon had no desire to draw out this learning process. Instead, the horse needed to be calmly and firmly guided into

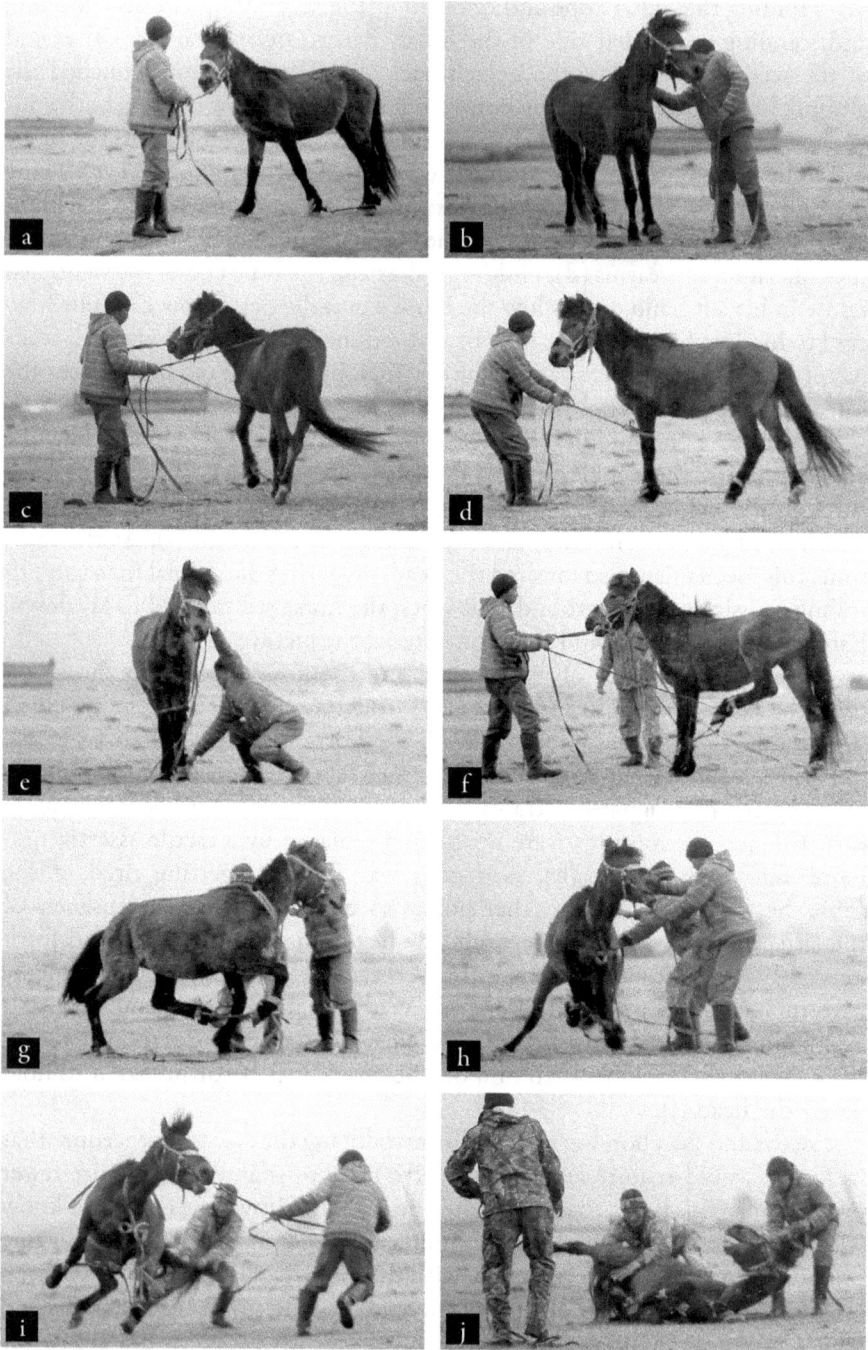

Illustration 5.1. Laying down a horse, steps a to j. Photographs by the author.

the final position of these movements. He had to be put on his side; aided by his master (Rus. *khoziain*) to overcome his anxiety.

With the colt still on his side, Borzhon and Badma tied his right and left front and rear fetlocks together, removing the hobble (k). While Borzhon's final jerk on the tail may be read as a kind of power assertion over the horse, it can also be seen to stand in line with Bator's sensitive roping technique. What began as a delicate dance with Bator had culminated in a series of denser but no less controlled movements with Borzhon. Throughout, the colt was learning the meaning of these ropes, and the goal of this exercise. If he were to be selected for training over the course of the next three years or so, these movements would eventually become second nature.

It was time to castrate the colt (Illustration 5.2). The men rolled the horse onto his back (l) and proceeded to wash his groin with soap and warm water from an iron pail. Three men were now holding the colt in position, using ropes (m), while Badma dried the skin surface with a clean towel (n). He then held the right testicle in his left hand, using the other to rub a disinfectant on the outside of the scrotum (o). By squeezing the scrotum from under the testis, its outer skin was tensed. Badma quickly pulled a two-inch top to bottom incision with a scalpel handed to him by Borzhon (p). With pressure from his left hand, Badma squeezed one of the testes out from the scrotum and passed it on to Borzhon who held it up with his right hand, pulling down the vas deferens with his left.

Meanwhile, Badma reached for a prepared string and tied off the vas deferens well below the testis by making a series of knots to cut circulation to the testis (q). With the scalpel, Badma separated the testis from the vas deferens just above the tie off. Then he put more disinfectant on the wound (r). After repeating the same procedure for the left testis, Badma used both hands to scoop excess blood from the groin area and open scrotum (s). With the incisions tinctured one last time, the horse's fetlocks were carefully untied, and held in place by the halter leash. The new gelding was now allowed to stand (t), even if he was still toggled.

TRAINING HORSES AND REINDEER

Once castrations had been completed at the hands of an experienced veterinary worker, individual geldings would be selected to be trained for riding. This process often began at the winter pasture after horses had been rounded up for the summer, and it would be continued at summer pasture. Shortly before our household was going to trek to summer pasture, my summer host, Tsydyp, told me how, prior to getting married to Dagzama, he had been training horses semi-professionally. It had been a good source of income, as he seemed to have a special knack for the task, and friends were sending their horses to him paying

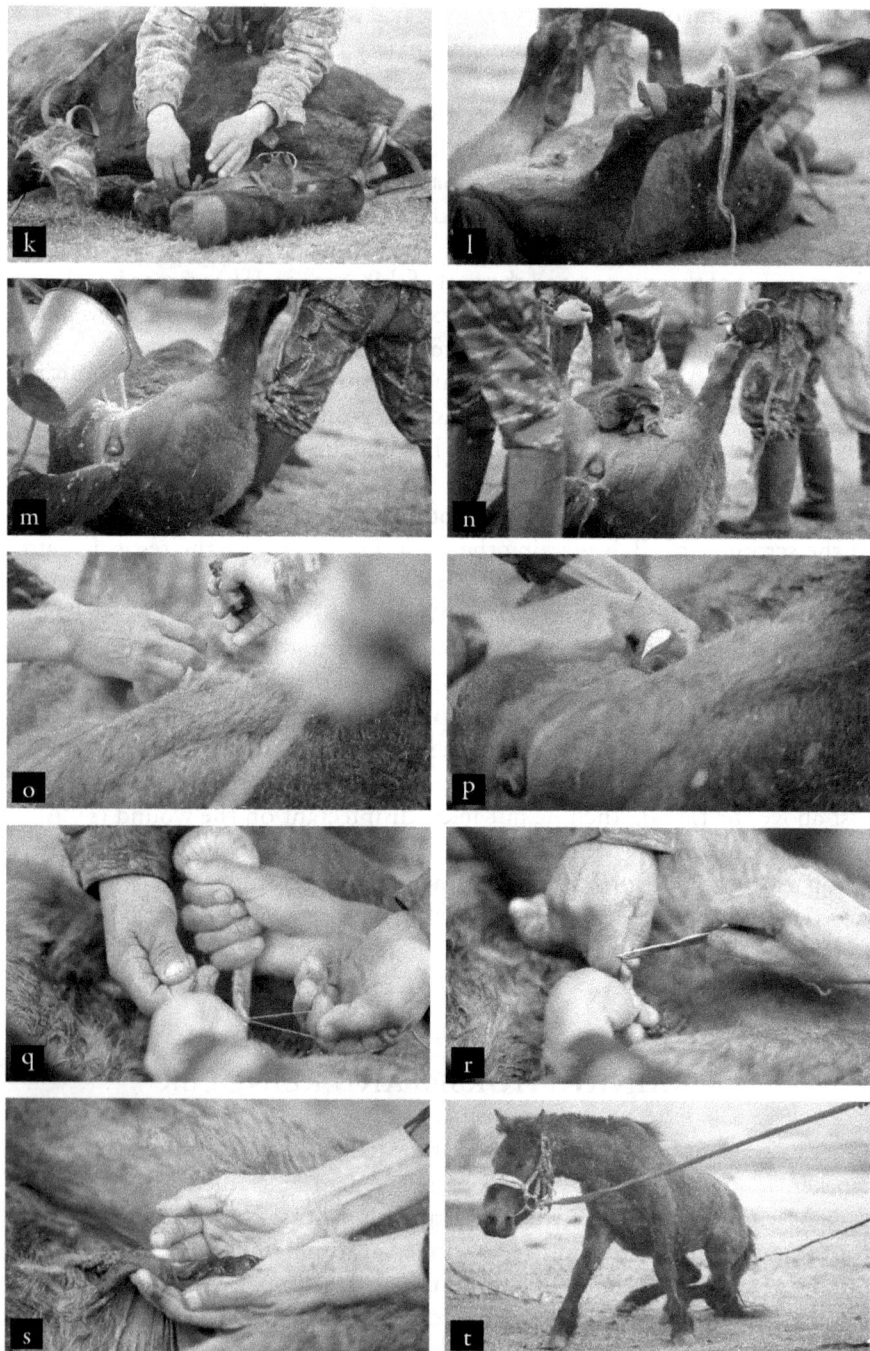

Illustration 5.2. Horse castration sequence, steps k to t. Photographs by the author.

for his services with forty liters of gas or a bottle of vodka per day of training. On average, he had a horse broken within three to five days.

Some of the work had been conducted inside his father's corral, but the majority of training had taken place out in the open taiga. Until 2005, Tsydyp had also been herding reindeer, and I was especially curious to learn how his experience of training reindeer compared to training horses.

Training reindeer was much easier than training horses, Tsydyp recalled. His older brother and reindeer herder, Iumzhap, was still actively training reindeer at his camp on the Onot River, and he was doing the same with his horses at his summer camp on the Tustuk River. Training horses and reindeer in tandem was thus an ongoing practice in the family, as much as it was for my Tofa friends from Alygdzher. For Tsydyp, training reindeer was easier because they were smaller and therefore easier to mount and steer, and they listened to the signal of reins as carefully as horses. But unlike horses, reindeer were more compliant with their riders. As a disciplinary measure, a rider would gently tap an antler with a stick, a sensation "reindeer dislike very much." And reindeer who were uncertain about a rider's intended direction would merely walk in tight circles, quite unlike half-broken horses who might bolt under similar circumstances, even if the terrain was rugged or steep.

Although several people still owned older style wooden reindeer saddles, in more recent years lightened horse saddles had been used. These were trimmed down to their wooden bars and steel cantle and fork, and covered with bear or other hide to soften the ride. In some models cantle and fork were still wooden. These saddles were more comfortable for the rider of a reindeer on longer treks through mountainous terrain, and they were lighter than full horse saddles, which is an asset when riding an animal with an average carrying capacity of around seventy kilograms (e.g., Zhigunov 1961).

Unlike other Siberian regions (see Vainshtein 1980a: 131), where reindeer breeds are on average smaller and ridden over the upper thoracic vertebrae, the Karagass breed is strong enough to be ridden from the center of the back, that is between thoracic and lumbar vertebrae, much like a horse. Nonetheless, great care is taken not to fracture the fragile spine, even in Karagass reindeer. The relatively small size of the Buriat-Mongolian horse breed used in Oka, and the comparatively large size of Karagass reindeer, reduces size discrepancy between the two species as compared to other regions. This relative similarity in size further helps explain the ease with which some saddle designs have been transferred from one species to another, calling only for minor adjustments.

This co-presence of horses with reindeer, and the experience of training both for riding and packing purposes is not unique to Soiotiia or Tofalariia. Drawing on an archived report by Wenkel (1916 as mentioned in Vainshtein 1980a), and writing about Tozhu reindeer hunter-herders, Vainshtein (1980a:

129) reiterates that, "a large proportion of deer-herding households had horses." In fact, 40 percent of all households are said to have had horses; the poor having one or two, and the rich having five to ten. It is unclear, however, what Wenkel means when he speaks of "one or two horses." Presumably these are trained horses, suggesting there may have been a harem from which to select. In either case, it appears residents of the larger Altai-Saian region have long relied on both species in conjunction.

Rather than taking time off to train a horse, most horse work in Oka was conducted as part of activities that had to be done anyway, such as commuting between village and camp, or traveling between more distant camps. For Borzhon, the best way to train a fresh gelding was to round-up, tack, and begin riding it almost right away. Yet, not all geldings were broken to ride right after they had been castrated. In some cases, several years would pass before a horse received training. Once an animal had been selected, Borzhon would ride it for most of the day—the main goal being to tire it out. Like other herders, he found that an exhausted horse was much more pliable and willing to learn. Come rest time, he would hobble the gelding to prevent him from running off as soon as he had rested up. Throughout each riding exercise, Borzhon would use his hands to signal to the horse in which direction to move. But Borzhon would also rely on the reigns as a way of signaling, which horses seemed to "understand from the get-go." He would never use any sounds or commands to communicate with his horse verbally, other than "trrrr"—equivalent of the English "whoa"—which meant to slow the horse, bringing it to a halt, or "chu" for "go."

During the summer I witnessed this method in action: Danzan, a younger brother of my host mother, told me one morning that he was going to ride to Khan-Modon, the remote homestead discussed in chapter 4. He was planning to help his friend Sasha look after his yak herd. I had been observing Danzan train a difficult new gelding over several days. He had tacked him repeatedly to establish a predictable pattern for the horse, tethering him to the family's *serge*. Then he would release the animal from the *serge*. Together, the two would slowly walk in large circles through a pasture, before Danzan would tether the horse to his brother-in-law's *serge* again.

The following morning, having put on bridle and hobble the night before, Danzan finally saddled and mounted the young gelding. After a cautious round through the back of our pasture, the two forded the Iakhoshop River, and rode off to Khan-Modon. Danzan knew the trail well. He had estimated the trip to take roughly four hours, and he was going to follow the river upstream and uphill without taking any major breaks so as to purposefully tire the horse. Ten days later, Danzan returned from Khan-Modon. Neither horse nor rider had taken injury, and the family were well on their way to yet another riding horse.

Not only geldings were trained for riding. In fact, Borzhon actually preferred riding mares. If a young mare had rejected her foal in her first year of bearing, Borzhon would train her for riding instead of mothering. If she had another foal the following year, it was more likely that she would take to mothering it. Thus, training a mare for transportation was a way to prepare the animal to become a good mother in a harem. But Borzhon's preference for mares had to do with the fact that they rode "much smoother than most geldings." Riding a mare, "you don't know if you're sitting in a car, on a sofa, or in a boat," he told me jokingly.

It was not uncommon for an Oka horse to live to its thirtieth birthday, although most trained horses served their riders only to the age of twenty-five. As working horses aged, their eyesight grew weak and they began to stumble in difficult terrain. With impaired vision and hearing, horses were also more easily spooked. Emergence of such signs would mark the end of their career. This often resulted in their slaughter and consumption. But in the experience of one female informant (b. ca. 1955), the slaughter of a retired horse could be an exceedingly difficult task for the family. Members of the household had become emotionally attached to the animal over the years, for which reason, some let their retired horses die a natural death.

This was certainly the case among Tofas when it came to retired working reindeer. Out of respect (Rus. *iz za uvazhenia*) for their faithful service over many years, frail riding and transportation geldings were often released rather than slaughtered. Tofa hunter-herder Nikolai Semenovich Kangaraev, never slaughtered any of his retired geldings after they had served him faithfully for years. But what was considered an appropriate and dignified end for a faithful animal varied from household to household.

ANTICIPATING NEW SHOES

I had left my cabin one morning to walk over to Borzhon's home, where I found him sitting in the kitchen, drinking tea with Grandfather Dorzho. Both were going to switch the summer shoes on Grandfather's gelding to winter shoes for the autumn hunt. Shoeing required at least three people—one to hold the head, another to keep the body down, and a third to perform the hoof work. I was invited to join the action, but more as an observer than a reliable participant. Grandfather took a last sip, set down his empty cup, and slipped into his boots. Then he rode over to Tsydyp's house to call for more hands. Borzhon and I fired up the old outdoor steel hearth in front of his house. The fire was increasing in heat as we consistently fed it with dry pieces of wood. We heated up two pairs of newly smithed shoes, which Grandfather and I had prepared in his shop—a procedure the significance of which I will describe in the next chapter. Minutes later, Tsydyp and Dagzama arrived on their old Belarusian motorcycle. Dagzama went inside to visit with the women, as the men readied their tools outside: an empty oil barrel, two eight-foot-long boards, a blanket, an array of various pieces of synthetic and organic webbing, various nippers, pliers, an aluminum pan filled with horseshoe nails, a hammer, an axe, and a sheathed knife.

Following the procedure for laying down horses, albeit with much greater ease than with the colt described above, Borzhon, Tsydyp, and Grandfather managed to bring the gelding to his knees, from where he was rolled onto his back, and then onto his left side. After the pasterns were released from the hobble, Borzhon reached across the horse's spine and flank, to draw together and cross his right front and rear cannons. Grandfather then tied them together with heavy webbing. Next he brought two blankets. One blanket he lay over the horse's exposed flank. On this Grandfather seated himself, with his legs held between girth and hooves. The second blanket he lay over his own knees. Onto these he drew the horse's tied right front and rear legs. This position provided controlled access to the soles, which Borzhon had previously cleaned with a small hammer.

Running back and forth between hearth and Grandfather's set-up, Borzhon would pass the glowing shoes to Grandfather for hot shoeing. Grandfather would press the hot iron to the foot, using nippers and hammer. This method sent a column of beige smoke into the wind each time the glowing steel of the shoe made contact with the horn of the hoof. Borzhon and Grandfather worked quickly, attempting to keep the horse on the ground for as little time as necessary. Meanwhile, kneeling over the animal's neck, Tsydyp gently pressing the gelding's jaw onto a third blanket. Unlike the young colt described previously, this seasoned gelding was not actively resisting. Instead he was breathing heavily, moaning audibly.

With the horn of the hoof melted to fit the shoe, the shoe was taken off again and set in a snow patch to cool. The next horseshoe was held in place to shape the second hoof. Grandfather now placed his feet on the left cannons near the ground and lifted the right cannons onto his knees, thereby creating the space required to work safely on the lower left hooves. Once all four feet had been leveled for their corresponding shoes, Borzhon brought in two eight-foot-long boards. These he laid down at a ninety degree angle to the horse's body. He then placed a blanket on the section that would hold up the horse's right front and rear legs, and pushed one end of the doubled boards under the tied cannons and onto the blanket covered flank.

To further raise the upper hooves, he lifted the other end of the boards and rolled an empty oil barrel under it. As Grandfather held up each shoe, Borzhon drove the nails, alternating between right and left branches of the shoe. With each strike—six nails per rear shoe and eight nails per front shoe—he used pliers to guide each nail in such a way as to curve it through the outer hoof wall. Then he twisted off the extruding tip of the nail with his pliers. Shoes attached, Borzhon set them by shortening the toe to ease breakover, using knife and hammer. Finally he tightened the shoes by bending the clipped nail endings, driving them face down into the outer wall of the hoof. With one side complete, the men flipped the horse onto its other side, attaching the other two shoes.

After the job was done, cigarettes were lit and all rested their eyes on the horizon. The freshly shoed gelding was grazing calmly in the pasture ahead of us. As we were standing there, Borzhon pointed out the ease with which the old horse had slipped into his new shoes. It had been the tenth time for Grandfather's horse to transition into winter shoes, and he seemed to be treading with great confidence. This could not be said of new geldings who needed time to become accustomed to the feeling of walking on the sharp toes and heels of a proper winter shoe. Perhaps it helped that the shoes on Grandfather's horse were spiked only at the heel.

Given the animal's seniority, Borzhon was contemplating aloud how it must have been wondering all this time: "When are they finally going to put winter shoes on my hooves? Snow and ice have been on the ground for a while now." Although a hint of humor seemed to ring in Borzhon's voice, as he gave us his take on the gelding's mind, the statement was consistent with an overall tendency I had observed at Uro. Animal-human encounters were often interpreted as taking place in answer to an anticipation that arose with the animal and not with the human. This applied not only to horses who, over the course of their lives, had become increasingly attuned to their households. It also applied to game in the forest. Grandfather's gelding had willed himself into Borzhon's ropes. He had anticipated the sure-footed gait that always followed the arrival of snow and ice. And the men were confident that in spite of his audible moaning, the horse was not actually resisting. Like game animals who run and hide and yet are understood to willfully render themselves to the hunter, so the moaning gelding in all his wiggling was seen to willfully endure the procedure. In fact, he was thought to have anticipated the routine long before anyone had the chance to carry it out.

CONCLUSION

This chapter started out by stressing the contemporary importance of the horse in mountain taiga households of the Eastern Saians. Furthermore, it suggested that tameness alone is not sufficient as a marker for domesticity in horses in this regional context. While Oka horses did not interbreed with their free running cousins, such as may once have been the *takhi*, they did exhibit traits associated with wild or feral populations. In Oka, several of these unruly traits increased a horses' suitability to the household, because they allowed the animal to remain self-reliant in an environment where people did not subsidize feed or provide shelter. Unruliness combined with other qualities was a desired trait for stallions, undermining the notion of tameness as a foundational feature of domestication.

To develop an alternative explanation for the local use of terms such as domestic and wild in horses, the chapter examined household affiliation in relation to range. A horse could willfully leave the range of its household and venture into that of another. Where this took place, a horse's ties to its original household were not necessarily severed. Instead, the master of the household whose range it had entered could offer to return the estranged animal. Consequently, there were no truly wild or even feral horses, although they could behave wildly or winterly. This observation speaks to the importance of the concept of range in Inner Asia, as well as to the role range may play in how we conceptualize domesticity, or belonging to the domus.

No matter a horse group's demeanor, horse sociality played itself out both within and without the human household. Bonds, animosities and hierarchies established in the taiga were recognized by human members within the household. Conversely, a household's breeding practices co-shaped the sociality of horses in the taiga. While Soiot breeders sought to strengthen independence and self-reliance in their horse groups, they also had to pay for these qualities during the annual spring time cajoling game during which dis-accustomed horses had to be reminded of their allegiance to the human household.

The second half of the chapter concerned itself more directly with the material implements facilitating horse-human interactions in the household. We looked at reproduction, transportation, and meat production, as well as at the criteria defining selective breeding, among them demeanor, gait, and coat color. Particular emphasis was put on the similarities that existed between training and riding horses and reindeer, which in the Saians has made interchangeable some of the material implements used for both. Descriptions of laying down a horse for the first time were followed by more invasive human practices, such as castration. The use of hobbles, lassos, ropes, and scalpels represented modes of physical contact aimed at forging mutual familiarity. At the same time, these encounters were also actively shaping the society of horses.

Finally, we followed the hot shoeing procedure of an experienced gelding, which illustrated how habituation to material implements could progress from first encounters to subsequent encounters. Here the horse was understood to act upon the established associations it had with material implements of the household. Horses willed themselves into ropes and lassos of their human-masters, much as deer willed themselves into the hands of their hunters.

Geldings anticipated new shoes. They were looking forward to the affordances of a steadfast grip on ice, as much as deer sought to feed their hunters' families, receiving new bodies. Soiot horse handling then illustrates what seems to run through all northern domestication relationships: a soliciting hand that aids us in overcoming our resistance to crossing thresholds between ways of being, time and again.

CHAPTER 6

READING WOLVES

By mid-October, the weather had cooled off significantly. In spite of the cold, the Sorok River was still flowing vigorously. In the morning, I walked across the valley to borrow a pair of waders from Borzhon. If I were careful enough, the long rubber boots would allow me to cross the river in a shallow spot on foot. Holding a pair of dry boots above my head, I successfully emerged from the waters on Burged and Marina's (b. ca. 1975) side of the river. Whenever I came to help them clean out their stables, or gather dried yak manure in the valley, Burged would reward my labor with insightful chats over tea afterward. Today was no different, and after having worked up a sweat in the compound, we went inside to eat some of Marina's white bread, scraping each morsel through hardened cream and dipping it in sugar.

Sitting in their kitchen, Burged told me the story of how a wolf couple had worked together one summer, harassing the stock at summer pasture. The male had approached several Mongolian cows on the far side of the pasture, well in sight of the cabin where the family were gathered. He was crouched down in tall grass, as if ready to attack any of the cows calmly grazing nearby. The wolf's overt posing called for the attention of the householders who quickly rushed across the pasture, chasing away the wolf. What they could not see from their vantage point was the predator's female partner, who in their absence had entered the pasture behind the cabin. As the family slowly returned to their home, they found the freshly torn carcass of one of their cows behind the cabin.

To Burged it was clear that his household had been tricked. The male wolf's crouching had been a performance intended to captivate the householders' attention. The wolf had lured them away in an attempt to put the cabin as a visual barrier between the staged and real attack. Even if someone had stayed behind at the cabin, their attention would have been drawn to the events at the far end of the pasture, not to what was going on behind their backs. The encounter that summer had been humiliating, but it had also been educational.

After all, this was how wolves collaborated. They were known to draw up effective schemes, and people had to be careful not to be misled by their movements.

Still in thought about the events of Burged's story, I was looking out of the rear kitchen window. A steep earthen slope, strewn with rocks, reached high into the blue sky. Like little dots perched on narrow terraces high above us, Burged and Marina's sheep were calmly grazing. How could they be so calm when wolves had come flying over the top so many times, picking sheep like apples from a tree? I would learn the answer to that question on another visit. As it turned out, sheep were thought to have a three-day memory. After three days, they would be out on the slope again, without a care in the world. Clearly, they were no match for animals who knew how to use built structures against people.

* * *

As hinted in the vignette above, the intent of this chapter is to provide a better understanding of how Soiot households negotiated their encounters with wolves. I have written about Soiot dog-human relations elsewhere (Oehler 2018a). A glance at the history of wolf-human relations in the Saians seems to suggest that people's attitudes toward this predator have depended on the species a household held at a given time, as well as on the households' degree of mobility within the landscape. Although wolves are highly symbolic animals in the folklore of Turkic peoples (e.g., Drompp 2011), the extent to which they have been sacralized in the Saians remains somewhat unclear. In Oka, there existed a connection between wolves and spirit-mastered households, but a stronger focus was placed on wolves as uniquely intelligent beings in their own right.

Seeing wolves in this light, they not only became enemies based on their capacity to take away stock from households. More centrally, they were seen as competitors in their capacity to learn and to anticipate concealed intentions. If material implements of the household come to serve as communicative devices between humans and horses or reindeer, then landscape modifications, intelligently designed features such as traps, and bodily movement between such features made up the means of communication between wolves and humans. Whether construed by people or by wolves, structures, devices, and movements could serve as tools concealing surprise. To avoid unnecessary physical confrontation, wolves—like humans—sought to infiltrate the other's social and material world under disguise of the familiar.

At the heart of Soiot-wolf relations lay the skill to read in the other's performance their true intentions. Riding through northwestern Mongolia in the wintery conditions of 1910, John H. Miller, a travel companion to British explorers Douglas A. Carruthers and Morgan P. Price, describes the stockherding nomads they encountered south of the Little Altai. "The camps of the

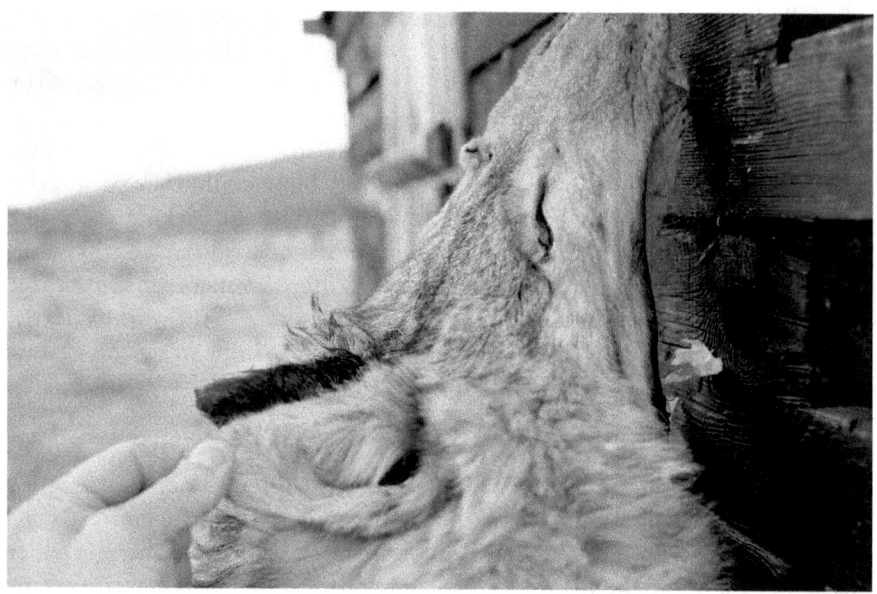

Illustration 6.1. Freshly shot and skinned wolf at Uro. Photograph by the author.

hardy herdsmen are now clustered in sheltered hollows; their owners' time is largely spent in waging war against the wolf-packs, which nightly harry their sheep-folds, and in interminable tea-drinking, smoking, and chatting round a meagre 'tezek' (dung-fed) fire" (Miller in Carruthers 1914: 320). Although this scene is specific to the southwestern corner of Uriankhai, it serves as a starting point in understanding the significance of wolves in the lives of pastoralists of northern Inner Asia.

Bernard Charlier's work on wolves' "absent presence" (2015: 2) in Uvs Province of northwestern Mongolia resonates with Miller's account. Charlier's interlocutors were actively guarding against wolves rather than purposefully hunting them. Yet killing a wolf was not exclusively a defensive mechanism. Shooting a wolf could also increase a herder's *hiimor'* (understanding). Understanding in this sense could also refer to the effectiveness with which one went about life, or with the closeness one enjoyed to the spirit master (Charlier 2012: 131).

Similarly, Natasha Fijn's work (2011) in Arkhangai and Bulgan Provinces of central and north central Mongolia resonates with Miller's account. Fijn describes "a war between respected parties," where a "large amount of the herder's time and energy is spent guarding and protecting the herds against wolf predation" with nighttime duties involving "men stay[ing] up guarding the animals in their pens" as they verbally respond to wolf calls, attempting to establish their location (2011: 210). Miller, Charlier, and Fijn provide us with a consistent picture of human-wolf interactions in the steppe lands just south of the Saians.

Moving up into far eastern Siberian reindeer country, staying up with herds to wait for the arrival of wolves is a rather foreign concept. Here the herds are large and far flung, quite unlike the sheep pens of Uvs Province. In Sebyan-Kyuel of the Republic of Sakha (Yakutia), where herds are kept for meat production, Piers Vitebsky describes how wolves were ruthlessly hunted by reindeer herders with little concern for their souls (2006: 271). According to Vitebsky, "the wolf [had] changed from competitor to looter" when reindeer were first domesticated (2006: 271). Like other wild animals belonging to *bayanay*, the spirit master, Eveny herders at Sebyan-Kyuel hunted wolves as part of an original bargain with wild reindeer to enter the domus (Vitebsky 2006: 27). Taking down wolves was inextricable from the responsibility of herding, even if this pitted herders against the spirit master.

The taiga herders described by Vitebsky, and the steppe shepherds encountered by Miller, Charlier, and Fijn seem to hint at a spectrum of herders' attitudes toward wolves. One is guarding against wolves, while hoping to acquire their sacral powers; the other is exterminating wolves as sly thieves, in spite of their sacral ties. It is doubtful, of course, that such a clear division would stand any test of nuanced ethnographic interrogation. Nonetheless, Vitebsky's and Charlier's herders did find themselves in distinct geographies, each guarding animal herds of species ideally matched to their respective environments. Since Oka herders were positioned at the intersection of Inner Asian steppe and Eurasian taiga, their herds were composed of animals from both regions. It is not a surprise then that the ruthlessness described by Vitebsky for Eveny-wolf relations, and the guarding attitudes described by Charlier, could both be found among Soiots.

Glowing memory of near-industrial grade eradication of wolf populations in the 1960s paralleled profound ideas about wolves as important balancing agents in the landscape. The thought of never again having to guard one's sheep through the night was sweet. But from an ecological-scientific standpoint, as well as in view of their being emissaries of a spirit master, people were equally convinced that wolves had an important part to play in the world. Total eradication of any species would represent a breach of the equilibrium that held the world together, whether one looked at it from the perspective of local cosmology or scientific ecology. Resentment and reverence were thus curiously mixed when it came to wolves.

For the anthropological observer this co-presence of ideas presented a unique opportunity to witness both ruthless wolf hunting at winter pastures and long-suffering herders as they would stay up night after night to scare wolves away from their sheep pens in the summer pastures. But this co-presence of attitudes toward wolves could also be traced in regionally diverse approaches to wolves that had historically existed in the Eastern Saian Mountains.

RAIDING WOLVES, FLEEING WOLVES

As mentioned above, historically the way people dealt with wolves in the Saians had to do with the kinds of animals that were being kept in particular locales and with the type of terrain they moved in. We know from Polish ethnographer Feliks Kon (1934 [1903]: 95–96) that transhumant cattle breeders of Eastern Tyva had organized systematic wolf raids at the turn of the century. Kon provides a detailed account of Tozhu cattle breeders, whom he calls Soiots.

> Hunting raids [on wolves] usually occur in response to the suggestion of a well-to-do Soiot whose stock has been under attack from wolves in the area. Nearby neighbors will join in the hunt. The better-to-do will join on their own horses, while the poor are provided horses by the initiator of the hunt. The group will set out early in the morning, some equipped with firearms, others with two-fathom-long lassos made of willow poles with a spiraled loop-like belt at their ends. To chase the wolves and for the purpose of self defense—if required—sharpened poles are used. Upon arrival at the site where wolves were reported to prowl, the stock owner, or one of the more experienced hunters, will appoint a position for each hunter to stand in. Hunters are placed in such a way as to leave open a level space in the landscape so that fleeing wolves can be pursued on horseback. Having positioned themselves in such a way, the hunters keep as quiet as they can, gradually creeping up on the wolf pack, in full anticipation of the perfect moment to attack, at which point they begin to shoot. If the wolf pack has noticed the hunters and is alarmed, the hunters' efforts are directed at blocking the wolves' way to the mountains and chasing them into wide open space. This is where the pursuit begins. It must be mentioned that Soiots are unable to shoot from their horses' backs, for which reason they must jump off in order to aim. Such a chase can take all day, until the horses are utterly exhausted. (1934 [1903]: 95–96)

Kon's account reflects the relative handicap of herders in steep hill country. Relying on their horses for transportation, they were unable to follow wolves into the hills. By directing wolves onto level ground, herders were able to pit the packs against the racing pace of their horses. But more importantly, Kon's account illustrates a concerted effort to pursue wolves, which stands in direct contrast to the way Tofas are said to have responded to wolves.

Although Bernhard E. Petri was able to visit Oka-Soiots in 1925, his most insightful account of wolves comes from observations he made with their Tofa neighbors to the north. Tofas responded to wolf population increases by moving camp. Petri's interlocutors reported that fifteen years prior to his visit there had only been a few wolves, but that their numbers had drastically increased over a period of twelve years, and that at the time of his visit, their appearance had once again decreased. The noted influx in their population had purportedly contributed to the decimation of Tofa reindeer herds (Petri 1927b: 19). Petri shows how increases in predation would lead people to consider packing up and moving camp earlier than usual.

> Karagas are highly ineffective in their battle against wolves. They do not use strychnine or traps. As soon as wolves appear and attack reindeer, [they] will vacate such a location and quickly migrate to another. While the wolves are engaged with the fallen reindeer, Karagas will attempt to move under cover of rain or snow in order to conceal their tracks and to prevent wolves from searching for them anew. Often the appearance of wolves will signal the end of summer migrations and usher a quick break up in multiple directions. (1927b: 19–20)

Of course we cannot know whether Tofas saw themselves as engaged in a "battle" with wolves, as Petri seems to suggest, or as did the pastoralists of most of Inner Asia, including the Soiots described by Kon. Neither can we know with any certainty whether these Tofas considered their own protective measures "inefficient," as Petri puts it. But it does make sense that they had refrained from the use of steel traps (Rus. *kapkan*) introduced by Russian settlers in their vicinity. The use of such traps had also been a taboo among their Oka-Soiot neighbors (Ayusheeva 2010: 309) for reasons that may have exceeded the possibility of reindeer being caught in them. Even during my own fieldwork at Uro, people still refrained from using steel traps in their fur hunting. Traps were associated with disrespect for the spirit master. In one instance, a Soiot hunter recalled how a Russian visitor had invited him to come and set steel traps for sable. The Soiot hunter accepted, if only out of curiosity. He had never previously used steel traps. Unsurprisingly, the hunt had not been successful.

In a later work, Petri (1928: 23) describes the Tofa method of moving camp in response to the arrival of wolves as a way of taking "flight" (Rus. *begstvo*). He attributes this running from wolves—rather than running after wolves—to underlying ritual motives. Given the political constraints of his time, Petri had likely not been at liberty to discuss the sacral nature of wolves in Tofa cosmology. More likely, his interlocutors were wise enough to conceal such details from the anthropologist. All Petri was able to record is the claim, shared by Tofa hunters, that "a Karagas [person] does not make his living from harvesting wolves" (Rus. *Karagas volka ne promyshliaet*) (1928: 23). However, the hesitation to confront wolves and kill them has also been recorded for the Altai (Potapov 1929: 145).

Here wolves served as the agents of spirit masters, sent to inflict retribution on herder-hunters who had engaged in unbalanced hunting activities. By sending wolves to kill animals from the domestic herds of human-mastered households, the spirit master was making up for animals that had been stolen from his herds (Broz 2007: 299). I encountered this principle also at Uro, where elder Soiot herder-hunter Iundun (b. ca. 1965) explained that "as much as you take from the spirit master during the summer [by hunting in excess], that many animals will he take from your herds in winter by way of wolves." According to Iundun, it was a cycle, a kind of give-and-take. In his view, a respectful hunter who ensured that all things were happening in balance and who would consequently leave game at rest during the summer would not suffer wolf attacks in winter. But not all would agree with Iundun. Borzhon later told me that even if a hunter had faithfully performed his hunting rituals to the spirit master, wolves would still come to claim from his stock in winter. Were the wolves really emissaries, or did they merely act on their own?

LEARNING LIKE A WOLF

"Who owns the wolves?" I asked Grandfather Tseren-Dorzho one day. "I don't know," he said. "They walk on their own—their legs feed them" (Rus. *Oni khodiat sami po sebe—volka nogi kormiat*). Then he continued:

> Each pack (Rus. *stai*) has its leader (Rus. *vozhak*), either a male or a female. Females (Rus. *volshitsy,* or *samki*)—leaders or not—are among the smartest of them. A pack consists of up to ten members, although pack size grows during the rut. At this time the wolves will bite each other, fighting over the female. They can travel between fifty and sixty kilometers in a day, and a single wolf will get to be about fifteen years of age.

Grandfather knew a lot about wolves, and he hated them passionately. His hatred was not aimed merely at wolves as a collective species. He had known individual wolves.

A particularly memorable wolf had followed him to his summer pasture one day, where eventually it stole a live lamb from his neighbor. The neighbor grabbed a rifle and pursued the wolf on her horse. When she had caught up with the wolf, she shot it dead and returned with her lamb. "One always resists a wolf," Grandfather concluded. And there seemed to be no limit to the cruelty permissible in that resistance. The men at Uro used to mix poison into ground horse meat (Rus. *kotletki*), which they would lay out in the woods. A wolf would die within thirty minutes of eating the bait. "Bleeding from its nostrils and mouth, it would scratch the ground, running from tree to tree, banging its head against the trunks. Eventually it would collapse. They would skin it and burn the flesh," he recollected.

Yet Grandfather's apparent contempt for wolves was also mixed with admiration. Wolves, perhaps, were not so much enemies as they were competitors. Not competitors for game. There was never a sense of competition over natural resources. The spirit master either gave, or he did not. Rather, they were competitors in skill and in the ability to learn quickly. Grandfather admired wolves for their ability to acquire and act upon fresh information. This was what made them so dangerous. They acquired knowledge and ability through attentive observation—second to none—except humans.

Grandfather himself was a man of many skills. He was an accomplished hunter and fisher, a skillful woodworker and birch bark carver. He was a mechanic and an electrician. These skills he had acquired through a sharp sense of observation and by trying them out on his own. He had built a large sawmill from an old moped outside his cabin. Each time he turned a dry log into boards, half a moped was moving along the cut. It was an ingenious invention. To receive cell phone service at his cabin, he had placed a hand-crafted metal dish at the top of a hill to extend the signal. His meat was hidden in a bear-proof cellar filled with ice in the slope of a river bend, and in his spare time he would contemplate new trap designs. Most of his inventions were not beautiful, but they were workarounds that solved real problems. Keen observation and experimental practice had made Grandfather the sought after man he was today.

Above all, Grandfather was sought for his fine work as an iron smith. People from the village placed orders ranging from bread baking pans to pliers, and from hoof nails to horse shoes. In his shop, he taught me how to make horseshoes. Although he could have given me verbal instructions, he preferred to perform each task, while I was to mimic each move as closely as I could. He would make an angled strike with a sledgehammer, then have me repeat it until I had it just right. Or he would fine tune an edge with the well-balanced strikes of a slender hammer, and I would work until I could repeat his moves. As my strikes became increasingly coordinated with his, we began moving back and forth as a team between fire and anvil.

His method and rhythm were beginning to make sense to me, and soon there emerged between us a natural workflow. After some time, Grandfather said, "You're like a wolf, Alex!" (Rus. *nu, Sashka, ty priam' kak volk!*). I looked at him with surprise. What did wolves have to do with working a smithy? But as my skills improved, and I was increasingly able to see ahead in the workflow, Grandfather would repeatedly use terms describing wolf behavior to commend my progress. "You're nimble like a wolf" (Rus. *nu tyi shustryi kak volk*) or "You think like a wolf" (Rus. *soobrazhaesh' kak volk*). Only later did it dawn on me: in Grandfather's experience wolves were able not only to follow sequences they had observed, they were able to anticipate the next step in yet incomplete sequences. They were able to see ahead and anticipate another's intent. In some sense, Grandfather was a wolf.

Like the wolf-birthed blacksmithing ancestors from the origin myth of the early Turks, who had once dominated Inner Asia (552–630 CE and 682–744 CE) (Drompp 2011: 516–17), Grandfather combined in his person an occupational tradition that had historically been linked with wolves. Grandfather had proclaimed himself to be a fervent atheist. But it was also known to all that according to Buriat cultural heritage the vocation of a blacksmith and that of a shaman were often considered one. Thus many Buriat blacksmiths had historically been healers (e.g., Dashieva 2013). The ability to see and foresee through one's practice of forging iron was thus well-established, no matter how little of this was directly disclosed to me or others by Grandfather Tseren-Dorzho.

INVISIBLE MOVEMENT, EMPATHETIC EVASION

Grandfather had been teaching me in his shop how to see like a wolf. And seeing like a wolf required putting yourself in the position of the one watching your movements. Burged's recollection of the wolf couple's deception, described at the beginning of this chapter, illustrates the wolf's keen awareness of the field of vision in other animals, including humans. It also speaks of the human awareness of this trait in wolves, an awareness I soon began to acquire for myself on my regular hikes between Uro and Sorok where I often encountered wolf tracks in fresh snow.

One autumn morning I noticed two adult wolf tracks running side by side. Both tracks were fresh, as it had snowed only an hour earlier. The couple were headed in the same direction as me, and so I followed their tracks until they approached an isolated winter cabin perched on a steep stretch of river bank. Judging by the lights, the family were home. Around the cabin they were keeping a few sheep, and cattle were walking about. Several of them were leisurely scratching away for forage. The cabin itself was surrounded by uneven, sparsely wooded, hilly terrain. Whenever the trail I had been following encountered a small rise in the ground, the tracks would depart from it to run a diversion, only to return to the trail behind the rise. At first I did not understand these maneuvers.

The cabin was now within rifle shot distance, and I was surprised that the wolves had ventured so close to human habitation in broad daylight. Curious to know what these wolves might have seen, I crouched down in their tracks. My eyes were now level with the height at which I suspected theirs had been. On my knees with my head lowered, I could no longer see the cabin. My body was now hidden from sight of someone who could have been looking from the north-facing window of the cabin. Had I followed the wolves' tracks in this ducking position all the way from the dense forest, I would have reached the cabin without once being exposed to the eyes of someone peering through the window.

I visited the same household two months later in the depth of winter, and I was told that wolves had recently been there at night. They had taken two sheep from inside their pen. This was quite a daring feat, I was assured, since the winter pen is located directly below the kitchen window. Judging by the wolves' tracks in the morning, the sheep had been heaved over the fence, down the slope, and into the forest. It was a rare thing that wolves would enter a pen and carry whole carcasses over a fence as tall as this one, the householders said. Looking back to my previous observations of the wolf tracks I had followed around the cabin, it seemed plausible the attack had been carried out by members of the same pack. Their earlier visits had afforded them an intimate knowledge of the terrain, and they had clearly established a path based on what they anticipated could be seen from the cabin's windows. They had empathetically circumnavigated the human gaze.

But not only were these wolves attuned to the ways in which humans looked for them in the landscape, they had also become aware of several of the implements people were using against them, and they had adjusted their movements accordingly. Uncle Borzhon remembered how he had joined a group of hunters who, under the leadership of the region's mayor, had rented a helicopter in 1989 or 1990 for hunting wolves. Flying over dense stands of bare larch crowns reaching toward the sky, the men had tracked a pack of wolves on a hillside. As the pilots lowered the aircraft for better aim from the air, the wolves slowed down, looking for shelter. Each of the wolves began hiding behind a tree. They stood on their rear legs, with their front paws propped up against the upright stem. Their bodies were flush with the trunks, and they maneuvered in relation to the hovering aircraft. Like the wolf couple approaching the cabin, these wolves had anticipated the human gaze, and more likely the flight line of bullets to come from barrels pointed at them through the helicopter's open sliding door. Borzhon never again hunted wolves from a helicopter. In later years renting them had become too expensive, and as the experiment had shown, hunting wolves from the air was an inefficient method. There was no concealed intent in the flying fortress of a Mil Mi-8 helicopter.

DESIGNS OF CONCEALED INTENT

Of less conspicuous design had been the old-fashioned wolf traps found around the Eastern Saian Mountains. If wolves knew how to position themselves in the landscape in such a way as to conceal their movement from the gaze of people, then humans had found ways to conceal their intentions from wolves in equally shrewd ways. Several of my interlocutors in Tofalariia remembered the use of what they called "wolf cages" (Rus. *volch'ia sadka*). This was a kind of trap well known throughout Eastern Siberia. It was only one among many different types of traps that had been used to kill wolves where poison was scarce or unadvisable. My friends in Oka described several other designs not mentioned here, and Larissa Pavlinskaia (2002: 128), in her field notes, describes additional designs.

Tofa hunters' descriptions of the trap design closely resembled Aleksandr A. Cherkasov's (1867: 179) account of a design that would be erected during the summer months. Wooden stakes were arranged in two circles—one inside another—to form a corridor of no more than ten to twelve inches in width. In autumn, live bait, such as a lamb, was placed inside the closed inner circle. A square opening in the outside wall allowed young and inexperienced wolves, drawn by the calls of the bait animal, to enter and familiarize themselves with the structure. Come winter, when the wolves had grown and their fur was thick, a door would be installed several inches wider than the corridor into which it opened. A habituated wolf could still enter the corridor, but in one direction only. With the wolf unable to turn in the narrow corridor, it remained trapped until a hunter would arrive on horseback to conceal his tracks. He would kill the trapped wolf inside the corridor without leaving the saddle, silently

Illustration 6.2. Ruins of a Tofa wolf trap. Photograph by the author.

strangulating it from above. Blood spill was averted to prevent disclosure of the purpose of the structure. But like other wolf trapping mechanisms that had been used in Oka and Tofalariia until the second half of the twentieth century (e.g., cross structured traps, iced slope traps, and concealed knife blades), the last remaining wolf cages were now rotting away.

According to Soiot and Tofa hunters, wolves had come to understand the danger associated with these human made objects. They were no longer venturing into these traps. Had wolves seen through the concealed intentions embedded in these structures? No particular historical cases were reported in which someone had used a wolf trap carelessly, compromising its efficacy, possibly revealing its purpose to wolves. Of course it is possible that improper use contributed to the discontinuation of traps in Oka and Tofalariia. But this possibility was never mentioned to me. If, as anthropologist Alfred Gell (1996: 29) suggests, traps "communicate the idea of a nexus of intentionalities between hunters and prey animals, via material forms and mechanisms," then wolves may be said to have identified this communication, or at least the danger of its concealed scheme had outweighed the lure of its unreachable bait.

Although constructed at a rate intended to habituate wolves to a trap's deceptive harmlessness, more recently the sight of traps had inculcated suspicion, leading wolves to avoid them, and eventually defeating the structure's hidden intent altogether. Riding through Tofalariian forest with Denis, we came across several sites which he indicated had once been prime wolf-trapping locations. All that was left were the rotten remains of intricate designs, abandoned in the taiga as monuments to an outdated human scheme.

Although traps are human made artifacts, and wolf dens a form of residential architecture, I will argue that both structures share a quality of hidden intent. At the very least, traps and dens share in the intent to hide something. Biologist Michael H. Hansell (2005: 2) groups homes, traps, foraging burrows, and other structures under the terms "animal architecture" and "animal-built-structures," grouping together in his comparison humans and other mammals with birds, fish, and insects in their ability to modify materials toward specific purposes. Humans may be the only vertebrates to construct traps (Hansell 2005: 21), while wolves rely on trapping prey by utilizing landforms in combination with strategic pack formation in their pursuits. But wolves do construct elaborate underground dens, many of which can hardly be described as simple shelters. They can be seen as architectural modifications of the landscape, the design of which originates with wolves and their predictions of patterns of movement in other animals. According to the hunters at Uro, wolf dens were built in part with the aim to evade humans. As most hunters in Oka would confirm, it is not easy to locate a wolf den. They were well hidden, and numerous stories accounted for the various tactics employed by experienced wolves in returning to their dens in fresh snow without leaving a direct track that could be followed.

In early autumn, one of Uncle Aiusha's (b. ca. 1965) healthy working horses had been grazing in the dead angle of a sharp bend of the Sorok River, just north of his cabin. When Aleksei, his neighbor, walked over to visit Aiusha one morning, he passed the spot where the horse had been grazing. All that was left of it now were blood stains in the fine dusting of the early snow. The horse itself had been torn into pieces. These pieces had been carried uphill, and into the woods. There was nothing left of the horse on the riverbank. Hobbled horses that were grazing near human households had not been targeted by wolves for a long time, and everyone in the valley was shocked by the news. Aiusha identified the incident as the work of the founding couple of a wolf "family" that he had been tracking for some time.

He had read their tracks, counting some nine or ten individuals. In this case, he figured the wolves had burrowed the meat somewhere in the forest as a stash for later winter use. Wolves did not normally take a complete animal, unless they were systematically building a food stash. Aiusha's and other hunters' knowledge of den locations was rarely exact, and even where it was precise, certainty was short-lived because wolves relocated or built new dens as soon as a location had been compromised. Aiusha believed that the wolf couple near his house was rotating between at least two dens, making it particularly difficult to track them. Annual rotation between dens, and sometimes within a single season, as well as the maintenance of multiple entrances to each den, were all part of a wolf's strategic maneuvering.

It was not likely, however, that Aiusha's wolf family was the one to blame for the loss of his horse. The herders at Uro had a general idea of the locations of several wolf dens within their vicinity, but these were not the dens of wolves bothering their stock. Although dens could be located near households, wolves frequenting a certain den were known to target only stock of more distant households. In the words of Buriat shaman Stepanovich, "wolves do not attack 'their' cattle—that is, cattle living within their territory. They tear [lit. take bites] (Rus. *kuski derut*) only from cattle located at a distance from their own home grounds." As a member of the Oka-Buriat wolf clan, Stepanovich attributed great sacrality to wolves. At his own cabin outside Orlik, he observed the life cycle of a single female who kept a den near his grounds. She had never attacked his stock, and he did not mind her presence. On the contrary, he enjoyed watching her coming and going from the den.

Den construction was not described to me directly as a weapon against humans, but herder-hunters at Uro understood den placement and positioning in the landscape as strategic and purposefully covert. Like human architecture, which fulfils many goals, wolf dens had to be seen as more than shelters. They could serve as concealed caches, as anchor points in extensive migrations, and as places to safely rear young. They were built on knowledge of prevailing winds, external visibility, optimal return routes, and proximity to water and game passes. They took into account the grazing patterns of domestic stock, vertical transhumance, and broader regional wolf migratory routes. Thus they were positioned much like traps. And like traps, which were meant to hide their ultimate purpose, these dens with their multiple entrances were edifices of illusion: a wolf could enter a den, apparently never leaving. In actuality, she would be gone before a hunter had discovered another exit.

Like a wolf trap, the den could become a nexus between hunter and wolf. Even if the den was not intended to trap a human in terms of physical containment, and although its material forms and mechanisms differed, it was built with the intent to remain hidden. And were it to be found out, the den's design would provide the wolf with options for escape or counterattack while built-in options remained concealed from the hunter.

THE DEN AS NEXUS

Aiusha's horse had been killed in autumn—the wrong time to locate a wolf den. Wolf dens had to be searched for in late spring, when the cubs were immature and dependent upon shelter. Their parents would roam in search of food, often leaving their young behind for days on end. In their parents' absence a litter was known to make noise near the den's entrance. Listening for such sounds could lead a careful hunter directly to a den, even in the absence of snow. Wolf cubs were also known to stray from their home, often returning to it in a straight line. At this point in the year, they had not yet acquired the skill of concealing their tracks through backtracking. If snow was still on the ground, the search was simplified.

Grandfather Tseren-Dorzho recalled an instance, ten years earlier, when together with a younger relative, he had come upon the tracks of an adult wolf in fresh May snow. As the two were following the wolf's tracks for many miles, they noticed it had caught a hare without breaking into a chase, or altering its path. From the grooves in the snow it was evident how the wolf had held the hare in its mouth, periodically setting it down to rest. Eventually, the men noticed how the wolf had begun to drag a bit. Shortly thereafter, both spotted five wolf cubs playing under a tall cedar tree.

Opposite the den, in the shade of the tree, blood covered the snow, and ripped pieces of hare flesh were laying about. Another hare had been brought to the den by a second adult wolf. Both mature wolves had taken off again. The men immediately killed the litter. According to the Soiot *seer*, or canon of traditional Soiot beliefs, to kill an entire brood of any species was prohibited, but by allowing the parents to live, the men had avoided the impermissible (Ayusheeva 2010: 309). They proceeded to skin each body, burying three of the carcasses and poisoning the flesh of the remaining two.

Grandfather left the poisoned carcasses by the den for the parents to eat upon their discovery of the raid. He knew about the revenge of wolves: "You must leave the little ones for them to eat. The meat will calm their fury. If one fails to calm the wolves after an invasion of this sort, they will track the hunter and catch up with him." He concluded, "A wolf is not a companion" (Rus. *volk ne tovarishch*). Grandfather's anticipation of the wolves' anger was in many ways indicative of the nexus of intentionalities represented by the den as an intentionally concealed structure. With its cover blown, the wolf would be infuriated. Grandfather did not know what had become of the adults they had intended to poison, but killing a litter only reduced the headcount for a season. Furthermore, cubs and single males were not the key players of this strategic yet opportunistic game.

Although all wolves represented a threat to domestic stock, and in spite of talk about mature and cunning males, it was the wolf-mother of a pack that had to be targeted during a hunt. It was she who held ties to a particular territory and its dens. Marina recalled her grandfather saying: "If you are going to kill wolves, preferably kill the female. If the female dies, then the male leader of the pack will abandon the gang and go away in search of another female." To Marina, this advice seemed quite applicable now.

> It seems that here in this territory there is a female. Here she has her house (Rus. *u nee svoi dom*), she gives birth to her little children here, and so she cannot leave (Rus. *detennoshek prinosit, i id'ti ne kuda*). And these males . . . they come and they go. . . . That is why Grandfather always said to kill the female. It is useless to kill the male. She will find another, and again they will terrorize [you].

To be truly effective, then, a herder-hunter had to find the lead female. Any kind of predictable wolf movement hinged on her, and her movements were anchored to at least one den. As it turned out, not only human hunters knew which members of a wolf pack had to be targeted for maximum efficiency. Wolves too had figured out which members of a human household had to be targeted or co-opted in order to best secure their own aims within a herding compound.

INFILTRATING DOG-HUMAN RELATIONS

Uncle Borzhon had vivid memories of one wolf in particular—a lone animal—which he described to me as "an abnormally obnoxious (Rus. *naglyi*) wolf." Several years ago, this wolf had harassed his household at the summer camp on the upper Sorok River. It had beset their stock day after day, and especially during the nights, over the course of two or three weeks while Borzhon had been in town and his wife Ranzhur and their sons had been taking care of their yak herd, cows, horses, and sheep. At night, the wolf would cross the fenced structure surrounding their summer compound. Once inside, it was reckless enough to frequent the narrow pathway between Borzhon's cabin and equipment shed where his hunting dogs were tied up for the night. During the first few nightly visitations, his dogs had barked insistently. But with time, Borzhon recalled, the wolf started "making friends" (Rus. *podruzhilsia*) with his dogs.

At first, I did not quite understand what Borzhon meant by "making friends" with his dogs, since all dog owners at Uro knew from experience that wolves were quick to kill watch dogs, particularly if they were on a leash, as Borzhon's were. It had been the dogs' job to warn the family of approaching predators, yet both dogs remained silent now as the wolf increased its visits to the encampment. Borzhon reasoned that perhaps his dogs had become "too scared" to bark. It seemed, they had been dealing with a young and especially strong wolf. After all, it had killed "one animal after another" over the course of these weeks.

Every night, following the slightest sound, the men would rush into the dark, rifles loaded—never able to take the wolf down. When Borzhon finally returned to the summer cabin on his horse, his family were quick to give him an account. He left immediately, riding back to Uro where he still had a secret batch of wolf poison from years past. Various people had hidden small stashes of barium that had survived the demise of the kolkhoz. At the time of my fieldwork, the majority of these hidden stashes had been exhausted and nobody could obtain any fresh poison since its ban. Back at the summer pasture, Borzhon inserted the old barium capsules into bait meat. The following morning Borzhon's sons found the dead wolf on a bend down river. Contrary to their expectations, the animal had not been young or energetic. Borzhon described him as old and haggard, but evidently it had been shrewd.

Singling out and isolating select animals for the purpose of preying on them may be one way in which wolves generalize their socially learned knowledge, applying it also to humans and their stock. But how does one account for what looks like systematic destabilization of the human-dog tie? According to ethologists Zsófia Virányi and Friederike Range (2014: 55–56): "Further research needs to examine . . . to what extent dog-human and wolf-wolf cooperation relies on the same mechanisms. Based on our current knowledge, we suggest that dog-human cooperation likely relies on the leading role of humans enhanced by the dependency of dogs on humans and by a steeper dominance hierarchy that characterizes dogs in comparison to wolves."

Clearly, the wolf in Borzhon's pasture did not have the same sense of subjugation as his dogs did vis-à-vis the household. Borzhon had spoken of the wolf as if it had recognized his dogs' subordinate function of reporting to their owner, a role in which dogs became their owners' eyes in the pasture. By "befriending" through frequent visitation at very close range and possibly by implying a threat to the dogs' lives, the wolf had infiltrated the hierarchical relationship uniting dogs and master. In effect, the dogs had temporarily become complicit in the intruder's agenda, averting their own deaths.

DEATH IN THE ODORLESS

To counter-infiltrate the sociality of wolves, a hunter not only had to be silent and invisible, but most importantly, he had to be odorless. One such hunter was Sasha, the yak herder from Khan-Modon who had lost a large part of his stock to wolves. When I asked him about the use of traps he only laughed. "They were of little help. You'd catch a few wolves that way, but from then on no wolf would step near that trap again." "Wolves are cunning," he said, and "they learn fast." If a method was to be efficient against wolves, it had to be odorless and invisible. The only weapon that had really worked was scentless poison, and this had never really been different as far as he could tell. Sasha proceeded to give me a little glimpse of the Soiot experience with natural poisons.

A Soiot elder once told him how their ancestors had used wolf poison long before the Soviet introduction of barium. This was an interesting fact for me, as I had read about encounters of wolf and fox poisonings in Feliks Kon's recollections of Soiots from Uriankhai (1934), recorded in pre-revolutionary times. I knew that poisons had been introduced by settlers under the tsar, but had there been prior indigenous use of poison? According to the elder, Soiots had been making their own poison from a local plant called *bal'shargana*. In Russian, Sasha referred to the plant as bear grass (Rus. *medvezh'ia trava*). He said that bears liked it. Entire hillsides were covered with it at Khan-Modon.

Bal'shargana was also a place name on the upper Tissa River, bordering with Tyva. Sasha's bear grass likely corresponds to what is commonly known in English as wolfsbane or *Aconitum*, a highly poisonous plant that has been used by indigenous hunters from East Asia to the Americas. David Jones (2007: 23) reports widespread use of *Aconitum* in various regions of China, including Tibet, into the twentieth century. While Tibetan medicine has long made use of the toxicity of the plant for healing purposes (e.g., Ma et al. 2015), there seems to be a gap in the literature on the use of *Aconitum* as a deterrent to predators, particularly for Inner Asia.

According to Sasha's elder, people would locate tiny buds of the plant before they bloomed. To make the poison, they had taken empty steel buckets to cover the shoots in their natural habitat. Rocks were then placed on top of the upturned buckets. This "lack of light seems to turn its juices into poison," said Sasha. Once the plant had grown to its full size inside the bucket, people carefully harvested the leaves, laying them out to dry and eventually crushing them down to a powder.

Mixed in with small bits of meat, and strewn in strategic locations in the forest, the powder was easily masked by the scent of blood or meat. Sasha reckoned that bear grass would have been much less powerful than factory prepared barium, and that wolves would have collapsed within only two or three days after repeatedly ingesting the powder. Although he was planning on putting the elder's memory to the test, he had not yet done so. However, given the dire circumstances of his herd, he was ready to try it out any time now. In a way, returning to his ancestors' pre-Soviet practice would allow him to circumnavigate the government's ban on the use of commercial wolf poisoning. At the same time, it would be a way of responding to the shrewdness of wolves who seemed to evade all other means of extermination. Although wolves were such keen observers and schemers, they had never been able to detect poison. For this reason—in Sasha's memory—there had been very few wolves during the Soviet years. The kolkhoz had "a really good thing going" with their poisoning methods, he recalled. Yak and other cattle herds were growing substantially then. For Sasha, the old Soiot way of concealing death in odorless self-grown poison, which the Soviet method of barium had merely intensified by a few times, "was the way to go" even now.

CONCLUSION

I attempted in this chapter to provide several examples to characterize the encounters between Soiot households and wolves. Multiple encounters with wolves took place during my fieldwork, most of which I decided not to include in this book. The examples I did select relied primarily on recollections of past encounters, intersections between wolves and people during which I had not personally been present. The reason for this is that the time that had passed between the event and its recollection actually allowed people to make sense of their encounters. I have tried to show how decisions regarding wolves were made in retrospect of past encounters. This retrospective view also allowed me to establish what seemed to lie at the heart of Soiot human-wolf relations: the skill to read in another's performance their actual intentions.

I introduced this concept of pedagogy with a vignette of a collaborating wolf couple in a summer pasture. Only in retrospect did the observed behaviors make sense. Looking not only to the past, but also to neighboring regions, I reviewed divergent approaches to wolves among small and large scale herders of northern Mongolia and northeastern Russia. Historically, there seem to have existed two main regional approaches in dealing with wolf predation, one being the periodic organization of systematic raids on horseback, and the other a kind of agreeable "flight" from wolves by moving one's camp prematurely. The latter approach still requires additional insight into the potential cosmological meanings that may have been ascribed to wolves by Tofas a century ago.

Although cosmological explanations for wolf behavior played an important role for some Soiots, my own observations suggest that wolves were known primarily as shrewd learners who anticipated the intentions of others through careful observation of routine movement. This became especially clear through the blacksmithing experience with Grandfather Tseren-Dorzho, who taught me many things about wolves in Soiot context, not least to view wolves as active learners. To illustrate their capacity to watch for observational skills in others, I described two wolves who had empathetically evaded the human gaze from a cabin's window by using the relief of the ground for visual shelter.

Hidden intent, it seems, stood at the center of wolf-human interactions in Oka. Traditional wolf trap designs were one material form in which humans deliberately disguised their intentions from wolves. Wolf dens, on the other hand, were known to be no less cunning in their concealment of intent through design. Traps and dens both represented a nexus between hunters and wolves, the one directed by wolves against humans, the other by humans against wolves. The chapter concluded with what may be two pinnacle aspects of wolf-human relations in Oka. The first of these two was the wolf's known ability to infiltrate the hierarchical sociality of the dog-human interface. This peculiar skill rendered the herder nearly powerless. The second aspect was the herder's ability to conceal a lethal strike in odorless poison. Only poison circumnavigated a wolf's keen senses, suspending its skill as an expert learner.

CONCLUSION

I set out, in the introduction, with Tim Ingold's observation that it is possible to have animals that are domesticated, yet not obviously so in any morphological sense. In this view, some forms of domestication are better expressed in terms of an animal's belonging to a household than in its altered phenotypic expression. This kind of domesticity, for Ingold, is marked by tameness (Ingold 1980: 82). Not all animals may physically express changes as the result of a life spent with or near human households, but their countenance toward humans and other animals will be affected. What Ingold refers to as tameness, I have described for Oka in terms of establishing and breeding for approachability or mutual relatability.

The reindeer, yak, and horses described in these pages support Ingold's point in several ways. Soiot and Tofa reindeer clearly had the ability to interbreed with their cousins in the taiga; their coat color, stature, and physical prowess often differed little from that of their counterparts under the auspices of local spirit masters. Even animals that no longer had a wild counterpart in the landscape maintained many of the features conventionally expected to be present outside domestication relationships. The sociality of Oka horse groups in many ways closely resembled the descriptions of ethologists who have studied feral and wild horse populations in places like Mongolia and North America. Furthermore, in Oka yak were deliberately bred to maintain the dark coat color of their wild relatives in places such as northern China, and it was important to breeders that their herds maintain social dynamics suitable for extensive ranges.

What scholars often seem to gloss in their attempts to broaden our understanding of domestication relationships is a finer qualification of the concept of tameness. What does it actually mean to become tame? The phenotypic characteristics of animals implicated in diverse domestication relationships may or may not be altered, sometimes depending on the material style of the relationship. But even where animals retain features associated with a state of wildness, their domestic relation may be expressed through a sense of familiarity or approachability. This approachability should not be mistaken for a constant state of docility. As we have seen in the chapters of this book, approachability is an attribute that often requires seasonal re-solicitation. Tameness, thus, is a nuanced beast.

Ebb and flow in the proximity of interspecies relations is not a weakness in the Oka style of domestication relationships. Other scholars confirm similar findings across pastoral societies of Inner and North Asia (see Ferret 2014; Marchina 2016; Stépanoff et al. 2017). Soiot and Tofa breeders were not only intent on maintaining in their herds the phenotypic features found in herds belonging to spirit masters; but they would, on occasion, select for unruly traits in reproductive bulls—features that came to thrive during seasonal increases in the proximity between animals and humans. Because of the seasonal nature of these proximal intervals, memory of previous encounters was never lost in their animals. In fact, herders purposefully built upon their animals' recollection of encounters in previous years, allowing for a shared history between animals and people. Part of this history, from the herders' perspective, was the passing on of particular traits from one generation of herd animals to the next.

Unruliness, as a case in point, allowed reproductive males to protect their family groups against intruding males in unfenced country, while also equipping them to fend off predators in lieu of human protection. In this sense, Soiot domestication relationships with yak, horses, and reindeer were in part sustained by deliberately fostering select animals' headstrong and autonomous qualities. Where the carrying capacity of a home range could sustain only limited concentrated grazing, animals relied on broader ranges—as well as ranges at different elevations—inevitably implicating them in regular encounters with predators. It may be more accurate then to speak of approachability and relatability than of tameness or docility as markers of domesticity in the Saians. Approachability and tameness differed also in cosmological terms.

For Ingold (2015: 24), "all it takes to trigger the shift from hunting to pastoralism is a transfer of control over herds from the animals' spiritual masters to humans." This was not entirely true in Oka, where animals that had been transferred to the control of human households (e.g., reindeer), or which had no counterpart in spirit-owned herds (e.g., yak, horses, dogs) remained indirectly subject to the benevolence of local spirit masters. A herder might not have been obliged to ask the spirit for permission to slaughter a yak, but he would depend on the spirit's good will to sustain the yak's life, to make its pastures grow, and to hold back predators. The same could be said of human members of the household, whose lives were subject to various intangible agents. Good will in all things had to be actively sought through a life of deliberate balance.

To understand this balancing act, we must return to chapter 2 in which I tried to show how shamanist and Buddhist approaches to the landscape differed. It was the lama's role to facilitate a divine encounter, and thus to bury the seed of divine desire within an animal or spirit so as to allow it to develop a yearning for a future revisitation with the entity of that first encounter (i.e., a kind of imprinting). It was also his duty to periodically revisit the creature, reminding it of its allegiance and commitment—its belonging. By caring for the creature or spirit in this way, the lama helped groom its state of tameness, a state that may be equated to the securing of benevolence and the gradual abolishment of ambiguity in the creature's demeanor. While the lama's revisitations seem to resemble herders' resolicitation of approachability in animals, the nature of these two encounters is not identical.

The herder—like the lama—reminds the animal of the part it plays in this shared more-than-human history, but not with the intention of alienating it from its other affiliations, its sense of autonomy, or its ability to act in line with a rationale not governed by human intention. The shamanic approach, by contrast, emphasized bi-directional communication—be it by playing cards to entertain the whims of ambiguous spirits or in flashing desirable consumables. In either case, it was a matter of haggling for collaboration in the taking of life, which relied on the presence of autonomous motives and the ability of others to respond. Coming from such divergent angles, it should be evident why for many of my friends at Uro a clear division into either wild or tame could not do justice to their daily experiences.

DOMESTIC CROSS-SPECIES RELATIONS

In her book on Matsutake mushrooms, anthropologist Anna Lowenhaupt Tsing (2015: 258) describes Japanese volunteers who "make themselves part of perhaps-helpful landscape disturbance as they wait to see what happens." The goal of these volunteers is to create pockets of forested land that is favorable to the natural growth of their coveted mushroom. The conditions they generate through their labor are only "perhaps-helpful" because humans have no real control over the mushroom. The attitude of these volunteers, described by Tsing, is reminiscent of the retrospective sense-making we encountered in chapter 2. Facilitating new assemblages or encounters between species is always a matter of hopeful experimentation.

The households at Uro were quite familiar with this type of experimentation. People had gradually introduced a number of new species into their folds without knowing how well these animals would live side by side. This process of multispecies experimentation was ongoing, with the newest introduced species being egg-laying hens. At Uro, several households purchased chickens from a traveling merchant in the spring. The poultry survived the harsh mountainous winter by moving into the covered winter sheep stables, spending the long season perched on top of the sheep. In this symbiotic arrangement the chickens kept warm, while feeding on the sheep's ticks. The cash investment for householders was minimal, and the addition of eggs was welcome.

However, not all experimentation with new combinations of species turned out as favorably. As mentioned in chapter 3, introducing dairy cows to reindeer summer encampments in the early 2000s had resulted in reindeer contracting an unidentifiable cattle-borne disease causing many reindeer to die. In spite of their initial surprise at the peaceful relations between dairy cattle and reindeer at Uro, the herders proceeded to remove the deer to a remote location in the mountains. Not only did this separation of deer from cattle prevent further disease transfer, the deeper snow at higher elevation also shielded the deer from wolf attacks common within the home ranges of yak and sheep. The failure of this experiment, however, had far-reaching consequences for Soiot households at Uro, who were now no longer able to rely on reindeer for transportation in their autumn and winter hunts.

In terms of seasonal rhythms, the combination of horses and reindeer formed a near ideal pairing for Tofas, who were still heavily reliant on both species during my visits. As recounted in chapter 3, the divergent altitudinal and seasonal preferences of horses and reindeer made possible a seamless transition between modes of transportation from winter to summer. Although Tofas kept some dairy cattle in the settlement, the total number of cows was smaller, and their seasonal encounters with reindeer were purposefully kept brief. The functional fit between Karagass reindeer and Mongolian horses was also reflected in the cultural heritage of material implements, such as saddle structures, which had been minimally adapted to fit both species.

There were other animal combinations that had either failed or had never been seriously pursued. One of them being the use of dogs in herding yak, reindeer, and sheep. Unlike the Sámi, or even Inuvialuit, who have used dogs in herding reindeer (e.g., Hart 2001: 66–67; Voujala-Magga et al. 2011: 231), my Soiot friends had never used dogs to herd any of their animals, not even sheep. Dogs were used to alarm householders of intruders, and they were trained to hunt sable and other fur-bearing prey. Retrieving fur bearers required great care, as an inexperienced dog could easily puncture a precious sable pelt with its fangs. As I have described elsewhere (Oehler 2018a), some dogs had been selected specifically for their lack of aggression around yak and other cattle. But none of them had been expected to take part in herding activities. It remains unclear to me whether serious experimentation with dog-assisted herding ever occurred in the Saians.

Perhaps the most profound example of unanticipated incompatibility of species within households of Oka emerged from the experimental combination of reindeer with yak and dairy cattle. While it was easy enough to keep cattle and reindeer separated to prevent the transfer of disease, it was much more difficult to allocate sufficient labor from each household to satisfy the demands of hay and lichen dependent ruminants. The extensive hay harvest required to sustain dairy cattle through the winter pulled labor away from distant reindeer-herding camps. Furthermore, the sheer distance and difficulty of access to viable reindeer habitat from Uro discouraged households from engaging with the herd on a regular basis.

Another interesting and perhaps unforeseen pairing of species among the multispecies constellation of Oka households was dogs and wolves. As I have described elsewhere (Oehler 2018a), dogs could become a herder's eyes in the field, or a hunter's accentuated sense of smell during a sable hunt. Wolves, too, were known to occasionally take a leading role in directing the action of dogs belonging to human households. In chapter 6, this translated to two watch dogs becoming a lone wolf's collaborators. By way of coerced complicity resulting from nightly wolf-dog encounters, the wolf refrained from killing the watch dogs, thus being afforded the ability to take down stock under the protection of the dogs' silence.

The reader may wonder how wolves fit into this picture of south Siberian domestication relationships. Clearly, the wolf who "befriended" the dogs had infiltrated the human household, posing a threat and not a conducive or sustainable relationship. And, clearly, wolves have never been part of the human household in the way that selectively bred stock have. Yet, in Oka, wolves and bears were often seen as the hunters of the spirit household. Much like human members of a household, who fulfill their duties of herding, milking, breeding, braking, and hunting, predators of the spirit household fulfilled their role in maintaining balance between human and spirit households. In this sense, wolves were integral members of a mirrored household and part of domestication relationships.

Wolves helped establish the balance required of any household. A human hunter might ask a spirit master for a gift of a prey. Belonging to one of the spirit masters' herds, prey was tied up in a domestication relationship of its own. In gratitude for a spirit master's untethering of the animal, the herder-hunter would reciprocate by extending from his own herd products unavailable to the spirit master, such as fermented and distilled milk (i.e., dairy vodka). Other times exchanges consisted of animals in the direct sense—a life for a life. In this economy, human masters supplicated to receive gifts they would collect with their rifles or traps. Conversely, spirit masters collected as and when they saw fit. Not in need of traps or rifles, they would act through wolves, bears, or inclement weather. But even such divine collection rarely occurred without negotiation.

NEGOTIATING DOMESTICATION RELATIONSHIPS

I have tried to emphasize the role of negotiation within and between households and those belonging to them. In Oka, belonging to a household—whether spirit or human-mastered—was defined through one's relationship with a master. Interspecies relationships were established and sustained not so much through spoken language as through mutual observation and material-tactile engagements. At the heart of these domestication relationships lay the assumption that all members of the household possessed some autonomy of movement that made possible a degree of resistance. Coercing or dominating others was not valued because such actions denied an animal's ability to respond and remain self-reliant. Communicative capacity and self-reliance lay at the heart of every household's ability to maintain animals beyond the confines of pastured land.

Domestication relationships were consequently not about the elimination of resistance, but about haggling for collaboration, finding ways to align wills and sometimes about severing ties. In all cases such relationships were communicative, involving the reading of intentions in others, no matter which household an animal belonged to. To make a life together, one had to be able to read the intentions of others and to find workable ways of communicating one's own intentions. Instead of relying on linguistic features that would preclude the participation of most animals, the herder-hunters at Uro were fluent in what Erin Manning and Brian Massumi (2014) call "thinking in the act." What the authors have in mind is a collaborative mode of thinking in which one does not prescribe meanings to actions before they occur, but in which meanings are composed through dialogue and interaction between beings, actions, and objects.

To Manning and Massumi, "every practice is a mode of thought, already in the act. To dance: a thinking in movement. To paint: a thinking through colour" (2014: vii). In this view, "the practice that is philosophy has no exclusive claim to thought or the composition of concepts" (2014: vii). Neither do writing or speaking command the domain of idea production. Drawing on Gilles Deleuze and Félix Guattari (2012: 34), Manning and Massumi assert, "one writing alone is already a crowd" (Manning and Massumi 2014: viii). Thinking and communicating thought in Oka often seemed to involve a crowd of humans and nonhumans. A common mode for collective thinking was the positioning of bodies in relation to other bodies in a shared landscape.

In a taiga context, characterized by unpredictability and ambiguity, wolves were feared and revered for their shrewd or nimble positioning. The Cambridge Advanced Learner's Dictionary defines shrewd as a "clear understanding and good judgment of a situation, usually resulting in an advantage" (2008). Hunters of Oka saw it as a trait that allowed one to take advantageous shortcuts. But a deliberate shortcut can be taken only by one who understands the two paths they are connecting in the shortcut. Crossing from the known to the not-yet-known requires foresight. The process of continuously developing foresight (often through accumulation of recollections of past encounters) is a kind of pedagogy. In the Soiot context, shrewdness was thus the ability to learn from careful nuanced observation. Watchfulness as a learner's tactic equipped herder-hunters with a literacy beyond the spoken or written word. Watchfulness was the ability to read the positioning of bodies to deduct imminent movement.

In the case of wolves, careful observation involved what I have called empathetic evasion, the ability to anticipate what another will see and willfully to withhold from them the privilege of seeing. This can be referred to as trickery that requires one's own pre-calculation. Sensory and evolutionary ecologist Martin Stevens (2016) refers to this as animal "cheats and deceits." The traps described in chapter 6 can be explained as a form of human trickery in which intentions remain purposefully concealed. However, in the context of Oka's wolves, a much more promising perspective comes from looking at these relations in terms of their non-linguistic communicative potential. Allowing others to anticipate and then betray their anticipation, arguably lies at the heart of any lively conversation.

This is not to say that all conversations amount to games of mutual trickery, of course. We are drawn to music because it establishes a predictable pattern through rhythm and melody, allowing us to follow along. Yet, entirely predictable patterns become repetitive and do not hold our attention. Musical breaks, by contrast, call for a sense of anticipation. They signal the beginning of a new part, either transitioning the listener to a section they have been joyfully awaiting, or exciting them by foreshadowing what is yet to be revealed. In so doing, musical breaks instill variety in an arrangement, but they also trip up the listener. By setting up a predictable pattern, the composer or performer builds up a position of power to surprise the listener's anticipation, thereby holding the listener's attention. The multi-month wolf trap construction in chapter 6 is such a communicative composition. Here wolves are lulled into a predictable pattern, only for the hunter-composer to perform a musical break, which is then followed by a lethal change in rhythm.

In domestication relationships the communicative change in rhythm is clearly not always lethal. And yet I would render a deeply distorted picture of these connections if I were to argue that social relations are by proxy mutually benevolent or even harmonious. In her recent book, *Matters of Care: Speculative Ethics in More than Human Worlds*, author María Puig de la Bellacasa (2017: 78) brings this realization to a point:

> Relationality is all there is, but this does not mean a world without conflict or dissension. An ontology grounded in relationality and interdependence

needs to acknowledge not only... essential heterogeneity, but also that "cuts" create heterogeneity. For instance, attached and intense focus on an object of love also creates patterns of identity that reorder relations through excluding some. In other words, where there is relation, there has to be care, but our cares also perform disconnection.

The care of Uro's herder-hunters performed many cuts, and so did that of their animals and spirit masters. The traps, dens, nets, trails, fangs, corrals, blades, lassos, and hobbles that facilitated much interspecies communication also lent themselves to musical breaks or cuts.

SHARING THOUGHT IN THE ACT

Like other residents of the mountainous taiga, my friends in Oka rarely spoke while hunting sable or herding yak. Perhaps this was because speaking or thinking in nonambiguous terms is dangerous where the environment has access to spoken words and unspoken thoughts alike. It would potentially allow others the type of advantageous shortcuts that true shrewdness affords. More likely, sparseness of speech reflected the rich availability of nonspoken ways of thinking and communicating across species.

This observation finds parallel in the thinking of French philosopher François Laruelle, for whom "thought is not the intrinsic property of humans that must serve to define their essence, an essence that would then indeed be 'local'; it is a universal milieu" (Laruelle 2012: 340 quoted in Ó Maoilearca 2015: 34, 235). Certainly the ability of herders and their stock to share ideas would seem to support this assertion. Yet, for Laruelle, the animal's "possible utterance" of their part of this milieu "remains a fiction." John Ó Maoilearca—one of Laruelle's louder voices in the anglophone world—confirms this relegation to fiction by asking: "What is it to imagine—or posture—an animal philosophy?" (Ó Maoilearca 2015: 235). From the etho-ethnographic point of view that I have taken in this book, these questions strike one as odd. For the herders at Uro, it was not important to know the shape or color of an animal's philosophy. Philosophy came together as the result of a mutual doing—a doing of life, together.

The question then is not whether animals have a philosophy of their own, or whether people can possibly know such a philosophy beyond mere posturing or imagining. Instead, it is a question of whether the lifeworlds of diverse beings afford sufficient mutual intelligibility (call it imagination or fiction) to co-construct a useful assemblage. Explorations into material nexuses, such as Gell's (1996) traps, or even the roping mechanisms described in the context of horses, provide the physical interstices in which Uexküll's *Umwelten* of multiple species collide productively. Domestication relationships and their material implements can thus become sites of communicative interstices, whether or not the perceptive world of creatures can be known beyond one's own. If thought emerges in collective nonspoken acts, and if participation in such acts draws on multiple species, then we are dealing in multispecies thought.

John Ó Maoilearca uses the term "sympathetic imagination" to refer to "the fictional placing of oneself in another creature's place" (2015: 235). Sympathy seems an odd choice for a posthuman thinker trying to distance himself from anthropocentrism. But whether sympathetic or empathetic, Ó Maoilearca's human thinker merely imagines the thoughts of the animal thinker. His human thinker does not think together with the animal thinker. Donna Haraway has pointed out that animals (i.e., dogs) are not only "good to think with" but also to be "lived with" (Haraway 2003: 5). Is living with not also thinking with? Oka's wolves empathetically evade the humans they live among. Unlike Ó Maoilearca's human thinker who imagines the position of another, these wolves have entered the physical thinking spaces of others, including humans. They think through emplacement. A shrewd human hunter, like a wolf, engages the same tactics whereby the hunter not only imagines the thoughts of the other, but acts upon their mind as it is being lived out.

MOVING FORWARD

Writing about animal-human relations from the perspective of human households has been an eye-opening experience for me. It has challenged my thinking about anthropology in several ways. Primary among these has been a critical reassessment of the assumed supremacy of human reason. Not because I have found other reasoning to be more powerful, but because I can no longer envision our reasoning in a vacuum. The herders and hunters at Uro, some of whose experiences I have described in this book, introduced me to a communicative openness that actively engaged nonhuman beings in the making of thought and of life. I strongly suspect that their openness was in no way unique, and similar openness can be found around the world, including in my own backyard here in Western Canada.

Spending time with human and other persons in another place has helped me realize how intertwined our lives, our thoughts, and our histories as human and other creatures really are. I can no longer think of human history on its own. Perhaps, a history of life is more fitting. Anthropologist Eduardo Kohn has spoken of an "anthropology of life," which for him is concerned with our entanglements with other life forms (2007: 4); entanglements in which we are yet another constituent, and which include death (2007: 229). Anthropologist

Tobias Rees expresses a similar sentiment, suggesting an "anthropology of the actual." Such an anthropology immerses itself in the world to "find out if (some of) the categories that order our knowledge, that are constitutive of the human and/or the nonhuman as we know it, are breaking open, with the effect that the human and/or the nonhuman lose their coherence" (Rees 2018: 103). He calls such immersive observations "moments of irreducible openness" (Rees 2018: 103).

This takes me back to the introduction of this book and to the Western Canadian Arctic, where my Inuvialuit friends first introduced me to their relationship with caribou and reindeer. When the first reindeer from Alaska arrived at the Inuvialuit corrals of Kitigaaryuit on 6 March 1935 (North 1991: 259), they entered not a barren land but a complicated meshwork of species living along the shores of the Beaufort Sea. Mangilaluk, visionary first chief (*umialiq*, lit. sponsor of a whaling crew) of Tuktoyaktuk (Morrison 1997: 40), had accepted the government's request to bring the herd to the mouth of the Mackenzie River in an effort to alleviate the recent loss of caribou (Hart 2001: 21). Accepting reindeer, in that sense, was an act of openness. It was a willingness to experiment with a new variant of animal-human relationship within the broader context of small-scale fisheries and hunting of beluga pods, bowhead whales, seals, waterfowl, muskrats, and ptarmigan, as well as extensive trapping and trading activities.

By 1965, Mangilaluk's invitation had resulted in seventy men receiving training in reindeer herding techniques (Hart 2001: 13). Many of these herders and their families had not only opened up to experiment with a new way of relating to an introduced species, but also transferred their concept of relationships—rooted in a heritage of hunting—to this new way of living with rangifer. In an Inuit way of knowing, referred to in Nunavut as Inuit *Qaujimajatuqangit*, "the ultimate goal of becoming human is to be as capable as possible in every area of life, but to also know the importance of respectful relationships and to value reliance on and support for others," including nonhumans (Karetak and Tester 2017: 6). Such respect makes sense in light of Ann Fienup-Riordan's (1990: 168 quoted in Laugrand and Oosten 2016: 9) description of the Alaskan Inuit perspective in which "humans as well as animals possess awareness (*ella*), which allow individuals a sense of control over their destiny."

I wonder what greater openness toward a more unbounded humanity/animality will mean for the future of our shared earth. Will the failures of anthropocentrism eventually lead us to embrace a stronger interspecies perspective? Will greater awareness of the co-constitution of thought, of common and intertwined histories, change animal-human relations? What will it mean to care? And when I say care, I have in mind "everything that we do to maintain, continue and repair 'our world' ... [that] which we seek to interweave in a complex, life sustaining web" (Tronto 1993: 103 quoted in Puig de la Bellacasa 2017: 69). How then would a renewed ethic of care reconfigure existing and future animal-human relations? If I have learned anything from my Soiot herder-hunter friends, it is that our relations with others will be sustainable only as long as they remain mutually negotiable.

REFERENCES

AAMO — Arkhiv Administratsii Munitsipal'novo Obrazovania "Okinskii Rai'on" [Administrative Archive of the Municipal Formation "Okinskii District"].
AAMO. 1995 38-1-183: 1-9. Organizatsionno-Plemenennaia Rabota v Olenevodstve v Kolkhoze 50 Let Oktiabria na 1995-2000gg. Vedenie/Spravka. [Organizational and Breeding Work in Reindeer Husbandry at the '50 Years of October' Kolkhoz for the Period 1995–2000. Management/Reference.]
_____. 1931 1-1-11: 21. Plany, Zadania po Dokhodam Kolkhoznikov Khoshunia za 1931 god. [Plans and Income Objectives for Kolkhozes of the Khoshun (district) for the year 1931.]
_____. 1962 2-1-165: 1. Postanovlenie Biuro RK KPSS Aimispolkoma. [Decree from the Office of the RK KPSS Regional Executive Committee.]
Alekseenko, E. A. 1980. "Ketskaia Problema" [The Ket question], In *Etnogenez Narodov Severa* [Ethnogenesis of the Northern Peoples], ed. S. I. Gurvich. Moscow: Nauka.
Anderson, D. G. 2002. *Identity and Ecology in Arctic Siberia: The Number One Reindeer Brigade*. Oxford: Oxford University Press.
Anderson, D. G., K. S. Kvie, V. N. Davydov, and K. H. Røed. 2017. "Maintaining Genetic Integrity of Coexisting Wild and Domestic Populations: Genetic Differentiation between Wild and Domestic Rangifer with Long Traditions of Intentional Interbreeding." *Ecology and Evolution* 7(17): 6790–802.
Aronsson, K. A. 1991. "Forest Reindeer Herding AD 1–1800: An Archaeological and Palaeoecological Study in Northern Sweden." Ph.D. dissertation. University of Umeå.
Ayusheeva, A. D. 2010. "The Ecological Traditions of Soyots." In *Ecology, Spiritual, Social and Economic Perspectives for the Development of the Baikal Region, The Second Samaev Readings: The Readings of the International Scientific and Practical Conference Dedicated to the Memory of Lama-Gelong Dazan-Khaybzun Samaev*, 308–12. Ulan-Ude: The Publishing House of RB MPH RCME SHI.
Badmaev, S. G. 2007. "Ekologo-Etologicheskie Osobennosti Iaka v Vostochnom Saiane." Ph.D. dissertation. Ulan-Ude: Buriat State University.
Bagirov, V. A., E. A. Gladyr', L. K. Ernst, P. M. Klenovitskii, N. A. Zinov'eva, and Sh. N. Nasibov. 2009. "Sokhranenie i Ratsional'noe Ispol'zovanie Geneticheskikh

Resursov Iaka (Bos mutus)" [Preservation and efficient use of genetic resources of yak]. *Sel'skokhoziaistvennaia Biologiia* (2): 37–42.

Baldaev, F. 2001. "Legenda o Iakakh" [Legend of the yak], trans. K.D. Tuluev. *Akha Newspaper*, P2.

Batomunkueva, S. R. 2011. "Traditsiia Pochitaniia Gor v Buriatii" [The Mountain Veneration Tradition in Buriatia]. In *Istoricheskii Opyt Vzaimodeistviia Narodov i Tsivilizatsii (Sbornik Nauchnykh Statei)* [Historical experience of the interaction between peoples and civilizations (An anthology of scientific essays)], ed. B. V. Bazarov, 156–9. Ulan-Ude: Pravitel'stvo RB.

Bellacasa, M. P. 2017. *Matters of Care: Speculative Ethics in More than Human Worlds*. Minneapolis: University of Minnesota Press.

Bellezza, J. V. 2017. "The Swastika, Stepped Shrine, Priest, Horned Eagle, and Wild Yak Rider—Prominent Antecedents of Yungdrung Bon Figurative and Symbolic Traditions in the Rock Art of Upper Tibet." *Revue d'Etudes Tibétaines* 42: 5–38.

Bichurin, N. I. 1950. *Sobranie Svedenii o Narodakh, Obitavshikh v Srednei Azii v Drevnie Vremena* [A collection of data on the peoples inhabiting Central Asia in ancient times]. Moscow: Nauka.

Bird-David, N. 1999. "'Animism' Revisited: Personhood, Environment, and Relational Epistemology." *Current Anthropology* 40: 67–91.

Boyd, L. E., D. A. Carbonaro, and K. A. Houpt. 1988. "The 24-Hour Time Budget of Prewalski Horses." *Applied Animal Behavior Science* 21: 5–17.

Broz, L. 2007. "Pastoral Perspectivism: A View from Altai." *Inner Asia* 9(2): 291–310.

Budiansky, S. 1992. *The Covenant of the Wild: Why Animals Chose Domestication*. London: Yale University Press.

Burla, J.-B., A. Ostertag, A. Patt, I. Bachmann, and E. Hillmann. 2016. "Effects of Feeding Management and Group Composition on Agonistic Behavior of Group-Housed Horses." *Applied Animal Behavior Science* 176: 32–42.

Cambridge Advanced Learner's Dictionary. 2008. Cambridge: Cambridge University Press.

Carruthers, D. 1914. *Unknown Mongolia: A Record of Travel and Exploration in Northwest Mongolia and Dzungaria* (Vols. 1 and 2). London: Hutchinson & Company.

Cassidy, R. 2007. "Introduction: Domestication Reconsidered." In *Where the Wild Things Are Now: Domestication Reconsidered*, ed. M. H. Mullin and R. Cassidy, 1–25. Oxford: Berg.

Castren, M. A. 1856. *Reiseberichte und Briefe aus den Jahren 1845–1849*. Saint Petersburg: Anton Schiefner.

Charleux, I. 2002. "Padmasambhava's Travel to the North: The Pilgrimage to the Monastery of the Caves and the Old Schools of Tibetan Buddhism in Mongolia." *Central Asiatic Journal* 46(2): 168–232.

Charlier, B. 2012. "Two Temporalities of the Mongolian Wolf Hunter." In *Space and Time in Languages and Cultures: Language, Culture, and Cognition*, ed. L. Filipova and K. M. Jaszczolt, 121–42. Amsterdam: John Benjamins Publishing.

———. 2015. *Faces of the Wolf: Managing the Human, Non-Human Boundary in Mongolia*. Leiden: Brill.

Cherkasov, A. 1867. *Zapiski Okhotnika Vostochnoi Sibiri (1856–1863)* [Records of an Eastern Siberian hunter (1856–1863)]. Saint Petersburg: Izdanie Knigoprodavtsa S. V. Zvonareva.
Chernetsov, V. N. 1973. "Etnokul'turnye Arealy v Lesnoi i Subarkticheskoi Zonakh Evrazii v Epokhu Neolita" [Ethno-cultural areals in forested and subarctic zones of Eurasia in the Neolithic Era]. In *Problemy Archaeologii Urala i Sibiri* [Case studies in the archaeology of the Urals and Siberia], 10–17. Moscow: Nauka.
Childe, V. G. 1958. *The Prehistory of European Society*. Nottingham: Spokesman Books.
Chysyma, R. B., and B. K. Kan-ool. 2016. "Osobennosti Ekster'era Iakov Selektsionnogo Stada" [The features of yaks of selection herd exterior]. *Vestnik Krasnoiarskogo Gosudarstvennogo Agrarnogo Universiteta* 12: 64–8.
Clutton-Brock, J. 1989. *The Walking Larder: Patterns of Domestication, Pastoralism, and Predation*. London: Routledge.
Cohen, R. S. 1989. "Naga, Yaksini, Buddha: Local Deities and Local Buddhism at Ajanta." *History of Religions* 37(4): 360–400.
Conaty, G. T., and L. Binder. 2003. *The Reindeer Herders of the Mackenzie Delta*. Toronto: Key Porter Books.
Cooper, K. F. 2007. "Closely Watched Households: Visibility, Exposure and Private Power in the Roman Domus." *Past & Present* (197): 3–33.
Cronin, M. A., J. C. Patton, N. Balmysheva, and M. D. MacNeil. 2003. "Genetic Variation in Caribou and Reindeer (Rangifer Tarandus)." *Animal Genetics* 34(1): 33–41.
Dashibalov, B. B. 2000. "Iz Proshlogo Okinskogo Kraia: O Drevnostiakh Oki" [From the past of the Oka region: About Oka's antiquities]. In *Krai Podnebesnykh Dolin* [Valleys in high places], 4–6. Ulan-Ude: Resp. Tipografiia.
Dashieva, N. B. 2013. "Kuznechnyi Kel't Buriat: Istoriko-Kul'turnye Istoki" [The Blacksmith's Cult of Buriats: Historical and Cultural Roots]. *Vestnik Vostochno-Sibirskoi Gosudarstvennoi Akademii Kul'tury i Iskustv* 1(4): 7–18.
Deleuze, G. and F. Guattari. 2012. *A Thousand Plateaus*. London: Bloomsbury.
Dimitriev, N. G., and L. K. Ernst, eds. 1989. *Animal Genetic Resources of the USSR, FAO Animal Production and Health Paper*. Rome: Food and Agriculture Organization of the United Nations.
Donahoe, B. 2003. "A Line in the Sayans: History and Divergent Perceptions of Property among the Tozhu and Tofa of South Siberia." Ph.D. dissertation. Bloomington: Indiana University.
_____. 2012. "'Trust' or 'Domination'? Divergent Perceptions of Property in Animals among the Tozhu and the Tofa of South Siberia." In *Who Owns the Stock? Collective and Multiple Property Rights in Animals*, ed. by A. M. Khazanov and G. Schlee, 99–120. New York: Berghahn Books.
Dong, S. K., and D. Pariya. 2009. "Indigenous Yak and Yak-Cattle Crossbreed Management in High Altitude Areas of Northern Nepal: A Case Study from Rasuwa District." *African Journal of Agricultural Research* 4(10): 957–67.
Drompp, M. R. 2011. "The Lone Wolf in Inner Asia." *Journal of the American Oriental Society* 131(4): 515–26.
Dugarov, B. S. 1983. "O Proiskhozhdenii Okinskikh Buriat" [About the Origins of Oka-Buriats]. In *Etnicheskie i Istoriko-Kul'turnye Sviazi Mongol'skikh Narodov* [Ethnic and

historical cultural connections of Mongolian peoples], 90–101. Ulan-Ude: Buriatskii Institut Obshestvennykh Nauk.

Dumont, L. 1970. *Homo Hierarchicus: The Caste System and Its Implications*. Chicago: University of Chicago Press.

Elverskog, J. 2003. "Excerpt from the Jewel Translucent Sutra: Altan Khan and the Mongols in the Sixteenth Century." In *The History of Mongolia (vol. 3)*, 527–37. Leiden: Brill.

Endres, J. 2015. *Rentierhalter: Jäger. Wilderer? Praxis, Wandel und Verwundbarkeit bei den Dukha und den Tozhu im Mongolisch-Russischen Grenzraum*. Stuttgart: Franz Steiner Verlag.

Even, M.-D. 1991. "The Shamanism of the Mongols." In *Mongolia Today*, ed. S. Akiner, 183–205. London: Kegan Paul International.

Ferret, C. 2014. "Towards an Anthropology of Action: From Pastoral Techniques to Modes of Action." *Journal of Material Culture* 19(3): 279–302.

Fijn, N. 2011. *Living with Herds: Human-Animal Coexistence in Mongolia*. Cambridge: Cambridge University Press.

———. 2015. "The Domestic and the Wild in the Mongolian Horse and the Takhi." In *Taxonomic Tapestries: The Threads of Evolutionary*, ed. A. M. Behie and M. F. Oxenham, 279–98. Acton: ANU Press.

Finley, M. I. 1973. *The Ancient Economy*. Berkeley: University of California Press.

Fitzhugh, W. W. 2009. "Stone Shamans and Flying Deer of Northern Mongolia: Deer Goddess of Siberia or Chimera of the Steppe?" *Arctic Anthropology* 46(1/2):72–88.

———. 2017. "Mongolian Deer Stones, European Menhirs, and Canadian Arctic Inuksuit: Collective Memory and the Function of Northern Monument Traditions." *Journal of Archaeological Method and Theory* 24: 149–87.

Fowler, C. 2016. "Relational Personhood Revisited." *Cambridge Archaeological Journal* 26(3): 397–412.

Fraser, R. 2010. "Forced Relocation amongst the Reindeer-Evenki of Inner Mongolia." *Inner Asia* 12: 317–45.

Frolov, A. N., O. A. Zav'ialov, and A. V. Kharlamov. 2018. "Produktivnye Kachestva Bykov Simmental'skoi Porody Razlichnykh Genotipov [Productive Qualities of Simmental Breed Bulls of Diverse Genotype]." In *Puti Realizatsii Federal'noi Nauchno-Tekhnicheskoi Programmy Razvitiia Sel'skogo Khoziaistva na 2017–2025 gody* [Pathways to the Realization of a Federal Scientific Technical Program of Agricultural Development for 2017–2025], 732–36. Orenburg: Federal State Budgetary Scientific Institution, Federal Research Center for Biological Systems and Agro-Technologies Russian Academy of Sciences.

Galdanova, G. R. 2000. "Okinskii Krai: Istoria, Obychai i Traditsii (po Polevym Materialam)" [The Oka Region: History, practices and traditions (based on field materials)]. In *Krai Podnebesnykh Dolin* [Valleys in high places], 17–41. Ulan-Ude: Respublikanskaia Tipografiia.

———. 2009. "Serge v Traditsionnoi Kul'ture Buriat [The *serge* in the traditional culture of the Buriat]." *Tal'tsy* 2(33): 47–55.

Gaunitz, C., A. Fages, K. Hanghøj, A. Albrechtsen, N. Khan, M. Schubert, A. Seguin-Orlando, et al. 2018. "Ancient Genomes Revisit the Ancestry of Domestic and Przewalski's Horses." *Science* 360(6384):111–114.

Gell, A. 1996. "Vogel's Net: Traps as Artworks and Artworks as Traps." *Journal of Material Culture* 1(1): 15–38.
Gomboev, V. T. 2002. "Pochitanie Dukhov Gor u Okinskikh Buriat [Mountain spirit veneration among Oka-Buriats]." *Etnograficheskoe Obozrenie* 2: 69–77.
Gregory, C. A. 1997. *Savage Money: The Anthropology and Politics of Commodity Exchange*. Amsterdam: OPA.
Grøn, O. 2011. "Reindeer Antler Trimming in Modern Large-Scale Reindeer Pastoralism and Parallels in an Early Type of Hunter-Gatherer Reindeer Herding System: Evenk Ethnoarchaeology in Siberia." *Quaternary International* (238): 76–82.
Guo, S., P. Savolainen, J. Su, Q. Zhang, D. Qi, J. Zhou, Y. Zhong, X. Zhao, and J. Liu. 2006. "Origin of Mitochondrial DNA Diversity of Domestic Yaks." *BMC Evolutionary Biology* 6(1): 73.
Hahn, E. 1896. *Die Haustiere und ihre Beziehungen zur Wirtschaft des Menschen*. Leipzig: Drucker & Humbolt.
Hallowell, A. I. [1960] 2002. "Ojibwa Ontology, Behavior, and World View." *Readings in Indigenous Religions* 22: 17–49.
Hansell, M. 2005. *Animal Architecture*. Oxford: Oxford University Press.
Haraway, D. 2003. *The Companion Species Manifesto: Dogs, People and Significant Otherness*. Chicago: Prickly Paradigm Press.
Harvey, G. 2006. "Animals, Animists, and Academic." *Zygon* 41(1): 9–19.
Hart, E. J. 2001. *Reindeer Days Remembered*. Inuvik: Inuvialuit Cultural Resource Centre.
Hatt, G. 1918. "Rensdyrnomadismens Elementer." *Geografisk Tidsskrift* 24: 241–69.
Heissig, W. 1953. "A Mongolian Source to the Lamaist Suppression of Shamanism in the 17th Century," *Anthropos* 48(1/2): 1–29.
_____, W. 2004. "The Lamaist Suppression of Shamanism." In *Shamanism: Critical Concepts in Sociology* (vols 1–3), ed. A. A. Znamenski, 1:227–44. London: Routledge.
Henze, D., and P. S. Pallas. 1967. "Vorwort." In *Reise Durch die Verschiedenen Provinzen des Russischen Reichs*, iii–xv. Graz: Akademische Druck- und Verlagsanstalt.
Higgs, E., and M. Jarman. 1969. "The Origins of Agriculture: A Reconsideration." *Antiquity* 43(169): 31–41.
Humphrey, C. 1995. "Chiefly and Shamanist Landscapes in Mongolia." In *The Anthropology of Landscape: Perspectives on Place and Space*, ed. E. Hirsch and M. O'Hanlon, 135–162. London: Routledge.
Ingold, T. 1974. "On Reindeer and Men." *Man* 9(4): 523–38.
_____. 1980. *Hunters, Pastoralists and Ranchers: Reindeer Economies and Their Transformations*. Cambridge: Cambridge University Press.
_____. 1987. *The Appropriation of Nature: Essays on Human Ecology and Social Relations*. Iowa City: University of Iowa Press.
_____. 2000. *The Perception of the Environment: Essays on Livelihood, Dwelling and Skill*. London: Routledge.
_____. 2011. *Being Alive: Essays on Movement, Knowledge and Description*. London: Routledge.
_____. 2013. "Anthropology beyond Humanity." *Suomen Anthropologi: Journal of the Finish Anthropological Society* 38(3): 5–23.
_____. 2015. "From the Master's Point of View: Hunting *is* Sacrifice." *Journal of the Royal Anthropological Institute* 21(1): 24–27.

———. 2017. "On Human Correspondence." *Journal of the Royal Anthropological Institute* 23(1): 9–27.
Isaac, E. 1970. *Geography of Domestication*. Englewood Cliffs: Prentice Hall.
Jacobsen, E. 1993. *The Deer Goddess of Ancient Siberia: A Study in the Ecology of Belief*. Leiden: Brill.
———. 2001. "Cultural Riddles: Stylized Deer and Deer Stones of the Mongolian Altai." *Bulletin of the Asia Institute* 15: 31–56.
———. 2015. *The Hunter, the Stag, and the Mother of Animals: Image, Monument, and Landscape in Ancient North Asia*. Oxford: Oxford University Press.
Jones, D. E. 2007. *Poison Arrows: North American Indian Hunting and Warfare*. Austin: University of Texas Press.
Kalinina, I. V. 2000. *Pravoslavnye Khramy Irkutskoi Eparkhii: 17 – Nachalo 20 Veka* [Russian Orthodox sanctuaries of the Irkutsk diocese: 17. to early 20. centuries]. Moscow: Galart.
Karetak, J., and F. Tester. 2017. "Introduction: Inuit Qaujimajatuqangit, Truth and Reconciliation." In *Inuit Qaujimajatuqangit: What Inuit Have Always Known to Be True*, ed. J. Karetak, F. Tester, and S. Tagalik, 1–19. Halifax: Fernwood Publishing.
Keay, M. G. 2006. "The Tsaatan Reindeer Herders of Mongolia: Forgotten Lessons of Human-Animal Systems." In *Encyclopedia of Animals and Humans*, 1–4. Retrieved 1 November 2019 from http://library.arcticportal.org/437/1/tsaatan_reindeer_herders.pdf.
Kertselli, S. V. 1925. "Karagasskii Olen' i Ego Khoziaistvennoe Znachenie [The Karagass reindeer and its economic importance]." *Severnaia Azia* 3: 87–92.
Khimitdorzhiev, Sh. B., and Ts. P. Vanchikova, ed. 2011. *Buriatskie Letopisi* [The Buriat chronicles]. Ulan-Ude: Respublikanskaia Tipografia.
Kol, N., and O. Lazebny. 2006. "Polymorphism of ISSR-PCR Markers in Tuvinian Population of Reindeer Rangifer Tarandus L." *Russian Journal of Genetics* 42(12): 1464–66.
Kon, F. I. 1934 [1913]. *Ekspeditsiia v Soiotiiu* [Expedition into Soiotiia], *Za Piat'desiat Let: Sobranie Sochinenii* [After Fifty Years: A Collection of Writings]. Moscow: Izd-vo Vsesoiuznogo Obshchestva Politkatorzhan i Ssyl'no-poselentsev.
Kohn, E. 2007. "How Dogs Dream: Amazonian Natures and the Politics of Transspecies Engagement." *American Ethnologist* 34(1):3–24.
Kosarev, M. F. 1991. *Drevniaia Istoriia Zapadnoi Sibirii: Chelovek i Prirodnaia Sreda* [Ancient history of Western Siberia: Humans and the natural environment]. Moscow: Nauka.
Kramer, F. L. 1967. "Eduard Hahn and the End of the 'Three Stages of Man.'" *Geographical Review* 57(1): 73–89.
Kropotkin, P. A. 1867. "Poezdka v Okinskii Karaul" [Voyage to the Oka Fore-Post]. *Zapiski Sibirskogo Otd. Russkogo Geograficheskogo Ob-Va*. 9: n.p. Irkutsk: IRGO.
Küçüküstel, S. 2018. "Living with Reindeer and Hunting among Spirits: The Dukha of South Siberia." Ph.D. dissertation. Berlin: Humboldt University.
Kyzlasov, L. R. 1969. *Istoriia Tuvy* [The history of Tuva]. Moscow: Nauka.
Laufer, B. 1916. "Burkhan." *Journal of the American Oriental Society* 36 (1916): 390–95.
———. 1917. "The Reindeer and Its Domestication." *Memoirs of the American Anthropological Association* 4(2): 91–147.

Laugrand, F., and J. Oosten. 2016. *Hunters, Predators and Prey: Inuit Perceptions of Animals.* New York: Berghahn Books.
Laurelle, F. 2012. *From Decision to Heresy: Experiments in Non-standard Thought.* Falmouth: Urbanomic.
Leach, H. M. 2007. "Selection and Unforeseen Consequences of Domestication." In *Where the Wild Things Are Now: Domestication Reconsidered,* ed. R. Cassidy and M. Mullin, 71–100. Oxford: Berg.
Leslie, D. M., and G. B. Schaller. 2009. "Bos Grunniens and Bos Mutus (Artiodactyla: Bovidae)." *Mammalian Species* (836): 1–17.
Lestel, D. 2002. "The Biosemiotics and Phylogenesis of Culture." *Social Science Information* 41(1): 35–68.
Lien, M. E., H. A. Swanson, and G. B. Ween. 2018. "Introduction: Naming the Beast—Exploring the Otherwise." *Domestication Gone Wild: Politics and Practices of Multispecies Relations,* ed. H. A. Swanson, M. E. Lien, G. B. Ween, 1–30. Durham, NC: Duke University Press.
Lkhagvasuren, I. 2012. *Altaiskie Uriankhaitsy: Istoriko-Etnograficheskoe Issledovanie Konets 19.- Nachalo 20. Veka* [Uriankhai Altaians: Ethnohistorical Research from the late 19th to the early 20th centuries], Senri Ethnological Reports. Osaka: National Museum of Ethnology.
Mannen, H., M. Kohno, Y. Nagata, S. Tsuji, D. G. Bradley, J. S. Yeo, D. Nyamsamba, et al. 2004. "Independent Mitochondrial Origin and Historical Genetic Differentiation in North Eastern Asian Cattle." *Molecular Phylogenetics and Evolution* 32: 539–44.
Maksimov, A. N. 2019 [1928]. "Proiskhozhdenie Olenevodstva" [The origin of reindeer herding]. In *Etnograficheskie Trudy: Izbrannoe.* [Ethnographic labors: Selected writings], by A. N. Maksimov, 200–29. Moscow: Iurait.
Ma, L., R. Gu, L. Tang, Z.-E. Chen, R. Di, and C. Long. 2015. "Important Poisonous Plants in Tibetan Ethnomedicine." *Toxins* 7(1): 138–55.
Manning, E., and B. Massumi. 2014. *Thought in the Act: Passages in the Ecology of Experience.* Minneapolis: University of Minnesota Press.
Mansheev, D. M. 2005. "Skotovody Vostochnogo Prisaiania v kontse 19 nachale 20 Veka" [Herders of the Eastern Pre-Saian between the late 19th and early 20th centuries]. *Vestnik Evrazii* (3): 71–88.
Marchina, C. 2015. "Faire communauté: Étude Anthropologique des Relations Entre Les éleveurs et Leurs Animaux Chez Les Peuples Mongols (d'après L'exemple Des Halh de Mongolie et Des Bouriates d'Aga, Russie)." Ph.D. dissertation. Paris: Institut National des Langues et Civilisations Orientales.
———. 2016. "'Follow the Horse': The Complexities of Collaboration Between the Lasso-pole Horse (*uurgach mor'*) and His Rider among Mongolian Horse Herders." In *The Meaning of Horses,* ed. D. Davis and A. Maurstad, 116–28. London: Routledge.
Mashkovtsev, A. A. 1940. "Saianskii Dikii Reliktovyi Severnyi Olen" [The Saian's wild relict reindeer]. *Doklady AN SSSR* 27(1): 78–80.
Mel'nikova, L. V. 1994. *Tofy: Istoriko-Etnograficheskii Ocherk* [Tofas: An ethnohistorical sketch]. Irkutsk: Vostochno-Sibirskoe Knizhnoe Izd-vo.
Miller, M. 1935. *The Great Trek.* Garden City, NJ: Double Day, Doran & Company Inc.
Mirov, N. T. 1945. "Notes on the Domestication of Reindeer." *American Anthropologist* 47(3): 393–408.

Mitypova, G. S. 2005. *Pravoslavie v Istorii i Kul'ture Buriatii* [Russian Orthodoxy in the History and Culture of Buriatia]. Ulan-Ude: Respublikanskaia Tipografia.

Morrison, D. 1997. "An Ethnohistory of the Inuvialuit from Earliest Times to 1902." *Revista de Arqueología*, 12: 29–54.

Mulk, I. M. 1994. "Sirkas — Ett Samiskt Fångstsamhålle i Förändring." Ph.D. dissertation. University of Umeå.

Mumford, S. R. 1989. *Himalayan Dialogue: Tibetan Lamas and Gurung Shamans in Nepal.* Madison: University of Wisconsin Press.

Myka, J. L., T. L. Lear, M. L. Houck, O. A. Ryder, and E. Bailey. 2003. "FISH Analysis Comparing Genome Organization in the Domestic Horse (Equus Caballus) and the Mongolian Wild Horse (E Przewalskii)." *Cytogenet Genome Res* (102): 222–25.

Nadasdy, P. 2007. "The Gift in the Animal: The Ontology of Hunting and Human–Animal Sociality." *American Ethnologist* 34(1): 25–43.

Nantsov, G.-D. T. 1998. *Materialy po Lamaizmu v Buriatii* [Materials on Lamaism in Buriatia]. Ulan-Ude: Institut Mongolovedeniia, Buddologii i Tibetologii SO RAN.

Nasatuev, B., B. Budazhanayev, and T. Khabiryanova. 2015. "Introduktsiia Iakov v Nizinnyi Eravninskii Raion iz Vysokogornogo Okinskogo Raiona Buriatii" [Introduction of yaks to lowland Evravinskii District from mountainous Okinskii District of Buryatia]. *Vestnik Buriatskoi Gosudarstvennoi Sel'skokhoziastvennoi Akademii* [Herald of the Buriat State Agricultural Academy] (2): 138–40.

Nefedev, E., and E. Gerasov. 1929. "Okinskie Soioty" [Oka Soiots]. *Zhizn Buriatii* [Life of Buriatia] 6: 38–43.

North, D. 1991. *Arctic Exodus: The Last Great Trail Drive.* Toronto: Macmillian of Canada.

O'Connor, T. P. 1997. "Working at Relationships: Another Look at Animal Domestication." *Antiquity* 71(271): 149–56.

Oehler, A. 2018a. "Hunters in Their Own Right: Perspectival Sharing in Soiot Hunters and Their Dogs." In *Dogs in the North: Stories of Cooperation and Co-Domestication*, ed. R. J. Losey, R. P. Wishart, J. P. L. Loovers, 40–56. London: Routledge.

———. 2018b. "Social Memory and Oka-Soiot Reindeer Herders: On the Challenges of Reindeer in Multi-Species Mountain Households." *Journal of Ancient Technology Laboratory* 14(3): 112–23.

Olsen, Ø. 1915a. *Et Primitivt Folk: De Mongolske Rennomader* [A Primitive People: The Mongolian Reindeer Nomads]. Oslo: Cappeln.

———. 1921. *Los Soyotos: Nomadas Pastores de Renos.* Madrid: Calpe.

Olsen, S. J. 1990. "Fossil Ancestry of the Yak, Its Cultural Significance and Domestication in Tibet." *Proceedings of the Academy of Natural Sciences of Philadelphia* 142: 73–100.

Ó Maoilearca, J. 2015. *All Thoughts Are Equal: Laruelle and Nonhuman Philosophy.* Minneapolis: University of Minnesota Press.

Ortner, S. B. 1978a. *Sherpas through Their Rituals.* Cambridge: Cambridge University Press.

———. 1978b. "The White-Black Ones: The Sherpa View of Human Nature." In *Himalayan Anthropology: The Indo-Tibetan Interface*, ed. J. F. Fisher, 263–86. The Hague: Mouton Publishers.

Oyun, N. Yu, E. A. Konorov, A. V. Urum, I. V. Artyushin, G. R. Svishcheva, C. Cendsuren, and Yu A. Stolpovsky. 2018. "Study of Genetic Diversity and Population Structure of the Yak (Bos Grunniens) in the Sayan-Altai Region." *Russian Journal of Genetics* 54(10): 1210–20.

Pavlinskaia, L. R. 2002. *Kochevniki Golubykh Gor* [Nomads of the Blue Mountains]. Saint Petersburg: Evropeiskii Dom.
Pedersen, M. A. 2003. "Tame from Within: Landscapes of the Religious Imagination among the Darkhads of Northern Mongolia." In *The Mongolia-Tibet Interface*, ed. U. E. Bulag and H. G. M. Diemberger, 175–96. Leiden: Brill.
Petri, B. E. 1927a. *Etnograficheskie Issledovaniia Sredi Malykh Narodov v Vostochnykh Saianakh: Predvoritel'nye Dannye* [Ethnographic research among the small numbered peoples of the Eastern Saians]. Irkutsk: Izdanie Irkutskovo Universiteta.
_____. 1927b. *Olenevodstvo u Karagas* [Reindeer herding among the Karagas]. Irkutsk: Izdanie Irkutskovo Universiteta.
_____. 1928. *Promysli Karagas* [Subsistence strategies of the Karagas]. Irkutsk: Izdanie Irkutskovo Universiteta.
_____. [1928] 2014. "Staraia Vera Buriatskogo Naroda" [The Old Faith of the Buriat People]. In *Vselennaia Sibirskogo Shamana – Istoria, Legendy, Obriady* [The Siberian shaman's universe: History, legends, rituals], ed. unknown, 58–135. Irkutsk: Irkutskii Oblastnoi Kraevecheskii Muzei.
Phillips, R. W., J. A. Tolstoy, and R. G. Johnson. 1946. "Yaks and Yak-Cattle Hybrids in Asia." *Journal of Heredity* 37(7): 207–15.
Pollan, M. 2002. *The Botany of Desire: A Plant's-Eye View of the World*. London: Bloomsbury Publishing.
Pomishin, S. B. 1971. "O Transportnom Ispol'zovanii Olenia Tofalarami [About the transport use of reindeer by Tofalars]." *Sovietskaia Etnografiia* 5: 128–31.
Potapov, L. P. 1929. "Okhotnich'i Pover'ia i Obriady u Altaiskikh Turkov' [Hunters' beliefs and rituals among Altaian Turks]." *Kul'tura i Pis'mennost' Vostoka* [Culture and literature of the East] 5: 123–49.
Prytkova, N. F. 1970. "Odezhda Narodov Samodiiskoi Gruppy kak Istoricheskii Istochnik" [Clothing of the peoples belonging to the Samoed group as a historical source]. In *Odezhda Narodov Sibirii* [Clothing of the peoples of Siberia], ed. S. V. Ivanov, 3–99. Leningrad: Nauka.
Qiu, Q., L. Wang, K. Wang, Y. Yang, T. Ma, Z. Wang, X. Zhang, Z. Ni, F. Hou, R. Long, and R. Abbott. 2015. "Yak Whole-Genome Resequencing Reveals Domestication Signatures and Prehistoric Population Expansions." *Nature Communications* 6: 10,283.
Radde, G. 1863. *Reisen im Süden von Ost-Sibirien in den Jahren 1855–1859* (vol. 2). Saint Petersburg: Kaiserliche Geographische Gesellschaft.
_____. 1865. "Extrait de L'ouvrage Intitule Notices Contribuant a La Connaissance de L'empire de Russie." In *Graphite de Siberie*, ed. M. J.-P. Alibert, 51–61. Paris: Imprimerie Poitevin.
Ragagnin, E. 2011. *Dukhan, a Turkic Variety of Northern Mongolia: Description and Analysis*. Wiesbaden: Harrassowitz Verlag.
Ransom, J. I., and B. S. Cade. 2009. "Quantifying Equid Behavior: A Research Ethogram for Free-Roaming Feral Horses." Paper 26. Publications of the US Geological Survey.
Rassadin, I. V. 1999. "Ob Olenevodstve u Okinskikh Soiotov [About the reindeer herding of Oka Soiots]." *Gumanitarnye Issledovaniia Molodykh Uchenykh Buriatii* 2(1): 23–28.
_____. 2005. *Khoziaistvo, Byt i Kul'tura Tofalarov* [Subsistence, way of life, and culture of Tofas]. Ulan-Ude: Izdatel'stvo BNTs SO RAN.

———. 2012. "O Kharaktere Olenevodstva u Okinskikh Soiotov" [On the particulars of Oka-Soiot reindeer breeding]. *Gumanitarnyi Vektor* 4(32): 214–17.

———. 2017. "Zhivotnovodstvo u Soiotov i Buriat: Sravnitel'no-Sopostavitel'nyi Analiz" [Animal husbandry among Soiots and Buriats: A comparative analysis]. *Gumanitarnyi Vektor* 12(4): 190–95.

Rassadin, V. I. 1971. *Fonetika i Leksika Tofalarskogo Iazyka* [Phonetics and lexicon of the Tofalar language]. Ulan-Ude: Buriatskoe Knizhnoe Izdatel'stvo.

———. 1996. "Zhivotnovodcheskaia Leksika v Iazyke Okinskikh Buriat i Soiotov [Animal terminology in the languages of Oka-Buriats and Oka-Soiots]." *Problemy Buriatskoi Dialektologii* [Topics in Buriat dialectology], eds. V. I. Rassadin, L. D. Shagdarov, and T. P. Bazhaeva, 45–57. Ulan-Ude: Russian Akademy of Sciences BNTs SO RAN.

———. 2000. "Osobennosti Traditsionnoi Material'noi Kul'tury Saianskikh Olenevodov-Tofalarov" [Particularities in the material culture of Tofalar reindeer herders]. *Etnologicheskie Issledovaniia* (1): 131–48.

———. 2003. *Soiotsko-Buriatsko-Russkii Slovar'* [Soiot-Buriat-Russian Dictionary]. Ulan-Ude: Respublikanskaia Tipografiia.

———. 2010. Soyotica. In *Studia Uralo-Altaica,* ed. V. I. Rassadin and B. Kempf. Szeged: University of Szeged.

———. 2012. *Iazyk Soiotov Buriatii* [The Language of the Soiots of Buriatiia]. Elista: Kalmyk University Press.

Rees, T. 2018. *After Ethnos.* Durham, NC: Duke University Press.

Rindos, D. 1984. *The Origins of Agriculture: An Evolutionary Perspective.* Cambridge, MA: Academic Press.

Rødven, R., I. Männikkö, R. A. Ims, N. G. Yoccoz, and I. Folstad. 2009. "Parasite Intensity and Fur Coloration in Reindeer Calves – Contrasting Artificial and Natural Selection." *Journal of Animal Ecology* 78(3): 600–7.

Røed, K. H., Ø. Flagstad, M. Nieminen, Ø. Holand, M. J. Dwyer, N. Røv, and C. Vila. 2008. "Genetic Analyses Reveal Independent Domestication Origins of Eurasian Reindeer." *Proceedings: Biological Sciences* 275(1645): 1849–55.

Røed, K. H., Ø. Flagstad, G. Bjørnstad, and A. K. Hufthammer. 2011. "Elucidating the Ancestry of Domestic Reindeer from Ancient DNA Approaches." *Quaternary International* 238(1–2): 83–88.

Rose, D. B. 1996. *Nourishing Terrains: Australian Aboriginal Views of Landscape and Wilderness.* Australian Heritage Commission.

Rudenko, S. I. 1953. *Kul'tura Naseleniia Gornogo Altaia v Skifskoe Vremia* [The culture of the mountainous Altai in Scythian times]. Moscow: Izd-vo Akademii Nauk SSSR.

———. 1970. *Frozen Tombs of Siberia: The Pazyryk Burials of Iron Age Horsemen,* trans. M. W. Thompson. Berkeley: University of California Press.

Saller, R. P. 1984. "Familia, Domus, and the Roman Conception of the Family." *Phoenix* 38(4): 336–55.

Savinov, D. G. 1994. *Olennye Kamni v Kul'ture Kochevnikov Evrazii* [Deer stones in the culture of Eurasian nomads]. Saint Petersburg: Press of Saint Petersburg State University.

Schrempf, M. 1999. "Taming the Earth, Controlling the Cosmos: Transformation of Space in Tibetan Buddhist and Bon-Po Ritual Dances." In *Sacred Spaces and Powerful Places in Tibetan Culture,* ed. T. Huber, 198–226. Dharamsala: Library of Tibetan Works and Archives.

Sharastepanov, D. T.-B. 2008. *Oka: Gody i Liudi* [Oka: Years and people]. Ulan-Ude: Respublikanskaia Tipografia.
Shi, Q., Y. Guo, S. C. Engelhardt, R. B. Weladji, Y. Zhou, M. Long, and X. Meng. 2016. "Endangered Wild Yak (*Bos Grunniens*) in the Tibetan Plateau and Adjacent Regions: Population Size, Distribution, Conservation Perspectives and its Relation to the Domestic Subspecies." *Journal for Nature Conservation* 32: 35–43.
Shirokogorov, S. M. 1966. *Social Organization of the Northern Tungus*. Oosterhout: Anthropological Publications.
Shirokogorova, E. N. 1919. "Severo-Zapadnaia Mandzhuriia (Geograficheskii Ocherk po Dannym Marshrutnykh Nabliudenii) [Northwestern Manchuria (A geographic study based on observations made en route)]." *Uchennye Zapiski Istoriko-Filologicheskogo Fakulteta vo Vladivostoke* [Scientific proceedings of the historical-philological faculty at Vladivostok] 1: 109–46.
Sirelius, U. T. 1916. "Über die Art und Zeit der Zähmung des Rentiers." *Journal de La Société Finno-Ougrienne* 33(2): n.p.
Sirina, A. 2003. "Bernard Eduardovich Petri." *Anthropology & Archaeology of Eurasia* 42(2): 71–93.
Skeat, W. W. 1993. "Domus." In *The Concise Dictionary of English Etymology*, ed. W. W. Skeat. Hertfordshire: Wordsworth Editions.
Smith, A. T., Y. Xie, R. S. Hoffmann, D. Lunde, J. MacKinnon, D. E. Wilson, W. C. Wozencraft. 2010. *A Guide to the Mammals of China*. Princeton University Press.
Sodnompilova, M. M. 2009. *Mir v Traditsionnom Mirovozzrenii i Prakticheskoi Deiatel'nosti Mongol'skikh Narodov* [The world according to the traditional worldview and practical activities of Mongolian peoples]. Ulan-Ude: Izdatel'stvo BNTs SO RAN.
Star, S. L. 1991. "Power, Technologies and the Phenomenology of Conventions." In *A Sociology of Monsters*, ed. J. Law, 26–56. London: Routledge.
Stépanoff, C. 2012. "Human-Animal 'Joint Commitment' in a Reindeer Herding System." *HAU: Journal of Ethnographic Theory* 2(2): 287–312.
Stépanoff, C., C. Marchina, C. Fossier, and N. Bureau. 2017. "Animal Autonomy and Intermittent Coexistences: North Asian Modes of Herding." *Current Anthropology* 58(1): 57–81.
Stepanova, E. V. 2006. "Evoliutsiia Konskogo Snariazheniia i Otnositel'naia Khronologiia Pamiatnikov Pazyrykskoi Kul'tury [Evolution of horse harnesses and relative chronology of the monuments of the Pazyryk culture]." *Arkheologicheskie Vesti*, 13:102–50.
Stevens, M. 2016. *Cheats and Deceits: How Animals and Plants Exploit and Mislead*. Oxford University Press.
Stevensen, A, and M. Waite (eds.). 2011. "Household." *Concise Oxford English Dictionary: Luxury Edition*. Oxford: Oxford University Press.
St-Louis, A., and S. D. Côté. 2012. "Foraging Behaviour at Multiple Temporal Scales in a Wild Alpine Equid." *Oecologia* 169(1): 167–76.
Storli, I. 1996. "On the Historiography of Sami Reindeer Pastoralism." *Acta Borealia* 13(1): 81–115.
Suchet, S. 2002. "'Totally Wild'? Colonising Discourses, Indigenous Knowledges and Managing Wildlife." *Australian Geographer* 33(2): 141–57.
Swancutt, K. 2007. "The Ontological Spiral: Virtuosity and Transparency in Mongolian Games." *Inner Asia* 9(2): 237–59.

Taishin, V. A. 2015. "Poroda Iaka Domashnego (*Poephagus Grunniens L*) Okinskaia [Yak bull (*Poephagus Grunniens L*) of Okinsky breed]." *International Journal of Applied and Fundamental Research* (1): 84–85.

Taishin, V. A., and V. V. Anganov. 2014. "O Nasledovanii Fenotipicheskikh Priznakov Docher'mi Bykov Iakov (*Poephagus Grunniens L*) Zhelatel'nogo Tipa Porody Okinskaia [On the inheritance of phenotypic traits by daughters of yak bulls (*Poephagus Grunniens L*) of desired type of Okinsky breed]." *International Journal of Applied and Fundamental Research* (9): 83–85.

Tashak, V. I., and D. V. Kobylkin. 2015. "Issledovanie Peshchery Gorome na Okinskom Plato [The exploration of the gerome cave on the Oka plateau]." *Vestnik Buriatskogo Nauchnogo Tsentra Sibirskogo Otdeleniia Rossiiskoi Akademii Nauk* (4): 11–19.

Terentyev, A. 1996. "Tibetan Buddhism in Russia." *The Tibet Journal* 21(3): 60–70.

Thomas, N., and C. Humphrey. 1996. *Shamanism, History, and the State*. Ann Arbor: University of Michigan Press.

Treude, E. 1975. "Forty Years of Reindeer Herding in the Mackenzie Delta, NWT." *Polarforschung* 45(2): 121–38.

Tronto, J. C. 1993. *Moral Boundaries: A Political Argument for an Ethic of Care*. London: Routledge.

Tsing, A. L. 2011. *Friction: An Ethnography of Global Connection*. Princeton, NJ: Princeton University Press.

———. 2015. *The Mushroom at the End of the World*. Princeton, NJ: Princeton University Press.

Tsybenov, B. D. 2001. "Rasprostranenie Buddizma sredi Khori-Buriat [The spread of Buddhism among Khori-Buriats]." In *Narody Buriatii v Sostave Rossii: Ot Protivostoianiia k Soglasiiu* [Peoples of Buriatia in the Russian Alliance: From resistance to agreement], ed. E. M. Egorov, 39–47. Ulan-Ude: Respublikanskaia Tipografia.

Tsyrempilov, N. V. 2013. *Buriatskaia Buddiiskaia Obshchina v Rossii (XVIII – nach. XXV.)* [The Buriat Buddhist community in Russia (from the 18th to the early 20th centuries)]. Ulan-Ude: Institut Mongolovedenia, Buddologii i Tibetologii SO RAN.

Turov, M. G., A. Weber, and K. Maryniak. 2010. *Evenki Economy in the Central Siberian Taiga at the Turn of the 20th Century: Principles of Land Use*. Northern Hunter-Gatherers Research Series. Edmonton: CCI Press.

Tylor, E. B. 1873. *Religion in Primitive Culture*. New York: Harper.

Tybykova, L. N. 2005. *Altai Morphological Dictionary*. Gorno-Altaisk: Gorno-Altaisk Publishing House.

Uexküll, J. [1934] 2010. *A Foray into the Worlds of Animals and Humans: With a Theory of Meaning*. Minneapolis: University of Minnesota Press.

Ulturgasheva, O. 2012. *Narrating the Future in Siberia: Childhood, Adolescence and Autobiography among Young Eveny*. New York: Berghahn Books.

United Nations. 1992. *UN Convention on Biological Diversity*. Retrieved 28 September 2019 from https://www.cbd.int/.

Våge, D. I., M. Nieminen, D. G. Anderson, and K. H. Røed. 2014. "Two Missense Mutations in Melanocortin 1 Receptor (MC1R) are Strongly Associated with Dark Ventral Coat Color in Reindeer (Rangifer Tarandus)." *Animal Genetics* 45(5): 750–53.

Vainshtein, S. I. 1960. "K Voprosu o Sayanskom Tipe Olenevodstva i Ego Vozniknovenii [On the Saian type of reindeer husbandry and its origin]." *Institut Etnografii. Kratkie Soobshcheniia* 34: 54–60.

———. 1961. *Tuvintsy Todzhintsy* [Tuvinian Tozhus]. Moscow: Izd-vo Vostochnoi Literatury.

———. 1968. "Rodovaia Struktura i Patronimicheskaia Organizatsia u Tofalarov (do nachala 20. Veka) [Descent structure and patronymic organization among Tofalars (until the early 20th century)]." *Diskussii i Obsuzhdeniia* 3: 60–67.

———. 1972. *Istoricheskaia Etnografia Tuvintsev: Problemy Kochevogo Khoziaistva* [Ethnohistory of Tuvans: problems of nomadic economy]. Moscow: Nauka.

———. 1980a. *Nomads of South Siberia: The Pastoral Economies of Tuva*, ed. C. Humphrey. Cambridge: Cambridge University Press.

———. 1980b. "Proizkhozhdenie Saianskikh Olenevodov: Problema Etnogeneza Tuvintsev-Todzhintsev i Tofalarov [The emergence of Saian reindeer herders: Issues in the ethnogenesis of Tuvinian-Todzhas and Tofalars]." In *Etnogenez Narodov Severa* [Ethnogenesis of the northern peoples]. Moscow: Nauka.

Vasilevich, G. M. 1964. *Tipy Olenevodstva u Tungusoiazychnykh Narodov* [Types of reindeer herding among Tungus-speaking peoples]. Moscow: Nauka.

Vasilevich, G. M., and M. G. Levin. 1951. "Tipy Olenevodstva i ikh Proiskhozhdenie [Types of reindeer breeding and their origin]." *Sovietskaia Etnografiia* 1: 63–87.

Vasilu, A. 2004. "Domination." In *Dictionary of Untranslatables: A Philosophical Lexicon*, ed. B. Cassin, E. Apter, J. Lezra, and M. Wood, 227. Princeton, NJ: Princeton University Press.

Vilà, C., J. A. Leonard, A. Götherström, S. Marklund, K. Sandberg, K. Lidén, R. K. Wayne, and H. Ellegren. 2001. "Widespread Origins of Domestic Horse Lineages." *Science* 291(5503): 474–77.

Virányi, Z., and F. Range. 2014. "On the Way to a Better Understanding of Dog Domestication: Aggression and Cooperativeness in Dogs and Wolves." In *The Social Dog: Behavior and Cognition*, ed. J. Kaminski and S. Marshall-Pescini, 35–64. San Diego: Academic Press.

Vitebsky, P. 2006. *The Reindeer People: Living with Animals and Spirits in Siberia*. Boston, MA: Houghton Mifflin Harcourt.

Viveiros de Castro, E. 1996. "Images of Nature and Society in Amazonian Ethnology." *Annual Review of Anthropology* 25: 179–200.

———. 1998. "Cosmological Deixis and Amerindian Perspectivism." *The Journal of the Royal Anthropological Institute* 4(3): 469–88.

Voujala-Magga, T., M. Turunen, T. Ryyppo, and M. Tennberg. 2011. "Resonance Strategies of Sámi Reindeer Herders in Northernmost Finland During Climatically Extreme Years." *Arctic* 64(2): 227–41.

Webster, N. 1913. "Domesticate." *Webster's Revised Unabridged Dictionary of the English Language*. London: G. Bell.

Weil, K. 2010. "A Report on the Animal Turn." *Differences* 21(2): 1–23.

Whitaker, I. 1981. "Tuvan Reindeer Husbandry in the Early 20th Century." *Polar Record* 20(127): 337–51.

Wiener, G., H. Jianlin, and L. Ruijun. 2003. *The Yak (2nd edn.)*. Bangkok: Food and Agriculture Organization of the United Nations.

Wiklund, K. B. 1918. "Om Renskotselns Uppkomst. [About the Origin of the Reindeer Herd]" *Ymer* 3: 249–73.

Willerslev, R. 2004. "Not Animal, Not Not-Animal: Hunting, Imitation and Empathetic Knowledge among the Siberian Yukaghirs." *Journal of the Royal Anthropological Institute* 10(3): 629–52.

⸺. 2007. *Soul Hunters: Hunting, Animism, and Personhood among the Siberian Yukaghirs*. Berkeley: University of California Press.

Wilson, D. E., and D. M. Reeder, eds. 2005. *Mammal Species of the World: A Taxonomic and Geographic Reference*. Baltimore, MD: John Hopkins University Press.

Winter, H., and U. Tshewang. 1989. "The Cross Breeding of Yaks in Merak-Sakten (Bhutan)." *Reproduction in Domestic Animals* 24(3): 116–22.

Wright, B. 1999. "Equine Digestive Tract Structure and Function." Ontario Ministry of Agriculture, Food and Rural Affairs, retrieved 1 September 2018. http://www.omafra.gov.on.ca/english/livestock/horses/facts/info_digest.htm.

Zaksheeva, E. O. 2009. "Serge v Traditsionnoi Kul'ture Buriat" [The *serge* in traditional Buriat culture]. *Tal'tsy* 2(33): 47–55.

Zeder, M. A. 2006. "Central Questions in the Domestication of Plants and Animals." *Evolutionary Anthropology: Issues, News, and Reviews* 15(3): 105–17.

Zeuner, F. E. 1963. *A History of Domesticated Animals*. New York: Harper & Row.

Zhigunov, P. S. 1961. *Severnoe Olenevodstvo* [Northern reindeer herding]. Moscow: Nauka.

Zhukovskaia, N. L., and A. P. Derevianko. 1988. *Kategorii i Simvolika Traditsionnoi Kul'tury Mongolov* [Categories and symbolism of the traditional culture of Mongolia]. Moscow: Nauka.

Zolotarev, A. M., and M. G. Levin. 1940. "Concerning the Antiquity and Origin of Reindeer Breeding." *Probl. Proiskhozhd. Evoliuts. Porodoobraz. Domashn. Zhivotn.* [Problems in the Evolutionary Origins of Breeds of Domestic Animals] 1: 171–89.

INDEX

Abbott, R., 181
Aberdeen, University of, xi
agriculture, collective farms, farming, 5, 9, 39, 72–73, 78, 80, 83–84, 89, 91, 93, 101, 109, 111; kolkhoz system, 67, 77, 82–84, 90–91, 101, 106, 108, 110–12, 128, 157, 159. *See also* plants
Ala-Su River, 6
Alar' regions, 11
Alaska, ix, 2–3, 170
Albrechtsen, A., 176
Alekseenko, E. A., 10, 173
Alibert, Jean-Pierre, 8
Alkyadyr Mountain, 85
Alps, European, 12
Altai Gobi, region, 98–99
Altai, Republic of, 98, 104
Altai-Saian. *See* Saian
Altan-Khan. *See* Khan
aluminium. *See* mining, metals
Alygdzher, 65–66, 75, 78–80, 83, 85, 127, 135
Amazonian, "animal mask" view, 35
America. *See* North America
Amerindian perspectivism, 35
Amur Orochens, 36
Anderson, David G., xii, 4, 173, 184
Anganov, V. V., 105, 184
animal sacrifices, 26, 45, 52–53, 59, 63, 70, 92. *See also* animals; death; domestication; spirits

animals. *See* bears; boar; camels; cattle; caribou; chipmunks; deer; dogs; donkeys; foxes; goats; hares; horses; Khainak; lynx; musk deer; muskox; muskrats; pigs; reindeer; sable; seals; sheep; squirrels; whales; wolves; yaks. *See also* birds; fish; insects; veterinary services; zoology
anthropocentric, 29–30, 32, 38
anthropology, anthropologists, 1, 3–5, 7, 9–10, 17–18, 22, 29, 32, 36, 40, 43, 47, 49, 54–55, 59, 69, 71, 89, 98, 102, 106, 112, 147, 153, 163, 169; fieldwork, methods, 17–18. *See also* archaeology; archives; ethnography
archaeology, 1, 4, 8–11, 29–31, 33–34, 69–70, 102, 116; Gorom Cave, 102; petroglyphs, rock art, 103; zooarchaeology, 30
archives, archival sources, 7, 9, 17, 42, 60, 82–85, 98, 111, 135
Arctic ix, 2–3, 170; Arctic Domus Project, xii
Arkhangai Province, 144
Aronsson, K. A., 68, 173
Artyushin, I. V., 180
astrology, 52, 61. *See also* cosmology
atheism, 150
Australia, 32–33
Ayusheeva, A. D., 147, 155, 173

Bachmann, Iris, 174
Badmaev, Sergei G., 73, 106–108, 173
Bagirov, V. A., 104, 173

Baikal, Lake, 102, 112; region, 46, 82, 104
Bailey, E., 180
Baldaev, F., 95, 174
Baldorzho, lama, 45, 60–64, 108
Balmysheva, N., 175
barium. *See* mining, metals
Batagol Mine, map, xv; River, 8
Batomunkueva, S. R., 41, 174
bears, 20, 24, 27, 47–49, 95–96, 112–14, 135, 149, 158–59, 165; bear grass, wolfsbane, 158–59
Beaufort Sea, 170
Belaia River, 87
Belarus, 138
Bellacasa, Maria Puig de la, 167–68, 171, 174
Bellezza, J. V., 174
Beluga whales, 170
Bering Strait ix
berries. *See* plants
Bhutan, 105–106
Bichurin, N. I., 10–11, 174
Binder, Lloyd, 2–3, 175
birch. *See* trees
Bird-David, N., 174
birds, 8, 47–48, 153; chickens, 16, 18, 121, 124, 163–164; eagles, 39–40; ptarmigan, 170; waterfowl, 170
Birius River, 71
Bjørnstad, G., 182
blacksmith. *See* mining, metals
boar, 96–97
Bokson, 45, 60, 72; map, xv
Bon-Po. *See* Buddhism
Boreal woodland caribou. *See* caribou
Bowhead whales, 170
Boyd, L. E., 37, 174
Bradley, D. G., 179
Britain, England, United Kingdom, xii, 6, 21–22, 31, 68, 136, 143, 158
bronze. *See* mining, metals
Broz, Ludek, 47, 49, 51, 148, 174
Buddhism, lamas, x, xii, 40–46, 52–64, 92, 103, 163; astrology, 52, 61; Bon-Po masters, 55; Dalai Lama, third, Sonam Gyatso, 53; Dalai Lama, thirteenth, 56; reincarnation, 61; tantric practices, 43, 45, 54–55, 60–64

Budiansky, Stephen, 32, 174
Buduun Lharampa, lama, 56
Bukha-Gorkhon, 9
Bulagats, 12
Bulgan Province, 144
Bureau, Nicolas, 183
burial. *See* death
Buriatiia, Republic of, Buriatia, Buriats, ix–x, xii–xiii, 7–9, 11–12, 22, 25–26, 40–43, 46–48, 51, 53, 55–56, 60, 62–63, 65, 67–68, 71–73, 82, 84, 90, 92–93, 95, 98–99, 104, 114, 121, 130, 135, 150, 154; language, xiii, 11, 22, 25–26, 40, 42, 62, 84, 121; map, xv. *See also* Evenki; Soiots
Burkhan, Burkhan Baabai, deity, 8, 43, 46–50, 52, 56, 58, 61; Shargai-Noion, 56
Burkhany, 56
Burla, Joan-Bryce, 37, 174

Cade, B. S., 119–20, 181
camels, 96–98, 106
Canada, ix, 2–3, 169–70. *See also* Inuit; Inuvialuit; Mackenzie River; Northwest Territories; Nunavut
Carbonaro, D. A., 174
caribou, ix, 2–3, 170; Boreal woodland, 2; Dolphin, 2; Northern Mountain, 2; Peary, 2; population, 2; Union, 2
Carruthers, Douglas, 6–7, 68, 143–44, 174
Cartesian. *See* Descartes
Cassidy, Rebecca, 29–30, 33, 174
Castrén, M. Alexander, 9, 174
cattle, cows, dairy cattle, x, 5, 7, 10, 12–13, 15–16, 20, 22, 25, 27–28, 51, 64, 69, 71–74, 81–82, 86, 88–89, 91, 93–103, 105–11, 114–15, 117, 120, 128–29, 142, 146, 150, 154, 157, 159, 164–65
Caucasus, North, 104
caves, Gorome, 102; photo, 85; sacred, 54–55, 57–58, treasure, 48–49
cedar. *See* trees
Cendsuren, C., 180
Charleux, I., 54, 174
Charlier, B., 174
Chemitevich, Vladimir, 111–12
Chen, Z-E., 179
Cherkasov, A., 152, 175

Chernetsov, Valeri N., 9, 175
chickens. *See* birds
Childe, V. Gordon, 29, 175
China, Chinese, 10–11, 36, 53, 101, 158, 161; map, xv; Qing empire, 53
chipmunks, 11
Christianity. *See* Russian Orthodox
Chukotka, Russia, ix, 3
Chysma, R. B., 104, 175
Clutton-Brock, Juliet, 30, 175
Cohen, Richard S., 42, 175
collective farms. *See* agriculture
communism. *See* Russia
Conaty, G. T., 2, 175
Cooper, Kate, 21, 23–24, 175
cosmology, 35, 40, 63–64, 68, 92, 145, 147, 160, 162; astrology, 52, 61
Côté, S. D., 119, 183
cows. *See* cattle
Cronin, M. A., 2, 175

Dag-Ezi. *See* spirits
Daidyn-Ezhin-Daiban-Sagan-Babai, 93
dairy cattle. *See* cattle
Dalai lama. *See* Buddhism
Dambaev, Dasha Dorzhievich, 88
Darkhad people, 59, 69, 90
Darzheevich, Dondok (shaman), 49–50, 52–54
Dashibalov, Bair B., 9, 54, 175
Dashieva, N. B., 150, 175
Davydov, Vladimir N., 173
death, animal, 114, 123, 158–59, 169; animal sacrifices, 37, 42, 84, 124, 163, 176, 195, 237; burial, 70, 155; mass killings of reindeer, 83. *See also* poison
death, human, 39–40, 48, 54, 60, 137–38, 158; burial, 70, 39; 39, 70; gods of death, 103. *See also* religion
deer, 24; Siberian red deer, 70. *See also* reindeer
Delaplace, Grégory, xii
Deleuze, Giles, 166, 175
Derevianko, A. P., 41, 186
Descartes, Rene, 32; Cartesian approach, 85
Di, R., 179
Dimitriev, N. G., 101, 175

dogs, 6, 13, 16, 27–28, 36, 48, 65, 73, 87, 113, 129–30, 143, 157–58, 160, 162, 164–65, 169
Dolphin caribou. *See* caribou
domestication of animals: definitions, 28–31; horses, 27; reindeer, 3–6. *See also* references throughout
domus. *See* Arctic Domus Project; Roman
Donahoe, Brian, 7, 49, 78, 91, 175
Dondok. *See* Darzheevich
Dondokov, Badma Khorluevich, and family, 12, 14, 39, 44–45, 52–54, 128–30, 133; photo, 44
Donokov, Baianbata, and family, 12–14, 18, 20, 61–62, 121, 129–30
Donokov, Borzhon, and family, 13–14, 19–21, 28, 37–38, 50–52, 81–82, 109, 114, 121–22, 124–25, 127–31, 133, 136–39, 142, 148, 151, 156–57; photo of fishing, 37; photo of home, 14
Dondokov, Tsyren-Dorzho, 85
Dong, S. K., 175
donkeys, 96
Dorzho. *See* Dondokov
Doshpok River, 87
Drompp, M. R., 143, 150, 175
Duba Aimag, 10
Dugarov, Bair S., 11–12, 175
Dugol'ma River, 66
Dukhas (people), 7, 70–71, 78, 90, 97, 102–103
Dumont, Louis, 21, 23, 176
Dwyer, M. J., 182

eagles. *See* birds
Echzhi Aimag, 10
education, schools, 3, 13, 16, 42, 45, 53, 60, 84, 90, 112. *See also* universities
eezi. *See* spirits
Ellegren, H., 185
Elverskog, J., 53, 176
Endres, Jürg, 7, 78, 176
Eneolithic Botai culture, 27, 118
Engelhardt, S. C., 183
England. *See* Britain
English language, 21–22, 68, 136, 158
Engorboi, 12

Enisei (Yenisei) River, 19
Erdene-Zuu monastery, 54
Erlik-Khan. *See* Khan
Ernst, L. K., 101, 173, 175
ethnography, xi, 1, 5–9, 17–18, 24, 33, 46, 50, 68–69, 79, 88, 90–91, 145–46, 168
ethology, 18, 119, 157, 161
Eurasia, ix, 2–3, 68–69, 91, 145
Europe, European, 2, 6, 32, 101; Alps, 12; Eurocentric, 32–33; Research Council, xii. *See also* names of countries
Even, M.-D., 54, 176
Evenki, Orochens (peoples), 10, 36–37, 42, 102, 145, 159, 238. *See also* Tungus
ezen, ezi. *See* spirits

Fages, A., 176
farming. *See* agriculture
Fennoscandia, 3
Fenup-Riordan, Ann, 170
Ferret, C., 162, 176
Fijn, Natasha, 22, 118, 144–45, 176
Finley, Moses I., 21, 176
Finno-Ugrian, 10
fish, fisheries, 6–8, 13, 24, 46–47, 149, 153, 170; photo, 37; poison, 8
Fitzhugh, W. W., 70, 176
Flagstad, Ø., 182
Folstad, I., 182
forests. *See* trees
Fossier, Camille, 183
foxes, 158
Fowler, C., 24, 176
France, French, xii, 8, 36, 168
Fraser, R., 24, 176
Frolov, A. N., 101, 176
fur. *See* animals

Galdanova, G. R., 22, 41, 176
Gandan-Darzhalin, 56–59
Gargan River, 9, 11
Gaunitz, C., 27, 118, 176
Gell, Alfred, 153, 168, 177
Gelug school, Tibetan, 53
Gelupga Buddhist church, Mongolian, 60
Genghis Khan. *See* Khan
geographers, 8, 32, 116

Gerasov, E., 93, 180
German, Germany, xiii, 8, 29, 34
Gimadeev, Aleksandr Viktorovich, 66, 74–76
Gladyr', E. A., 173
goats, 7, 16, 25, 73, 97–99, 109, 120; Siberian ibex, 25
Gobi region, 98–99
gold. *See* mining, metals
Gomboev, V. T., 41, 177
Gorome Cave, 102
Götherström, A., 185
government. *See* Mongolia; Russia
graphite. *See* mining
Greece, Greco-Roman, ix; Greek language, domus, 21
Gregory, C. A., 23, 177
Grøn, O., 66–67, 78, 177
Guattari, Félix, 166, 175
guns. *See* hunting
Guo, S., 98, 177
Guo, Y., 183
Gurung shamans, lamas, 43, 60, 70
Gutara, 80
Gwich'in communities, 2, 248
Gyatso, Sonam. *See* Buddhism

Hahn, Eduard, 29–30, 32, 177
Halbi River, 9
Hallowell, A. I., 44, 177
Hanghøj, K., 176
Hansell, Michael H., 153, 177
Haraway, Donna J., 169, 177
hares, 155
harlag. *See* yaks
Hart, E. J., 164, 170, 177
Harvey, G., 24, 177
Hatt, Gudmund, 68, 177
Heidegger, Martin, 4
Heissig, W., 54, 177
Henze, D., 8, 177
herding. *See* animals
Higgs, E., 31, 177
Hillmann, Edna, 174
Himalayan mountains. *See* Tibet
Hoffmann, R. S., 183
Holand, Øystein, 182

horses, xi, 6, 10, 13, 15–16, 19–20, 22, 25, 27–28, 36–37, 39–40, 64–65, 67–70, 73–75, 77, 82, 85–86, 89–91, 94–98, 103, 106, 110, 112–13, 116–41, 143, 146, 148–49, 152, 154–55, 157, 159, 161–62; aging, lifespan, 120, 137; Mongolian horses, 67–68, 70, 118, 135, 164; origin, DNA, genetic makeup, 118, 122, 126; photos, 16, 37, 132, 134; population, 97–98, 118, 126, 140, 161; Przewalski (wild horse), 27, 118; training, 136–37
Hoshun River, 9
Hou, F., 181
Houck, M. L., 180
Houpt, K. A., 174
Hufthammer, A. K., 182
Humphrey, Caroline, 40–41, 43–44, 54, 177, 184
Hun Empire, 10
hunting, firearms, guns, rifles, 39, 61, 87, 113, 144, 146, 149, 150, 157, 165. *See also* animals

Ia River, 74
Iakhoshop Ridge, 88; River, 85, 87–88, 110, 112, 128, 136; Valley, 20
ibex. *See* goats
Ims, R. A., 182
Indo-Iranian, 10
Ingold, Tim, xii, 3–4, 35, 50, 161–62, 177
innoculations. *See* veterinary services
insects, 12, 80, 153; mosquitoes, 96; ticks, 164; warble fly, 80
Inuit, ix, 2–3, 170
Inuvialuit (peoples, region), ix, 2–3, 164, 170
Inuvik, 2
Iran, 10
Irkit clan, 11–12, 73
Irkut River, map, xv
Irkutsk Oblast, Irkutskaia, 7–9, 74, 84, 105; Ecclesiastic Seminary, 42; map, xv; University of Irkutsk, 9
iron. *See* mining, metals
Isaac, E., 30, 178

Jackson, Sheldon, Dr., 2–3
Jacobsen, E., 70, 178

Japan, 163
Jarman, M., 31, 177
Jianlin, H., 185
Johnson, R. G., 181
Jones, David E., 158, 178
juniper. *See* trees

Kalikhman, Arkadiy D., xii
Kalinina, I. V., 42–43, 178
Kamarski Orochens, 36
Kan-Ool, B. K. 104, 175
Kangaraev, Nikolai Semenovich, 74–79, 137
Kara-Buren River, 65–66
Karagass (peoples), 8, 26, 147; language, 9; reindeer, 71, 117, 135, 164. *See also* Tofas
Karagassia, 8
Karasuk, tribes, 69
Karetak, J., 178
Kazakhstan, 27
Keay, M. G., 71, 178
Kertselli, Sergei V., 26, 69, 178
Ket language, peoples, 10
Khaasut clan, 11
Khainak, hybrid yak, x, 21, 72, 93–115, 120. *See also* yaks
Khakass, Khakassia, 10–11, 69
Khan, Kanate (political entity), 10–11; Altan-Khan, 53–54; Erlik-Khan, 46; Genghis Khan, 11; Khan-Shargai-Noen-Babai (spirit master), 93; Khormus Khan, 56
Khan-Modon region, Rivers, 73; map, xv; valley, 112–13, 136, 158
Khan, N., 176
Khanate. *See* Khan
Khangai (spirit), 94, 144
Kharinskii, Artur V., xii
Kharlamov, A. V., 176
Khimitdorzhiev, Sh. B., 53, 178
Khoito-Gol, 56
Khonchon, map, xv; River, 8, 73, 85
Khorluevich, Badma. *See* Donokov
Khormus-Khan. *See* Khan
Khövsgöl Aimag, district, 7
Khubsugul. *See* Lake Khubsugul
Khukhein Khada, sacred site, 54
Khusaev, Darma Khontoevich, 12
Khustai Nuruu National Park, 118

Khuzhir, map, xv
Khuzhirtai-Gorkhon, 94
Kiakhta, Treaty of, 11
Kitigaaryuit, 170
Kitoi River, map, xv
Klenovitskii, P. M., 173
Kobylkin, D. V., 102, 184
Kohn, Eduardo, 169, 178
Kohno, M., 179
Kol, N., 178
Kon, Feliks I., 146–147, 158, 178
Konorov, E. A., 180
Kosarev, Mikhail F., 10, 178
Kramer, F. L., 29, 178
Krasnoiarsk Krai, 8, 69
Kropotkin, Piotr A., 8, 178
Küçükçüstel, Selcen, 7, 102–103, 178
Kudai, 46
Kunlun mountains, 98
Kvasha, Anastasia, xv
Kvie, D. G., 173
Kyren, 56
Kyzlasov, Leonid R., 11, 178

Lake Baikal. *See* Baikal
Lake Il'chir, map, xv
Lake Khubsugul, 12; region, 99
lamas. *See* Buddhism
lambs. *See* sheep
language. *See* Buriatiia; English; Greece; Karagass; Ket; Latin; Mongolia; Russian; Samoyed; Sanskrit; Soiots; Tibet; Tofas; Tozhus; Turkic; Uralic
larch. *See* trees
Laruelle, François, 168
Latin language, domesticus, 21
Laufer, Berthold, 43, 68, 178
Laugrand, F., 170, 179
Laurelle, F., 179
Lazebny, O., 68, 178
Leach, Helen M., 31–32, 179
Lear, T. L., 180
Leonard, J. A., 185
Leslie, D. M., 98, 179
Lestel, Dominique, 36, 179
Levin, Maksim (Maxim) Grigorievich, 10, 68–69, 185–86

lichen. *See* trees
Lidén, K., 185
Lien, Marianne Elisabeth, 29, 179
Liu, J., 177
Lkhagvasuren, I., 106, 179
Lomov, Vitalii (Vitka), 65–66, 75, 77, 79–81
Long, C., 179
Long, M., 183
Long, R., 181
Lunde, D., 183
lynx, 79

Ma, L. R. Gu, 158, 179
Ma, T., 181
Mackenzie River, delta, 2–3, 170
MacKinnon, J., 183
MacNeil, M. D., 175
Maksimov, A. N., 179
Manchuria, 10–11, 36
Mangilaluk, Inuvialuit chief, 170
Mannen, H., 27, 179
Männikkö, I., 182
Manning, Erin, 166, 179
Mansheev, D. M., 106, 179
Marchina, Charlotte, xii, 22, 162, 179, 183
Marklund, S., 185
Maryniak, K., 184
Marxism, 4
Mashkovtsev, A. A., 69, 179
Massumi, Brian, 166, 179
Matsutake mushrooms. *See* plants
Mel'nikova, Larisa V., 7, 46, 48, 68, 76, 78–79, 179
Meng, X., 183
metals. *See* mining
Milige Aimag, 10
Miller, John H., 6, 68, 143–45
Miller, M., 3, 68, 144, 179
Mills, Martin, xii
mining, metals, minerals, 8, 49; aluminium, 138; barium, 157–159; blacksmith, smithy, xi, 149–150, 160; Bronze age, 10, 70; gold, 8, 48; graphite, 8; iron, 99, 121, 133, 138, 149–150; Iron Age, 10; salt, xi, 22, 32, 36, 66, 75, 79–80, 85, 121–122, 125; silver, 48; steel, 15, 62, 135, 137–138, 147, 158
Minusin Hollow, 70

INDEX

193

Mirov, N. T., 68, 179
Mitypova, G. S., 42, 180
Modon. *See* Khan-Modon
Mondy, 42; map xv
Mongolia, Mongols, 6–8, 11, 27, 41–43,
 45–46, 53–54, 56, 59–61, 69, 93, 95, 98,
 102, 143–44, 159; Empire, 11; language,
 11, 43, 53; map, xv
Mongolian cattle, reindeer, 20, 22, 27, 71, 73,
 81, 91, 95, 98–99, 101–103, 105–109,
 142
Mongolian horses, 67–68, 70, 118, 135, 164
Morrison, D., 170, 180
mosquitoes. *See* insects
Mt. Munku-Sardyk, map, xxv
Mt. Richin-Khumbe, map, xv
Mulk, I. M., 68, 180
Mumford, Stan Royal, 43, 60, 69–70, 180
Munku Sardyk. *See* Mt. Munku Sardyk
mushrooms. *See* plants
musk deer, 79
muskox, 98
muskrats, 170
Myka, J. L., 118, 180

Nadasdy, Paul, 50, 180
Nagata, Y., 179
Nantsov, G. D., 56, 180
Narin-Kholoiskii, 11
Nasatuev, B. B., 104, 180
Nasibov, Sh. N., 173
Nefedev, E., 68, 93, 180
Nekliudov, in Sodnompilova, 54
Neolithic Age, 10, 29, 118
Neoplatonic philosophy, 29
Nepal, 43, 60, 105
Ni, Z., 181
Nieminen, M., 182, 184
Nizhneudinsk District, 7, 82
Norbu, of Puntsognamdolling datsan, lama,
 42–43, 53
North America, 1–2, 120, 158, 161;
 indigenous peoples, 2, 158. *See also* Alaska;
 Inuit; Inuvialuit
North, D., 3, 180
Northern Mountain caribou. *See* caribou
Northwest Territories, 2

Norway, Norwegian, 3, 6, 68
Nukhen Daban, 41
Nunavut, 170
Nyamsamba, Yeo D., 179

Ó Maoilearca, John, 168–169, 180
O'Connor, T. P. 30, 180
Oehler, Alex Christian, 65, 129, 143, 164–65,
 180; family, 18
Oka (district, place), x, xii–xiii, 7–13, 21–23,
 25–28, 31, 40–43, 45–46, 48, 50, 52–55,
 60–61, 63, 65–67, 71–74, 78, 81–88,
 90–91, 93, 97–99, 101–108, 111–13,
 116–19, 135–37, 139–40, 143, 145–47,
 152–54, 160–62, 164–69; photo, 55;
 Valley, 93
Oka-Buriat mountain cult, 41–43, 60
Oka-Buriats. *See* Buriatiia
Oka River, 8–11, 21; map, xv
Oka-Soiots. *See* Soiots
Oka Valley, 93
Okhotsk, 3
Okinskii District, xii, 7; Arkhiv Administratsii
 Munitsipal'novo Obrazovanis (AAMO),
 85, 111, 173; map, xiv
Olsen, Ørjan, 6–7, 68–69, 180
Olsen, S. J., 102–3, 180
Onkhot clan, 11–12
Onot River, 89, 135; map, xv
ontologies, 32, 35, 167; colonial, 32;
 indigenous, 32
Oosten, J., 170, 179
Orkhoboomo, 41
Orlik, 12, 15, 42, 54, 63, 82, 85, 105, 128,
 154; map, xv
Orochens. *See* Evenki
Orthodox. *See* Russian Orthodox
Ortner, Sherry B., 43, 180
Ostertag, Anic, 174
oxen. *See* cattle; muskox
Oyun, N. Yu, 99, 180

Padmasambhava, 54
paleontology, 32
Pallas, Peter Simon, 8, 177
palynology, 116
Pariya, D., 105, 175

parks. *See* Khustai Nuruu National Park
pastoralism, pastoral, xi, 3–5, 10, 29, 69, 71, 93, 115, 144, 147, 162
Patt, Antonia, 174
Patton, J. C., 175
Pavlinskaia, Larissa R., 1, 7, 9–11, 72, 78, 83–84, 88–90, 98–99, 101, 106–107, 111, 152, 181
Pazyryk burials, 70
Peary caribou. *See* caribou
Pedersen, Morten Axel, 54, 59–60, 181
Petri, Bernhard Eduardovich, 1, 9, 46–47, 49, 68, 71–73, 83–84, 90, 112, 128, 146–47, 181
petroglyphs. *See* archaeology
Petrov, Mikhail, 42
Phillips, R. W., 101–102, 181
philosophy, philosophers, 29, 32, 36, 166, 168
pigs, 36
Plato. *See* Neoplatonic
plants, berries, 16, 39; hay, 12–13, 16, 20, 36, 73, 81, 85, 91, 99–101, 106, 110–12, 120, 165; mushrooms, 161, 163; rice, 52; vegetarian, 36, 86; wolfsbane, bear grass, 158–159. *See also* agriculture; trees
Pleistocene era, 31, 102
poison, 8, 79, 112, 114, 148, 152, 156–60; banned, 157
Poland, Polish, 146
Pollan, M., 13, 181
Pomishin, Semen B., 77, 181
Ponty, Maurice-Merleau, 4
Porphyry, philosopher, 29
Potapov, Leonid P., 147, 181
Prebaikalia, 12
Presbyterian missionary, 2–3
Price, Morgan P., 6, 143
Prytkova, Natalia F., 10, 181
Przewalski. *See* horses
ptarmigan. *See* birds
Pulk family, 3
Puntsognamdolling. *See* Norbu

Qi, D., 177
Qing empire, China, 53
Qiu, Q., 98, 181

Radde, Gustav, 8, 181
Ragagnin, Elisabetta, 71, 181
Range, Frederike, 157, 185
Ransom, J. L., 119–20, 181
Rassadin, Igor V., xii, 7, 26, 68, 83, 90–91, 99–111, 181–82
Rassadin, Valentin I., 10–11, 25–26, 68, 84, 90, 182
Reeder, D. M., 25, 186
Rees, Tobias, 1, 170, 182
reindeer: antlers, 66, 70, 75–77, 83, 130, 135; diseases, 79–80, 88–89, 164–165; Karagasss (breed), 71, 117, 135, 164; mass killing, 83; population size, 2, 83–85, 87–89; Tungus, 3, 10. *See also* caribou; Mongolian cattle, reindeer
religion. *See* atheism; Buddhism; Oka-Buriat mountain cult; Russian Orthodox; Presbyterian; shamans; spirits
rice. *See* plants
Richardson, reference, 60
Richin-Khumbe, Mount, map, xv
rifles. *See* hunting
Rindos, D., 30, 182
Rinpoche, Guru, 54
rock art. *See* archaeology
Rødven, R., 71, 182
Røed, K. H., 68, 173, 182, 184
Roman, Greco-Roman domus, ix, 21–24, 29, 38
Rose, Deborah B., 32–33, 182
Røv, N., 182
Rudenko, S. I., 70, 182
Ruijun, L., 185
Russia: communism, 9, 48; map, xv; Marxism, 4; Russian Empire, 53; Russian Federation, xii, 84, 104, 113; Russian revolution, 8–9, 46, 73, 78, 101, 158; Soviet religious oppression, 60; Soviet Northern Committee, 9, 84; Soviet school system, 60; Tsar, 158. *See also* agriculture, collective farms, kolkhoz system
Russian language, xiii, 21–22, 26, 112
Russian Orthodox Church, 42–43, 46; Holy Trinity Church, 42
Ryder, O. A., 180
Ryyppo, T., 185

sable, 11, 28, 147, 164–65, 168
Sahtú lands, 2
Saian Mountain Range, Saian Cross region, Saian-Altai region, ix–xi, 6–11, 24, 26, 28–29, 33, 40, 42–43, 46–47, 54, 60, 66–72, 85, 88–92, 97, 114, 117, 136, 139–40, 143, 145–46, 151, 162, 164
Saiany (settlement), 42–43, 54, 85, 88–90; map, xv
Sakha Republic, Yakutia, 145
Saller, R. P., 22, 182
salt. *See* mining
Sámi (peoples), 3, 6, 32, 68, 164
Samoyed language, peoples, 9–11, 69–70
Samuel, Geoffrey, 56
Sandberg, K., 185
Sandy Mountain, 56
Sanskrit language, 53
Sápmi, Fennoscandia, 3
Sariputra, 57–58
Savinov, Dmitri G., 70, 182
Savolainen, P., 177
Scandinavia, 3, 6, 68
Schaller, G. B., 98, 179
schools. *See* education; universities
Schrempf, Mona, 55–56, 182
Schubert, M., 176
seals, 170
Sebyan-Kyuel, 145
Seguin-Orlando, A., 176
Selenge Aimag, 93
Shakyamuni, 57–58
shamans, shamanism, x, xii, 39–41, 43–54, 59–60, 63–64, 70, 92, 100–101, 150, 154, 163
Sharaeva, Baatar, 85–86, 89–91
Sharaeva, Iumzhop, 14, 83, 85–86, 88–91, 125, 135
Sharaeva, Maria Manzaraksheevna, 90
Sharaeva, Tsydyp, 14, 88, 90, 133, 135, 137–138
Sharastepanov, Dasha T.–B., 11–12, 41, 52, 55, 99, 183
Shargai-Noion. *See* Burkhan Baabai
sheep, 7, 10, 13, 15–16, 52, 64, 73, 86, 89, 91, 94, 97–98, 101, 109–10, 120, 129, 143–45, 150–51, 157, 164; lambs, 59, 63, 148, 152; population, culling, 101
Sherpa people, 43
Shi, Q., 98, 101, 183
Shirokogorova, Elizaveta Nikolaevna, 36–37, 183
Shirokogorova, Sergei M. 4, 36, 183
Shumak River, village, 54
Siberia. *See* references throughout
Siberian ibex. *See* goats
Sikir River, 9
silver. *See* mining
Simmentel, cattle breed, 101
Sirelius, U. T., 68, 183
Sirina, A., 1, 183
Skeat, Walter W., 21, 183
Sliudianka, 112
Smith, A. T., 101, 181
Snellgrove, 60
Sodnompilova, Marina M., 54–55, 183
Soiots, Oka-Soiots (people) ix, x, xiii, 1, 7–9, 11–12, 21, 23–24, 26, 35, 38, 39–41, 43, 45–46, 48–50, 52–54, 58–59, 63–68, 70–74, 78, 81–84, 86, 88–95, 98–101, 103–105, 112–20, 128, 130, 135, 140–41, 143, 145–48, 153, 155, 158–62, 164, 167, 171; as indigenous people, 7; language, 11, 90; population, 83–84. *See also* Buriatiia
Sonopov, Dezhida Dambaevich, 12
Sorok, xii, 12–13, 39, 45, 53, 65, 82–83, 85, 87–89, 94–95, 106, 108, 110–12, 121, 128, 142, 150, 154; map, xv
Sorok River, 20, 88, 114, 156; map, xv; photo, 37
Sorokskii Range, 89
Soviet. *See* Russia
spirits, spirit masters ix–xi, 21, 24–26, 35, 38–41, 43–56, 58–59, 61–64, 91, 93–94, 103, 117–118, 143–145, 147–149, 161–163, 165–166, 168; cher eezi, 49; Dag ezi, 46; eezi, 46, 49; Erlik-Khan, 46; ezen, ezhen, 22, 24, 43; ezi, 46, 49; Sun-Ezi, 46; Yama, 103; Yamantaka, 103. *See also* animal sacrifices; religion; shamans
squirrels, 28
Star, S. L., 33, 183
steel. *See* mining

Stépanoff, Charles, xii, 7, 26, 28, 32, 68, 71, 87, 162, 183
Stepanova, E. V., 70, 183
Stepanovich, Buda-Khean (shaman), 47–52, 154
Stevens, Martin, 167, 183
Stevensen, A., 22, 183
Stolpovsky, Yu A., 180
Storli, Inger, 68, 183
strychnine, 147
Su, J., 177
Suchet, Sandra (Suchet-Pearson), 32–33, 183
Sun-Ezi. *See* spirits
Svishcheva, G. R., 180
Swancutt, K., 43, 183
Swanson, Heather Anne, 179
Switzerland, Swiss, 9

Tagar tribes, 69
taiga. *See* references throughout
Tailgata, 41
Taishin, V. A., 104–105, 184
Tajikistan, 104
Tan-Shu texts, 10
Tang, L., 179
Tashak, V. L., 102, 184
Tennberg, M., 185
Terentyev, A., 41, 184
Tester, F., 170, 178
Thomas, Nicholas, 40–41, 43, 184
Tibet, x, 41, 43, 53–56, 60–62, 95, 98, 101–103, 105, 158; Himalayan mountains, region, 12, 25, 43, 70, 74, 98; language, 53, 61–62. *See also* Buddhism
ticks. *See* insects
Thı̨cho lands, 2
Todzhinskii District, 7
Tofalaria, 7, 9–10, 65–66, 71, 74, 81, 83–85, 116–118, 127, 135, 152–153
Tofas (people), x, xiii, 7–11, 24, 26, 42, 46, 48–49, 65–68, 70–72, 74–76, 78–85, 87, 90–92, 97, 114, 116–18, 135, 137, 146–47, 152–53, 160–62, 164; language, xiii, 10–11, 49; photos: camp, 67; reindeer, 72; trap, 152. *See also* Karagass
Tolstoy, J. A., 181

Tozhus, Uriankhai (people, district), 6–7, 9–10, 46, 49, 68, 71, 74, 78, 84, 87, 90–91, 97, 106, 135, 144, 146, 158; language, 10
transhumance, 7, 12, 22, 90, 105, 146, 155
trees, forest, ix–x, 11–12, 15, 20, 24–26, 31, 38, 46–47, 51–52, 65–67, 75–76, 78, 86, 99, 101, 114–16, 119, 139, 150–51, 153–54, 159, 163; birch, 149; cedar, 80, 155; clear-cutting, 33; firewood, 15, 65, 123; juniper, 50; larch, 15, 39, 151; lichen, 78–79, 86, 165; sawmill, 149; willow, 146; woodwork, 149
Treude, E., 2–3, 184
Tronto, J. C., 171, 184
Tshewang, U., 105, 186
Tsing, Anna Lowenhaupt, 33, 163, 184
Tsuji, S., 179
Tsybenov, B. C., 42, 53, 184
Tsyrempilov, N. V., 184
Tsyrenov, Boris D., 106–108, 111
Tuktoyaktuk, 170
Tulaev, A. E., 71
Tuluev, K. D., 96
Tungus (people) 10, 69; reindeer, 3, 10
Tunka Valley, district, 8–9, 11–12, 42, 54, 56–57, 73, 106, 122
Turkic language, 9, 11, 43, 70, 89, 150; peoples, 10–11, 68–69, 84, 143
Turov, M. G., 78, 184
Turunen, M., 185
Tustuk River, 12, 18, 89, 109–110, 112, 128, 135; Valley, 8, 109
Tuva, 84, 99. *See also* Tyva
Tybykova, L. N., 47, 184
Tylor, E. B., 24, 184
Tyva, Republic of, 6–10, 12, 46–47, 49, 68–69, 71, 84, 97–99, 104, 106, 146; map, xv

Uda River, 71, 116; Upper Uda, 71
Uexküll, Jakob von, 34–35, 85, 168, 184
Uighur (people), 10–11
Ulan-Ude, 15, 47, 83
Ulturgasheva, O., xiii, 184
Umwelt, life-world (concept), 35–38, 85, 87, 92, 168
Union caribou. *See* caribou

United Kingdom. *See* Britain
United Nations Convention on Biological Diversity, 29, 184
universities: Buddhist university monasteries, 41; University of Aberdeen, xi; University of Irkutsk, 9; Zhelgenskii monastery university, 41
Upper Sorok. *See* Sorok
Uralic language, 10
Urda-Uro, 14, 19–20, 89, 124
Uriankhai. *See* Tozhus
Uro Valley, ix, xii, 7, 12–20, 22, 39–40, 45, 63, 65, 74, 81–82, 85–89, 94–95, 100, 103, 105, 108–109, 111, 119–20, 122, 124, 127–28, 130, 139, 144, 147–48, 150, 153–54, 157, 163–66, 168–69; photos, 14, 144
Urum, A. V., 180
Uvs Province, 144–145

vaccinations. *See* veterinary services
Våge, D. I., 71, 184
Vainshtein, Sevyan (Sevian) I., 9–10, 21, 46, 69–71, 98, 135, 185
Vanchikova, Ts. P., 53, 178
Varro, Marcus Terentius, 29
Vasilevich, Glafira, 10, 69, 185
Vasilu, A., 23, 185
Verkhneudinsk District, 9
veterinary services, 16, 26, 80, 128, 133; inoculation, vaccination, 15–16, 20, 73, 105, 119
Viktorevich, Iuri, 112–114
Vilà, C., 118, 182, 185
Virányi, Zsófia, 157, 185
Vitebsky, Piers, 145, 185
Viveiros de Castro, Eduardo, 35, 185
Voujala-Magga, T., 164, 185

Wang, K., 181
Wang, L., 181
Wang, Z., 181
waterfowl. *See* birds
Wayne, R. K., 185
Weber, A., 78, 184
Webster, N., 21, 185
Ween, Gro B., 179

Weil, K., 35, 185
Weladji, Robert B., 183
whales, whaling, 2, 170
Whitaker, Ian, 68, 185
Wiener, G., 20, 98, 102, 185
Wiklund, K. B., 68, 185
Wild Ridge, 71
Willerslev, Rane, 48, 50, 186
willow. *See* trees
Wilson, D. E., 25, 183, 186
Winter, H., 105, 186
wolfsbane. *See* plants
wolves, xi, 15, 19, 24, 27–28, 44, 51–52, 62, 79–80, 85–89, 94–95, 99, 102–103, 108, 112–114, 122, 142–160, 164–167, 169; dens, 155–158; photos, 144, 152; poisoning, strychnine, 79, 112, 114, 148, 152, 156–160; population, 79, 108, 114, 145–147; traps, 143, 147, 152–153, 155–158, 160, 165, 167–168; wolf pack size, 148
World War II, 79
Wozencraft, W. C., 183
Wright, B., 36, 186

Xie, Y., 183

yaks, x–xi, 5, 12–13, 15–16, 19–21, 24–28, 38, 40, 64, 68, 71–74, 82, 86, 90–115, 117–120, 123, 129, 136, 142, 157–159, 161–162, 164–165, 168; breeding, cryobank, 104; culling, slaughter, 112, 129; origin story, 96–97; photos, 97, 100; population, xi, 99, 101–104, 108, 113–114; wool, 13, 99
Yakutia, 145
Yama, deity, 103
Yamantaka, deity, 103
Yang, Y., 181
Yenisei. *See* Enisei River
Yeo, J. S., 179
Yoccoz, N. G., 182
Yurts, 8, 22, 39, 106

Zaksheeva, E. O., 22, 186
Zav'talov, O. A., 176
Zebu cattle, 105

Zeder, Melinda, 33–34, 186
Zeuner, Friedrich E., 30, 32, 186
Zhang, Q., 177
Zhang, X., 181
Zhao, X., 177
Zheelgenski datsan, 55
Zhelgenskii university monastery, 41
Zhemchug, 12
Zhigunov, P. S., 97, 135, 186

Zhom-Bolok (Zhombolok) River, 9, 11; map, xv
Zhou, J., 177
Zhou, Y., 183
Zhukovskaia, N. L., 41, 186
Zinov'eva, N. A., 173
Zolotarev, Aleksandr M., 68, 186
zooarchaeology, 30
zoology, 6, 68. *See also* animals

www.ingramcontent.com/pod-product-compliance
Lightning Source LLC
Chambersburg PA
CBHW051543020426
42333CB00016B/2072